WHY DID THE SOCIALIST SYSTEM COLLAPSE IN CENTRAL AND EASTERN EUROPEAN COUNTRIES?

Also by Jan Adam

ECONOMIC REFORMS AND THE WELFARE SYSTEM IN THE
USSR, POLAND AND HUNGARY (*editor*)

ECONOMIC REFORMS IN THE SOVIET UNION AND EASTERN
EUROPE SINCE THE 1960s

EMPLOYMENT POLICIES IN THE SOVIET UNION AND
EASTERN EUROPE (*editor*)

EMPLOYMENT AND WAGE POLICIES IN POLAND,
CZECHOSLOVAKIA AND HUNGARY SINCE 1950

PLANNING AND MARKET IN SOVIET AND EAST EUROPEAN
THOUGHT

WAGE CONTROL AND INFLATION IN THE SOVIET BLOC
COUNTRIES

WAGE, PRICE AND TAXATION POLICY IN CZECHOSLOVAKIA,
1948–70

Why did the Socialist System Collapse in Central and Eastern European Countries?

The Case of Poland, the former Czechoslovakia and Hungary

Jan Adam
Professor Emeritus of Economics
The University of Calgary
Alberta, Canada

First published in Great Britain 1996 by
MACMILLAN PRESS LTD
Houndmills, Basingstoke, Hampshire RG21 6XS
and London
Companies and representatives
throughout the world

A catalogue record for this book is available
from the British Library.

ISBN 0–333–57325–0

First published in the United States of America 1996 by
ST. MARTIN'S PRESS, INC.,
Scholarly and Reference Division,
175 Fifth Avenue,
New York, N.Y. 10010

ISBN 0–312–12879–7

Library of Congress Cataloging-in-Publication Data
Adam, Jan, 1920–
Why did the socialist system collapse in Central and Eastern European
countries? : the case of Poland, the former Czechoslovakia and Hungary / Jan
Adam.
p.   cm.
Includes bibliographical references (p.   ) and index.
ISBN 0–312–12879–7 (cloth)
1. Socialism—Europe, Eastern—Case Studies.   2. Socialism-
-Poland.   3. Poland—Economic policy.   4. Socialism—Czechoslovakia.
5. Czechoslovakia—Economic policy—1945–1992.   6. Socialism-
-Hungary.   7. Hungary—Economic policy.   I. Title.
HX240.7.A6A33   1995
335.43'0943—dc20
95–34283
CIP

10   9   8   7   6   5   4   3   2   1
05   04   03   02   01   00   99   98   97   96
Printed and bound in Great Britain by
Antony Rowe Ltd, Chippenham, Wiltshire

To Zuzana and Julie

Contents

List of Tables

List of Abbreviations

JOURNALS AND PAPERS

Czechoslovak

HN	Hospodářské noviny
NH	Národní hospodářství
PE	Politická ekonomie
PH	Plánované hospodářství (in 1990 it was replaced by NH)

Hungarian

F	Figyelő
KSz	Közgazdasági Szemle
Nsz	Népszabadság
TSz	Társadalmi Szemle

Polish

E	Ekonomista (Polish)
GP	Gospodarka Planowa
TL	Trybuna Ludu
ZG	Życie Gospodarcze

Soviet

P	Pravda

NATIONAL STATISTICAL YEARBOOKS

NK	Narodnoe khoziaistvo SSSR (Soviet)
MRS	Mały Rocznik Statystyczny (Polish pocket yearbook)
RS	Rocznik Statystyczny (Polish)
SE	Statisztikai Évkönyv (Hungarian)
SEzh	Statisticheskii ezhegodnik (CMEA)
SR	Statistická ročenka ČSSR (Czechoslovak)

MISCELLANEOUS TERMS

CC	Central Commitee of the Communist Party
CP	Communist Party
CMEA	Council for Mutual Economic Assistance
EM	Economic mechanism
KJK	Közgazdasági es Jogi Könyvkiadó (Hungarian publisher)
PWE	Panstwowe Wydawnictwo Ekonomiczne (Polish publisher)
PWN	Panstwowe Wydawnictwo Naukowe (Polish publisher)

Acknowledgements

I would first like to thank the Social Sciences and Humanities Research Council Canada for the extended research grants which enabled me to work on this study.

I am obliged to those who read parts of the original drafts and whose comments enabled me to improve the final version of this book. I would like to pay special tribute to professors Ch. Bruce, W. Brus, É. Ehrlich, H. Flakierski, I. Gábor, Z. Hába, Gy. Kövári, K. Kovari-Csoor, T. Kowalik, G. Révész, L. Rusmich, Z. Šulc, L. Szamuely, J. Timár and O. Turek. I have greatly benefited from consultations with scholars in my field. I am especially obliged to L. Antal, G. Bager, W. Baka, W. Brus, L. Csaba, É. Ehrlich, I. Gábor, M. Górski, D. Gotz-Kozierkiewicz, Z. Hába, K. Hagemejer, W. Herer, L. Herzog, I. Hetényi, M.Hrnčír, I. Illes, P. Juhász, C. Józefiak, M. Jurčeka, V. Kadlec, A. Karpiński, M. Kaser, E. Kemenes, J. Klacek, V. Klusoň, G. Kołodko, S. Kopatsy, K. Kouba, Gy. Kővári, K. Kővári-Csoor, A. Köves, T. Kowalik, W. Krencik, M. Krzak, J. Lipiński, A. Lipowski, K. Loránt, J. Mujżel, M. Pick, L. Podkaminer, M. Rakowski, G. Révész, L. Rusmich, E. Rychlewski, Z. Sadowski, V. Šafaříková, A. Sipos, A. Sopocko, K. A. Soos, Z. Šulc, L. Szamuely, B. Sztyber, I. Tarafás, M. Tardos, T. Tepper, J.Timár, O. Turek, F. Vencovsky, R. Vintrová and Zenkowski. Of course, the sole responsibility for the views expressed in this book, or any remaining errors, is mine.

Most of the materials for this book were collected in libraries and institutes in Europe. My thanks are due to the libraries and their workers: to the Radio Free Europe in Munich, Osteuropa Institut in Munich, Bundesinstitut for Ostwissenschaftliche and Internationale Studien in Cologne, Economic Institute of the Hungarian Academy of Sciences, and Institute for Comparative Economic Studies in Vienna.

I wish also to record my appreciation for the help contributed by my research assistants: Mmes K. Lukasiewicz and the late J. Adler-Vertes in collecting, processing and evaluating materials. Special thanks go to Mrs B. Blackman for the care and patience with which she improved the English of my typescript. To my wife, Zuzana, who encouraged me in my work and helped me to collect and process materials, I am very much indebted.

JAN ADAM

x

Preface

When I had progressed quite far in writing my book, *Planning and Market in Soviet and East European Thought* (1993), the socialist system in Poland, the former Czechoslovakia and Hungary, the countries which are discussed in my book, went out of existence. At that time I decided that research into the causes of the collapse in the three countries mentioned would be my next research project. My previous book is in a sense a sequel to my book on economic reforms (1989), and this new book which I am presenting to the reader is a sequel to the two mentioned books.

The rise of a socialist system in the former USSR and Eastern Europe and its collapse are two of the greatest historic events of the twentieth century. No doubt these events will be a frequent topic for many historians for a long time to come, all the more because socialist ideas are not going to vanish; many of the conditions which have brought them into being are still with us. This book is intended to be a modest contribution to an examination of the causes of the collapse.

Evaluations of political and economic events of historic importance can be more successful if they are performed a long time after the events. This usually gives access to more sources about the circumstances which led to the events. In addition, with the passage of time, the emotions generated by such events settle down and it is possible to view the events more objectively. This is especially true of such a hot topic as this book is dealing with, where propaganda makes it difficult to see many of the circumstances connected with the collapse in the right perspective. On the other hand, a book written after a step back in time, in this case five years, has the advantage of being able to catch the atmosphere in which the event occurred.

I have selected the three countries studied for my research for several reasons. Perhaps the most important was that all my books discuss these three countries and therefore I know them best of all the former CMEA countries. What was perhaps no less important was the fact that two of the countries, Poland and Hungary, were the first two to abandon the socialist system. True, I also include the USSR in most of my books, but this time I have decided to confine myself to one chapter, which is needed anyhow due to the role of the Soviet Union in the so-called socialist camp. It seemed to me that it would be too big a 'bite' to want to include the USSR. In addition, when I started to work on this book it was not clear what would happen to the USSR.

Considering that the socialist system was an economic, political and social system, it is clear that an examination of the causes of its collapse cannot be confined to economic analysis: to get a complete picture of the forces which brought down the system an analysis of the political and social factors is also needed. Therefore, though my book is predominantly an economic examination, I devote some attention to political and social factors.

I have given much thought to the structure of my book. In my other books, which are also comparative in nature, certain chapters discuss common and contrasting features of the aspects examined in the countries covered by the research and are followed by country studies chapters. This time I have opted for a different method. With the exception of Chapter 8, where I first discuss common features of economic development and then treat separately development in individual countries, in all the other chapters there is no such strict separation since I felt the problems discussed did not require it.

In this book I first discuss the unreformed economic mechanism and then the reformed. I do this partly because I do not share the view of some economists who believe that socialism in whatever form, the traditional or the reformed, had no chance for survival and who therefore have a tendency to deal with it as a non-restructured phenomenon. In my opinion, to put it with some simplification, the reformed socialist system did have a chance, provided it had had more time for experimentation.

The book is divided into three parts besides the Conclusions. Part I, which consists of only one chapter, can be regarded in a sense as an introduction. It gives a short survey of views about the causes of the collapse of socialism: on the one hand, these are views which predicted the collapse of socialism on the basis of a certain theory before the real collapse came about, and on the other hand, views expressed after the event happened.

Part II contains five chapters dealing with the unreformed economic mechanism which I mostly call the traditional system. For space-saving reasons and for readers' convenience, this principle is not applied consistently. In Chapter 2, which is the first chapter of Part II, the traditional system is briefly described. True, most of the readers of comparative economic systems are familiar with its principles, but there are many who do not have a definite knowledge. Chapters 3 and 4 examine problems to which the economic literature has devoted little attention. Chapter 3 discusses economic and social policy, primarily during the traditional system. As will be shown in this chapter, systemic and economic policy aspects should not be mixed up, though a very thin line separates them. In Chapter 4 labour–management relations are discussed. Here, as well as in Chapter 5, which discusses external economic relations, changes arising during economic reforms are also examined. The last chapter of Part II is devoted to the political and ideological factors of the collapse.

Part III contains four chapters. Chapter 7 deals with economic reforms in the 1960s and the 1980s and the views which held that the economic reforms brought down the socialist system. Chapter 8 gives a short survey of economic development and its effect on the standard of living, primarily from the second half of the 1970s, when, in all the countries under review, the economies took a turn for the worse. In Chapter 9 I examine the development of ownership relations since the seizure of political power. In the last chapter I discuss the role of the Soviet Union in the collapse of the socialist system in Poland and Hungary. As is known, the latter two countries, which headed the movement away from socialism, could only achieve their goal because the Soviets no longer stuck to Brezhnev's doctrine. The last chapter does not confine itself to the examination of the relationship between the Soviet Union and the countries under review here and its impact on the collapse of the socialist system in the smaller countries. To understand why the Soviet Union did not try to prevent Poland and Hungary from rejecting the socialist system it is important to be familiar with the situation in the USSR in the second half of the 1980s. Chapter 10 describes that situation.

Some definitions of terms used in this book are required. Before the socialist system collapsed the term 'socialist economic system' on the one hand, and the terms 'economic mechanism' or 'system of management of the economy' on the other hand were usually regarded as different terms. The two latter terms meant methods used for the operation of the socialist economic system. They included planning, regulation system and organisational system. The 'socialist economic system' was regarded as a broader term which also included ownership relations. I will use the terms in the book as described here.

The Soviet Union and Czechoslovakia no longer exist as state structures. When these terms are used it is understood that I refer to former state structures. The three countries under review as a group are often called 'smaller countries' or 'small countries' in this book.

JAN ADAM

Part I
Introduction

1 Thoughts on the Causes of the Collapse of the Socialist System

INTRODUCTION

In this first chapter I am going to present a broad spectrum of views about the causes of the collapse of the socialist system. Of course, this will be only a selected group of opinions. I will present not only authors who explicitly discuss the causes of the collapse after it occurred or just before, but also others who predicted the collapse on the basis of some theory. The viability of socialism was discussed even before it was established. Once Marx and Engels had formulated their historical materialism which tried to find regularities in the development of social systems, and had expressed the idea that capitalism would be replaced by socialism, and later by communism as the final system, the debate about the viability of socialism began.

I will start out with general views on the inevitability of the collapse and only later present views which deal with the concrete causes of the collapse in the countries under review. This division will not be fully applied consistently.

VIEWS ON THE INEVITABILITY OF THE COLLAPSE

Von Mises' Views

The idea of socialism had already been called into question in the nineteenth century. In the twentieth century perhaps the most intellectually powerful challenge came from the Austrian economist, L. von Mises. He launched his challenge in his study 'Economic Calculation in the Socialist Commonwealth', which was published in 1920 (1963) at a time when the Soviet model of a planned economy only existed in the minds of some economists. Therefore it is no wonder that Mises' model of socialism, which was the basis for his analysis,

3

was in many respects different from the Soviet model which came into being in the 1930s. In Mises' model of socialism, the means of production belong to the community which makes decisions about their use. Money and prices, as we know them, do not exist. The freedom to use earnings according to the preferences of the earners does not exist. Each citizen receives a bundle of coupons which he can redeem for a certain amount of specified goods within a certain period.

Mises believes that such a system cannot be efficient because it lacks the properties needed for a rational allocation of resources to possible alternative uses. He is not concerned about the lack of consumer market prices; these he believes will emerge spontaneously. Individuals have preferences for certain goods and as a result an exchange will develop. In this process exchange ratios (prices), determined by supply and demand, will arise. Not only this, but money too will arise: some consumer goods will serve as a medium of exchange. Of course, the role of the money will be limited to consumer goods.

To Mises the real obstacle to an efficient working of the socialist system is primarily the lack of market prices for producer goods (goods of a higher order). Without such prices it is, according to him, impossible to attach a rational value to producer goods and engage in a rational economic calculation, which has two prerequisites. Even a socialist community may have no trouble with one prerequisite, with the formulation of its needs, mainly the most urgent. According to Mises the problem is with the other prerequisite, the valuation of the means of production, which is the basis for the most efficient satisfaction of needs. Needs can be satisfied in different ways, and the means of production can be used for multiple ends. The solution to the problem is the existence of rational prices and an exchange medium (money) for producer goods which can arise only in market conditions.

Mises maintains that not just any price can be used for economic calculation. He argues that prices based on the labour theory of value are not fit for such a purpose. In addition, he maintains that 'Exchange relations between production goods can only be established on the basis of private ownership of the means of production' (p. 112).

He is a staunch advocate of private ownership. In one place he writes, 'Every step that takes us away from private ownership of the means of production and from the use of money also takes us away from rational economics' (p. 104). To him private initiative and responsibility, important factors for the efficient performance of the economy, are possible only under private ownership. Managers of private corporations work efficiently because their interests are tied to the interests of the corporation they work for. They are owners of a fraction of the shares of the enterprise they manage and have the prospect of placing their heirs in the company. All this is impossible in a nationalised unit, where it cannot be expected that the manager will act on his own initiative. First, the authorities set limits for initiative, and secondly it is impossible to transfer power 'for in practice the propertyless manager can only be held morally responsible for losses incurred' (p. 122).

Hayek's Views

As far as I know F.A. Hayek did not discuss the reasons for the collapse of the real socialist system. In his writings he tried, however, to show that a system different from the market economy cannot work well and is doomed to failure. He did so in his *The Road to Serfdom*, which criticised primarily the planned economy of Nazi Germany. In *Collectivist Economic Planning* (1963), a volume of studies on the possibilities of socialism (which included *inter alia* the study of von Mises) which he edited and contributed to, he tried to show that economic calculation under socialism is theoretically possible but practically impossible. Here I would like to discuss his *The Fatal Conceit, the Errors of Socialism* (1989).

In this book he tries to substantiate, mainly on a philosophical level, the viability of the market economy and the failure of the socialist system. He maintains that the market economy, which is the result of spontaneous development, is necessarily superior to an order deliberately produced and based on collective command, and that a competitive market economy can produce more wealth and prosperity than a socialist system. The former can work more efficiently than the latter because it follows moral traditions spontaneously developed in the course of many thousand years. To follow morality imposed by reason, which is the way of socialism, must necessarily 'destroy much of present humankind and impoverish much of the rest' (p. 7). To him socialism is based on a false premise, that of an uncritical theory of rationality, and though it is 'inspired by good intentions and led by some of the most intelligent representatives of our time, [it] endangers the standard of living and the life itself of a large proportion of our existing population' (p. 9).

One can pose the question: how did the author arrive at such conclusions? Hayek believes that the present social order is the result of a development which led mankind between Scylla and Charybdis, instinct and reason. Both instinct and reason played an important but not a decisive role. Decisive for the present social order are the rules of human conduct which evolved gradually. These rules (or more precisely, institutions), among which the author mentions private property, competition and gain, constitute morality, which is handed down from generation to generation by 'tradition, teaching and imitation' (p. 12).

The instinct of fear and danger led primitive people to combine into small groups where solidarity and altruism were the rules of behaviour. But these rules were not applied to other groups. The same is true about the present situation. 'An order in which every one treated his neighbour as himself would be one where comparatively few could be fruitful and multiply' (p. 13). Spontaneous cooperation between individuals develops, which owes little to instincts of solidarity and altruism. The cooperation is guided by the invisible hand.

'Man is not born wise, rational and good', writes Hayek. All these properties must be learnt. 'It is not our intellect that created our morals; rather, human interactions governed by our morals make possible the growth of reason and those capabilities associated with it. Man became intelligent because there was *tradition* – that which lies between instinct and reason – for him to learn' (p. 21).

To Hayek private property 'is the heart of morals of any advanced civilisation' (p. 30) and no civilisation can last long if the government does not see as its main objective protecting private property (p. 32).

Hayek criticises some of the rationalists who wanted to rearrange society according to ideas thought out in advance and thus to let reason play a decisive role in changing the order and in imposing new rules of behaviour on society. He subjected, *inter alia*, René Descartes, Jean-Jacques Rousseau, Karl Marx and John Maynard Keynes to criticism. (Rousseau was criticised for challenging the existing order by making private property suspect in his work *The Social Contract* and private property 'was no longer so widely recognised as the key factor that had brought about the extended order' (p. 50).) He also complains about the great influence of rationalism and maintains that the more an intellectual is educated the more likely he is at the same time not only a rationalist but also a socialist (p. 53).

What has been said up to now is on a very general abstract philosophical level. Hayek also tries to underpin his arguments against socialism with more concrete reasoning. He has primarily two arguments. One is that planners cannot have the necessary information in order to be able to issue correct commands. The second is that, when no rational prices exist because they can only arise in competitive markets, it is impossible to allocate capital efficiently among different uses (pp. 86–7).

Brzezinski's Views

Brzezinski's book *The Grand Failure* (1989) was written at a time when the European socialist camp was already in an economic and political crisis. The author was already sure that his old dream of communist destruction was becoming a reality. He called the chapter in which he summarised the reasons for the upcoming communist breakdown 'The Agony of Communism'. In it he maintained that communism found itself in a general crisis[1] which engulfed ideology and the nature of the system. To him the crisis lay in the Soviet system being no longer an attractive model and there being no longer a monolithic communist movement. Furthermore, the communist system was faced with an insoluble dilemma namely that 'economic success can only be purchased at the cost of political stability, while political stability can only be sustained at the cost of economic failure'. Finally, the author expressed the view that East European countries saw the elimination of Moscow's and the Communist Party's (henceforth CP or simply Party) domination 'as the necessary precondition to social rebirth' (p. 232).

Brzezinski admits that the communist regime achieved some progress (he is, however, not very specific), but the social costs were disproportionally high. He writes:

> Communism's grand failure has thus involved, in summary form, the wasteful destruction of much social talent and the suppression of society's creative political life; excessively high human costs for the economic gains actually achieved and an eventual decline in economic productivity because of statist overcentralization; a progressive deterioration in the overly bureaucratized welfare system which represented initially the principal benefit of Communist rule; and the stunting through dogmatic control of society's scientific and artistic growth (Brzezinski, 1989, p. 241).

In his book Brzezinski tried also to predict what kind of a regime would arise in the post-communist era. He was not very optimistic; he suggested that the 'totalitarian model of social organization' characteristic of Soviet-type regimes precluded political pluralism. Still he did not give up on East European countries: the emergence of a civil society in some of the countries and the use of modern mass communications by Western countries to break down the monopoly of communist propaganda might pave the way to democratisation. The transformation might be eased by the fact that pluralistic democracies have assimilated some constructive aspects of Marxism, a more developed social consciousness (pp. 252–7).

It is interesting that Brzezinski, who put forward a whole list, one can say, of crimes of the Soviet system, at the end gave communism some acknowledgement. 'The bitter but also hopeful irony of history may, therefore, be that for some communism will come to be ultimately viewed as an inadvertent, and costly, transition stage from preindustrial society to a socially developed pluralistic democracy' (p. 257).

Fukuyama's Views

When Fukuyama wrote his book *The End of History and the Last Man* (1992) socialism in East European countries had already collapsed, and the Soviet Union was on the brink of collapse. (He outlined in substance his views in an earlier article, 'The End of History?', in 1989 and therefore I present his ideas in this subchapter.) Unlike the three previous authors, he could back up the discussion of his philosophy of history with experiences from the collapse in the East. Fukuyama, like Marx, looks for a final social system which would meet human longings and aspirations. Marx believed that such a social system would be communism, whereas Fukuyama opts for liberal democracy. His philosophy of history consists of two fundamental elements: Marx's interpretation of history and Hegel's desire of people for recognition. He writes (p. 204)

The universal and homogeneous state that appears at the end of history can thus be seen as resting on the twin pillars of economics and recognition. The human historical process that leads up to it has been driven forward equally by the progressive unfolding of modern natural science, and by the struggle of recognition . . . capitalism is inextricably bound to modern natural science.

Though Fukuyama rejects Marx's communism, he nevertheless accepts more or less Marx's interpretation of history[2] as one of the driving forces in the development of mankind. Unlike many authors, who deny that any pattern exists in the development of mankind, Fukuyama, like Marx, believes that there is some regularity. From

Marx's assertions in his *Preface to a Contribution to the Critique of Political Economy* (see Marx–Engels Reader, 1978, p. 3) one can conclude with great certainty that he regarded production forces as the driving force of development. Marx was, however, not specific about the meaning of the term 'productive forces'. It is possible to agree with O. Lange (1975, p. 221) who defined productive forces as all the factors which determine productivity, including, of course, technology at a certain stage of economic development.

To Fukuyama modern natural science is the mechanism[3] of directional historical change. He believes not only in a pattern in economic development, as has been already mentioned, but also that there is constant progress in this development and that history does not repeat itself in the sense that a form of social organisation once abandoned is not readopted by the same society. He writes, 'if history is never to repeat itself, there must be a constant and uniform Mechanism or set of historical first causes that dictates evolution in a single direction' (p. 71). And such a uniform mechanism is to him natural science, which is the basis for technological progress. Military competition between nations and wars are an important accelerator of technology and modernisation. In order to withstand any threat to sovereignty, nations are forced to develop technology and adapt social structures accordingly.

The desire to satisfy growing human needs is another accelerator of natural science. Industrialisation, the instrument for satisfying these needs, is manifested in economic growth and this produces 'certain uniform social transformations in all societies' (p. 77). In this sense wars and industrialisation are a unifier of nations.

The second driving force of human development is psychological in nature. It is the desire for recognition, a concept taken from Hegel, as interpreted by the French–Russian philosopher, A. Kojeve. Human beings seek recognition by others; they want their worth, dignity and freedom to be respected. What we call economic motivation is, to the author, largely the desire for recognition. The desire for recognition has led to violence and unequal relations among nations (colonialism) and people, but at the same time it has made people aware of their situation. The choice of democracy is inspired by the desire for recognition and equality. Fukuyama states explicitly that there is no economic rationale for democracy because 'this is a drag on economic efficiency' (p. 205). In another place he maintains that democracy is not the result of a natural development; 'it must arise out of a deliberate political decision' (p. 220).

Modern natural science with its prerequisite, education, and its results, industrialisation and urbanisation, has helped people in subordinate position to fight the inequalities. Recognition links 'liberal economics and liberal politics' (p. 206).

To Fukuyama liberalism and democracy are two separate concepts. Democracy (the right to vote and to participate in politics) does not guarantee human rights and freedoms which are the essence of liberalism (pp. 42–3). As mentioned, he believes that liberal democracy, as it already exists in the West, is the last stage in political development, though he acknowledges that liberal democracy has competitors in Asia and in the Islamic world.

Liberal democracy in its economic manifestation is capitalism or the free market economy. To him this is the system which can best satisfy human needs and therefore was victorious in competition with socialism.

Fukuyama believes that one of the main reasons for the collapse of the Soviet system was its economic failure. This had such a far-reaching effect because the legitimacy of the system was based on the promise of a high standard of living. However, the most fundamental reason was the failure to control thought (pp. 28–9). He also believes that the failure to respect the desire of the population for recognition was one of the reasons for collapse (p. 205). He does not, however, criticise communism for its social engineering, as Hayek did, because he himself applies social engineering to some extent.

VIEWS ON THE COLLAPSE OF THE SOCIALIST SYSTEM

In my opinion, it is useful to distinguish three groups of theories about the collapse of the socialist system. One has some affinity with Hayek's ideas even if the authors do not mention his name or may distance themselves from him because of Hayek's adherence to *laissez-faire*. Hayek's underlying idea is that a system thought out behind a desk, by the mind, cannot succeed. All those who believe that social engineering cannot be successful must come to the conclusion that the socialist system was doomed, if they are consistent in their thinking. The second group includes views that the socialist system itself carried the seeds of destruction. Some simply believe that a system which is not based on market forces is not a viable system. Others believe that the reforms destroyed the socialist system. Most of this group's ideas will be discussed in connection with economic reforms but some in this chapter. In the third group I include divergent views about the collapse of the socialist system.

Social Engineering

N. Petrakov (1993) can be regarded as one of the representatives of the group explaining the collapse of the socialist system as due to social engineering. He juxtaposes a market economy with a socialist economy. The former is 'an evolutionary form of economic organization . . . [resulting] from a process of many centuries of natural selection of effective forms of interaction' whereas the socialist 'was purely speculative from the very beginning'. He criticises Marx and Engels' Marxism for confining itself to a suggestion that the capitalist system would be destroyed without presenting a concrete concept of transformation to a new society. Therefore he calls Marxism a 'pseudoscientific apologia for social destruction.' In Petrakov's view Lenin and Stalin, who formulated the socialist system, drew from the utopians of the seventeenth through to the nineteenth centuries.

Petrakov tries to complement his view of socialism as a utopia by analysing its working. To him the greatest shortcoming of the Stalinist system was the lack of incentives and the use of non-economic instead of economic coercion. The reform of the system had to collapse because the tradition of state control made decentralisation impossible.

If P. Murrell, who is an adherent of an evolutionary approach to the transformation of the socialist system to a market economy, is consistent in his views, he must necessarily take the position that one of the main reasons for the collapse of the socialist system was social engineering. He developed his evolutionary approach in several papers. In his 1992 paper he distinguishes two schools which provide underpinnings for an evolutionary approach to economic reform.[4] To both schools 'socioeconomic mechanisms are information processing devices' and therefore in the forefront of their interest is the examination of intellectual capacities and how they can be improved (p. 83).

The evolutionary approach is based on the idea that experience should be the guide for action. It views with 'skepticism reforms . . . derived purely from theory, particularly those that exhibit speed, irreversibility and large scale' (p. 90).

In his 1993 article Murrell develops in greater detail his theory of an evolutionary approach by contrasting it with the shock therapy applied in Poland's and Russia's transition to a market economy.[5] He argues that the difference between the evolutionary and shock therapy approaches is not only in the economic sphere, but, more precisely, is also foremost in the idea about how human societies function. Taking as an example Lipton and Sachs' paper of 1990, he shows that these two authors in conceiving their strategy did not take into consideration the existing institutional structures. Murrell, referring to the two authors, writes, 'History, society and the economics of present institutions are all minor issues [to them] in choosing a reform program' (p. 113). He characterises shock therapy as 'Utopian Social Engineering' (p. 115). He also tries to show through the example of Poland and Russia that the shock therapy model cannot be successful in the long run.

Murrell maintains that shock therapy comfortably fits the views of Plato, Rousseau and Preobrazhensky. It is known that Preobrazhensky's ideas about the transformation to socialism, expressed in his *New Economics*, were used by Stalin in the elimination of NEP and the introduction of the centrally planned economy.

Indigenous Reasons

In a 1987 paper, which was reprinted in a book (1990), I. Szelényi, a well-known Hungarian sociologist, expresses the view that the economic crisis in the 1970s and 1980s in the socialist countries, which he characterises as a general crisis, resulted from the difficulty of transition from an economy based on extensive growth to an economy based on intensive economic growth. The problem is how to ensure growth when surplus labour is exhausted. According to him capitalism was faced with a similar problem; he implicitly assumes that the origins of the Great Depression of the 1930s were also in the transition from extensive growth, an idea which I doubt is well-founded (1990, p. 410).

He called the period of the 1970s and 1980s, in which economic growth had stagnated or declined, the crisis of transition. It was a period when socialism was close to collapse. But he did not share the view of those who believed that an intensive type of economic growth was possible only under conditions of private ownership and therefore socialism was doomed to collapse. Rather, he believed that socialism would turn into a socialist mixed economy (1990, pp. 426–32). Taking into consideration his characterisation of the mixed economy, one can call it market socialism.

Szelényi appreciated primarily the rise of the second economy in the Hungarian reform. Such a rise was possible because the bureaucracy wanted to achieve political stability even at the price of giving up some of its power. The second economy started first in agriculture, spread later into services and affected industry too. Its expansion was the first step in the direction of a consumer society. To Szelényi this was the start of the process of embourgeoisement (1990, pp. 417-20). In his 1990a article the author maintained that embourgeoisement brought down the socialist system. (See more about this in Chapter 9.)

J. Staniszkis (1991), a well-known Polish sociologist, maintains that contradictions in political, economic and international relations created a very critical situation for the existence of the socialist system. Some 'chance events' caused the systemic contradictions to deepen and destroyed the socialist system. In the political sphere the contradiction lay in the claim of the CP to be the executor of objective laws of history and in the 'subjectivism and anarchy inexorably resulting from such a formula' (p. 2).[6] The lack of democracy and civil society encouraged people to act collectively during a crisis in order to defend their interests. In this way Solidarity was born.

In the economic sphere there were contradictions between the rise of state ownership and the impossibility of controlling the economic process. The working of a state-owned economy depends on effective structures of control. The absence of the market in such a system and the resulting lack of reliable information makes control of the economic process impossible.

To Staniszkis the contradiction in international relations lay in that socialist countries were in double dependency. The socialist bloc as a whole was dependent on capitalist countries and in addition on CMEA. The second dependency had to mitigate the first and to redistribute the cost of the first. Such adjustments enabled the 'empire' (meaning the Soviet Union) to be consolidated and engage in competition with capitalism (pp. 3 and 120). The socialist countries were dependent for technology on the West, but the latter blocked the export of important innovations to socialist countries. The dependency also had another effect: socialist countries suffered from the economic fluctuations in the West.

The bad situation was compounded in the 1980s by the fact that the application of methods used in the past (such as changes in investment plans, shifting of resources) to overcome crises was more difficult. Sources of extensive development were exhausted and the demand for energy and raw materials was growing (p. 5).

One of the chance events which intensified the contradictions was a change in the composition of élites in the Soviet Union and the ascendancy of Gorbachev with his reforms (pp. 10–17).

Divergent Views

The opinion of G. Therborn (1992) about the collapse can be regarded as a voice from the left of the spectrum of views. First, let me mention Therborn's view on the substance of socialism. To him socialism is the combination of a culture (which provides its members with an identity, world view and a set of values) and a set of institutional structures (p. 17). According to him socialism collapsed as the result of a political and economic crisis in the 1980s and three epochal shifts. One of the epochal shifts was the end of colonialism, which crucially affected the viability of classical socialism (the socialists played an important role in fighting colonialism) (p. 22). In my opinion, this did not play any role in the defeat of real socialism in Eastern Europe. However, the defeat of socialism in Eastern Europe and later in Russia had a devastating effect on the socialist movement in the Third World.

The second shift was the transition in the post-industrial society to services alongside the declining role of industry, and with it the decline of the proportion of industrial workers in the total work force. The post-industrial society also brought a change in the relationship between enterprises and markets. 'Socialist theory was predicated upon the tendency of the former to replace the latter.' Services concentrated in smaller facilities required more markets (p. 23). The third shift was from modernism, which was combined with concepts of progress and development, to post-modernism, which questions the possibility of predicting the future.

He mentions two reasons why socialism may be regarded as a failure. First, it was not applied in any advanced capitalist country, as Marx and Engels had assumed it would be. Second, socialist countries had failed to catch up with the most advanced capitalist countries economically and politically.

Nevertheless, Therborn believes that it would be wrong globally to characterise the socialist system as a failure. He advances figures about the development of socialist countries compared to advanced countries. In addition, he maintains that the socialist countries managed to achieve basic industrialisation and economic modernisation. However, they failed to develop mass consumption and services (p. 28).

Therborn takes the position that the socialist system was reformable and its demise in the USSR was conjunctural rather than systemic. The reforms in China and the rapid economic growth there are, according to him, the best proof of this. The postponement of reforms in the USSR was fatal for the regime (p. 21).

Finally, mention will be made of a line of reasoning about the collapse of the socialist system which cannot be directly linked to one author, but which is implicit in some views on the collapse and has popular support. Some believe that the traditional socialist system failed because it was in substance contrary to human nature. According to this view people are driven by selfishness, envy, greed, and the desire for property and wealth – in brief, qualities which breed individualist rather than collectivistic attitudes which were the philosophical foundation of the socialist system. However people are able to bring out the best in themselves when they are confronted with competitiveness and rivalry. The architects of the socialist system believed that it was possible to mould human nature and behaviour to be in tune with the requirements of some thought-out, ideal, social and economic system, and that, if people were properly enlightened about the intricacies and wrongs of the old system and about their interests, they might be won over to new ideas. Because the architects of the socialist system tried to suppress human nature and create a 'socialist man' (cf. Roemer, 1993, p. 91), it is argued, people were not motivated to work hard, produce quality products, assume initiative and behave responsibly. In East European countries, this argumentation was often expressed in a laconic and joking way: why did Marx not first try his ideas on animals?

The best proof of the fact that the architects of the socialist system did not take human nature sufficiently into consideration is found in the amount of stress put for a long time on moral incentives instead of money incentives. They did not see, or rather, did not want to see, that sacrifices which people are willing to bear in revolutionary periods cannot be expected in peace time.

Another evidence of the inability of the architects of the system to reckon with the nature of the people was their treatment of the intelligentsia. They must have known that the success of the system and its stability depended to a great extent on the intelligentsia. Nevertheless they did not do what was necessary to gain and maintain its support.

CONCLUDING REMARKS

I intend to comment briefly on some of the views. Much of what Mises and later Hayek argued about the importance of market prices for economic calculation and thus for the achievement of economic efficiency was correct. In his famous study 'On the Economic Theory of Socialism' (1956) O. Lange, who challenged Mises' views, wanted to achieve rational prices by letting the Planning Office simulate the market.[7] His suggestion was never applied in practice. Economic reforms, mainly in the 1980s, were supposed to rationalise prices gradually.

As has been noted, Hayek believes that a spontaneous system is superior to a system designed by human beings. To him private property, competition and gain are the foundations of morality and, to exaggerate a bit, altruism and solidarity are not part of it. In other words, in the book discussed and in other works, he pleads for a system in which the 'invisible hand' is not impeded by government interference. In this respect there is no difference between him and Mises. However, Hayek tries to underpin his *laissez-faire* principle also with philosophical arguments, whereas Mises confines himself to economic reasoning.

Needless to say, none of the advanced capitalist countries has fully adopted Hayek's views. The welfare system, applied in all countries, is the best proof of it. The whole trend in development, interrupted by some temporary backward movements, indicates that government interference in the economy will probably grow, despite strong opposition in some countries, mainly the USA.

The present democratic institutions in advanced capitalist countries are not the result of spontaneous forces but, as Fukuyama (see p. 9) indicates correctly, they are the result of deliberate political decisions or, more precisely, of a long-lasting fight which was not free of violence. Before the struggle for democracy started, its concept was already in the minds of its intellectual architects.

Fukuyama believes that liberal democracy is the final social system. When Marx talked about communism as the final social system, he assumed that this would be a system which would eventually prevail all over the world. In Fukuyama's concept the final social system is not final, because as he himself acknowledges, liberal democracy has competitors in Asia and the Islamic world.

Liberal democracy manifests itself in the economic sphere as capitalism, as Fukuyama himself mentions. Therefore it is legitimate to call this system capitalist democracy. But this term contains a contradiction. Capitalism, understood solely as an economic system, is undemocratic in its foundations. It is a system where a large proportion of the means of production and the media are in the hands of or controlled by a small segment of the population, and this gives it disproportionate power and influence compared to its size (cf. Miliband, 1992). Needless to say, this has a negative effect on the nature of democracy.

Those who argue that the socialist system was not in tune with human nature have a point, as has already been mentioned. The architects of the socialist system suffered from the illusion that it was possible to change overnight people's conduct acquired during a long epoch, in a way that is contrary to their interests. In the beginnings of the regime a great many intellectuals, maybe even a majority in Czechoslovakia, were attracted to the system which promised to right the wrongs of the past, eliminate exploitation and manipulation and create a system of social justice and equal opportunity. They were even willing to accept some limitations on their freedom. However, in the course of time most of the intelligentsia became more and more disillusioned. This was because the governments disregarded the traditional position of the intelligentsia in society, which was also reflected in pay, and a large proportion of the intelligentsia (physicians, engineers, lawyers) was put at the level of an average skilled worker in terms of remuneration. This was contrary to the principle, which the communists themselves propagated, that the distribution of income under socialism is carried out according to work performed. The disillusionment also resulted from the circumstance that the regime, being dictatorial, could not afford to cater to the requirements of the intelligentsia to develop and thrive and to fulfil itself.

Part II

The Traditional System and the Collapse

2 The Traditional Economic Mechanism

INTRODUCTION

The socialist system of management of the economy or the economic mechanism[1] was introduced in the USSR in the 1930s. Its foundation was designed before the start of the first five-year plan, but its building blocks were finally determined on the basis of the experience gained in the process of fulfilling the plan. The organisation of industry in particular went through many changes. The socialisation of the means of production, which was at the foundation of the system, started during the civil war and was completed in the first half of the 1930s with the completion of collectivisation of agriculture. Chapter 9 discusses problems pertinent to ownership relations.

The final shape of the management system was determined by several factors. The adopted strategy of economic development, namely the decision quickly to industrialise the economy with stress on heavy industry, played a paramount role. The objectives of such a strategy could not have been achieved by market forces: these would have pushed the economy in a different direction. This strategy was greatly influenced by the security considerations of the country. O. Lange (1973, Works 2, pp. 384–5) likened the Soviet system to a war economy.

The dictatorial system introduced by Stalin also had an influence on the shape of the management system. To make the centralisation of the political power effective it seemed to be advantageous to combine it with economic centralisation.

Finally, Marxist ideology, which predicted that the communist economy would be a marketless economy, backed up the process of centralisation. This is not to say that the Soviets always followed Marxist ideology; they were quite selective.

The Soviet management system is known under different names. In the West, mainly in the 1950s and 1960s, it was known as a command economy. In Eastern Europe many called it an administrative system, centralised system. All these names were intended to indicate that

21

under that system coordination of economic activities was carried out by administrative methods instead of by the market.

Some also call the unreformed system classical or traditional. These names are intended to distinguish between the system created in the 1930s and the system which emerged as a result of major economic reforms. I will use most of the names when talking about the unreformed economic mechanism. Both the traditional and the reformed economic mechanisms are regarded as a part of the socialist economic system.

I do not intend to discuss the traditional economic mechanism in any great detail. It has been discussed in many publications,[2] so here I will only give a short survey of its structure and focus more on its shortcomings.

THE MAIN PRINCIPLES OF THE TRADITIONAL SYSTEM

In the traditional system market forces played a very limited role. Planning was the coordinating mechanism: planners, with the help of annual plans, coordinated the economic activities of enterprises, took care of the distribution of producer goods and consumer goods and concerned themselves with macro- and microequilibrium. The annual plans were to ensure price stability, full employment and proper wage differentials. All this was done by imposing compulsory plan targets and limits on enterprises. The annual plan, which was supposed to be a proper part of the five-year plan, was disaggregated through the channels of the hierarchic management to enterprises.

In order to determine microeconomic targets, the planners had first, of course, to determine macroeconomic targets for the distribution of national income between consumption and accumulation, for the distribution of consumption between personal consumption and the collective consumption fund, and for the distribution of investment between the material and non-material sphere. As a result of these targets, the rate of growth of the economy and of individual sectors was determined to a great degree.

To make sure that enterprises were able to fulfil the plan targets, the planners allocated inputs, producer goods and labour to them in terms of quantity and quality. Thus there was no market for producer goods, but there was a limited labour market in the sense that workers had the right of choice of jobs,[3] and wage differentials played a role in the distribution of labour.

To make enterprises interested in the fulfilment and overfulfilment of plan targets, which were assigned to them as compulsory tasks, money and non-money incentives were used. Money incentives were made contingent on the fulfilment of these targets. The money incentives were expressed in terms of growth of the wage bill and the size of the bonus fund. If the assigned plan targets were fulfilled the actual wage bill was equal to the planned. If they were overfulfilled, the actual wage bill was higher, depending on the adjustment coefficient.

It is only natural that in such an arrangement enterprises would try to get soft plan targets (low output targets and maximum inputs including labour) because this enabled them easily to fulfil the plan. Knowing enterprise strategy and not having reliable information about enterprise capacity, the central planners used a simple method: they increased the plan targets each year by a certain percentage. In the literature this method is known as the ratchet principle.

The planned wage bill itself was a product of the planned number of employed, taking into consideration its required structure (white- and blue-collar workers) and skill mix, and the planned average wage. Planning of both factors meant taking into account all the changes over the previous year, including, of course, changes in the size of planned targets. The authorities encouraged enterprises to overfulfil the output plan, whereas in the case of employment they did the opposite. For enterprises the easiest way to overfulfil the plan was to employ more workers. But this was contrary to the interests of the economy because it might have negatively affected productivity. In addition, all socialist countries in the course of time, one earlier, the others later, had to struggle with labour shortages. Therefore the authorities imposed limits on enterprises with regard to the number of workers they were allowed to employ.

The central planners controlled not only the wage bill but also the wage rates. These were set from above and were binding on enterprises. They changed only after long intervals. By controlling the wage rates, the planners wanted to have a second defence line against the possible drift of wages and a good control over wage differentials.

Incentives in the form of bonuses went through many changes. Initially, bonuses were given to managers for the fulfilment of the plan. Workers used to get bonuses for saving material, energy, etc. In Hungary in 1957, perhaps for the first time in a socialist country, a profit-sharing scheme was introduced: workers were given year-end rewards. The size of the fund depended first on the achieved level of profitability compared to the target, and later on the amount of profit produced. In Poland in 1957 profit became the success indicator and the source of the incentive fund (for more see Adam, 1984, pp. 127–8).

The fulfilment of plan targets was measured by so-called success indicators. When the traditional system was introduced in the USSR, many indicators were physical, i. e. metres, gallons, tons etc. The planners soon observed that they had committed a blunder, as the physical indicators worked against economic efficiency. Soon the indicators in natura were kept only where they made economic sense; otherwise value indicators were introduced, primarily gross value of output.[4]

To make sure that the demand for inputs resulting from the set targets (including exports) was in equilibrium with the supply available (including imports), the planners used a great number of material balances for important products as a significant method for working out the plan. The material balances meant balancing demand for products with the possible supply. The balancing was done on the basis of technical coefficients which describe how much of a given input is required to produce one unit of a given output.

This was a very laborious and time-consuming method of formulating the plan, particularly at a time when computer technology was not yet available or was only available to a limited degree. If an important material balance (say for coal or steel) on which other balances depended, turned out be in disequilibrium (say because the expected production at home fell short of the target, and the shortfall could not be replaced by imports) it was necessary to rework many other balances. The cumbersomeness of the working out of material balances was the main reason for enterprises getting their plan targets late, after the planning year had already started.

The more comprehensive the regulation of the economy, the greater the number of balances. For example in the mid-1980s the Soviet planners compiled 1800 product balances for the annual plan and 405 for the five-year plan. In 1988 the number of balances declined to 950 (Spulber, 1991, p. 67). The material balances showed what it was possible to produce, but did not show what it was optimal to produce.

Besides material balances the central planners also compiled manpower balances and financial balances. The former were aimed at making sure that the demand for labour, including the needed skill mix, resulting from the output plans would be in line with the possible supply. The aim of the latter was to ensure a link-up between the production, distribution and circulation of goods on the one hand, and the formation and use of incomes in all spheres of the economy on the other hand.

One of the important features of socialism was the pivotal role played by physical planning in the total planning system. Material balancing was an important component of physical planning, but not the only one. The assignment of targets in physical units, the determination of norms of labour intensity of products and technical coefficients from the centre were also a part of physical planning.

It has already been mentioned that the market mechanism was of negligible importance in the traditional system. However, market categories, such as prices and interest rates existed (wages have already been discussed) but only in a passive capacity. Prices of products were mostly planned and thus were not the result of market forces. The price system was marked by some additional socialist specialities. Prices were inflexible and individual price circuits (price subsystems) were mutually separated.

Consumer (retail) prices were planned with the intention of regulating consumption in accordance with consumer demand and planners' priorities. When they were set, their level was planned with the objective of clearing the market. Once they were set, they remained stable for a long time: changes were made only when great disparities appeared. This approach to consumer prices was dictated by the desire not to allow inflation. The planners were willing to accept shortages and line-ups at stores rather than to accept inflation.

Industrial (wholesale) prices neither allocated resources nor influenced enterprises very much in their decisions about choice of technology and inputs. Resources were allocated by the plan. Wholesale prices performed more of an accounting function; the fulfilment of the plan was measured in terms of wholesale prices. These were rigid too; they changed only after long intervals.

Agricultural procurement prices (at which collective farmers sold their products to procurement agencies) were also set by the central planners. Unlike the wholesale prices, which had no bearing on incomes, procurement prices were one of the factors which determined the incomes of collective farmers. In state enterprises the wages (without bonuses) of workers were not dependent on the performance of enterprises, but on workers' individual performance, wage rates and skill grades, whereas the incomes of collective farmers depended to a great degree on the performance of the collective farm of which they were members. Collective farms were treated as genuine cooperatives when it came to incomes and investment. Otherwise they were more or less subordinated to the planning system like the rest of the economy.

The changes in one price circuit were not necessarily reflected in another, since there was a separation of price circuits. What was especially striking was that even big changes in wholesale prices did not show up in consumer prices.[5] Instead they were reflected in changes in the turnover tax or subsidies or a combination of both. Increases in agricultural procurement prices were mostly also taken care of by subsidies.

This separation had two goals. One was to separate domestic production, non-agricultural as well as agricultural, from consumption and from the influences of world markets. The idea behind this separation was that if enterprises did not have to consider consumer demand and developments in foreign trade, they would be able to concentrate fully on output targets. It was assumed that planners had assigned targets in a way that reflected consumer demand, modified by planners' priorities and foreign trade needs. The second goal was to shield the economy from inflation which might be generated domestically or imported.

Interest rates were planned too. Their level was determined primarily by the need to have a source of funding for the operations of the central bank and its branches. For this reason they were quite low and stable. Thus the interest rate was not viewed as a price for the use of credit, and it had a negligible influence on the size of the credit extended, not to say on investment decisions. The global size of credit was determined by the central planners.

Investments were not allocated on the basis of profit expectations, but on the basis of the plan. Enterprises were obliged to surrender all the profit (minus what was left to them for bonuses) and the amortisation fund (minus sums for maintenance and minor investments) to the state budget. The planners redistributed the funds according to the plan objectives without any consideration for the performance of enterprises. This meant that enterprises which made a lot of profit might not get funds for investments whereas enterprises which suffered losses might. In practice it often happened that light industry made huge profits which, however, were used for the expansion of heavy industry. What is also important to remember is that the distribution of investment funds was very much governed by political considerations, a topic which will be discussed in Chapter 3 in greater detail.

In banking the field was absolutely dominated by a huge state (national) bank with many branches scattered all over the country. The state bank fulfilled the function of a central bank and of a credit-rationing institution. Even the bank for external financial relations, if such existed in the country, was subordinated to the state bank. Economists, who labelled the Soviet banking system as a monobanking system, were correct.

The state bank also fulfilled a very important function in the management of the economy. It was entrusted with the task of supervising the performance of enterprises. To this end enterprises were obliged to conduct all their financial operations through the bank branch in their location. In addition, they were not allowed to extend loans to each other. The bank was allowed to apply sanctions *vis-à-vis* enterprises which did not fulfil the plan and which overdrew wage funds.

The state bank extended short-term credit to state enterprises for certain purposes only. It was, however, not allowed to extend long-term credit to enterprises for investment purposes since enterprises had to content themselves with investment funds allocated to them as grants. Collective farms, which had to finance investments from their own resources, could get long-term loans.

Foreign trade was also planned. In planning, imports were the point of departure. In considering imports the idea of self-sufficiency had a great impact, therefore import substitution was often practised. Imported commodities were primarily those which could not be produced at home for lack of know-how or for other reasons, or could be produced only at very high cost and were needed for the fulfilment of the plan. Of course, imported goods were also goods which could not be produced at home for geographical reasons. For more about foreign trade see Chapter 5.

Economic efficiency was to be achieved by the planning system itself, by employing all resources, including human, and by making the plan targets assigned to enterprises as taut as possible. In addition, the *khozraschet* (accountability) principle alone – which made enterprises financially quasi autonomous units in that they were expected to arrange their activities in a way to cover costs and make a profit – was also supposed to push enterprises to promote economic efficiency. The stress in socialist countries was on macroeconomic efficiency. The planners, as in many other cases, considered the economy as a huge enterprise belonging more or less to the state, and therefore the total result was primarily of importance to them. This is not to say that microeconomic efficiency was entirely neglected. It was to be achieved by the planning of technical coefficients, norms of labour intensity of products and performance norms for piece workers, and bonuses.

Market equilibrium was to be achieved by balancing the plans for the total purchasing power (minus expected savings) with the value of the supply of consumer goods plus services. For this purpose, the global wage bill as well as total non-wage incomes were planned for each year. In order not to exceed the global wage bill, wage bills in enterprises and organisations, as well as the size of the work force, were planned. The efforts to achieve market equilibrium combined with price rigidity and separation of price circuits were the main instruments in fighting inflation.

THE EVALUATION OF THE TRADITIONAL SYSTEM

I have briefly discussed the main principles of the traditional system. To understand the working of the socialist economic system and its impact on the economy it is also important to discuss the political and social system and the economic and social policies applied during the traditional system. All this will be covered in the next chapters. In this subchapter I would like to discuss the advantages and disadvantages of the traditional economic mechanism. Since the advantages of the system can be summarised in a short paragraph, I will start with them.

The traditional system had the advantage of being able to mobilise resources for priority projects quickly, as happened in the case of industrialisation, the space programme, etc. Who knows whether the USSR would have achieved as much progress in the industrialisation effort in such a short time without its centralised system? The traditional system was arranged in such a way that open inflation could be easily held within defined limits, provided the authorities were willing to accept the costs involved. Since the traditional system was a supply-constrained system, it largely contributed to full employment.

Planning in the Traditional System

The traditional economic mechanism had its logic and was to a great extent internally consistent; nevertheless it was inefficient because it was based on unrealistic assumptions. One such an assumption was that planners know best what the possibility and the needs of the economy and consumer preferences are, and that they are able to compile a plan which reflects all this and also ensures increasing economic efficiency. It can be shown theoretically, and experience confirms it, that this is impossible. The working out of such a plan presupposes a rational price system and *a very quick, permanent flow of truthful information about the production capacity of enterprises and about demand.* The price system, which was the work of the planners and was used for various purposes – among others, for the solution of certain social tasks – could only be and really was a distorted gauge of social cost and scarcity. One could argue that modern computer technology can master the information problem. The argument might be valid if computers could also force enterprises to provide truthful information. It is obvious that computers cannot fulfil such a role and enterprises were very often not interested in revealing their capacities for reasons which will be mentioned. From the foregoing it is clear that the assumption about planning was unrealistic.

There were also other problems which made microeconomic planning ineffective. Their common denominator was the enormous number of products with which the planners had to grapple in compiling the annual plan. The numbers were overwhelming even though the plan targets were formulated in groups of products in most cases. The planners had not only to see to it that all the products or groups of products in demand were produced, but also that the inputs needed for their production were on hand. Once it was decided that enterprises should be assigned output targets, allocation of inputs was a necessary consequence under conditions of shortages. The coordination of production and allocation of inputs turned out to be a job which could not be performed to the satisfaction of producers and consumers. The desire to plan everything was one of the sources of shortages (for more see Nove, 1991, pp. 78–91).

Macroeconomic planning was not effective either. The planners were not able to formulate an optimal long-term plan which would contain structural changes corresponding to the expected changes in technology and demand. On the one hand, the theory of planning was not sufficiently developed and on the other, the formulation of macroeconomic plans was much influenced by political pressures. Commencing with the 1960s, the planners increasingly relied on trends in the development of advanced capitalist countries when compiling long-term plans. On the one hand, this was a smart approach since the advanced capitalist countries were ahead in the development of technology; on the other hand, it shed an unfavourable light on planning. The planners' approach could be interpreted as the inability of the planned economy to get ahead of market forces when it came to predicting future priorities. Needless to say, this was a good argument even against reformers who believed that long-term planning had its justification and that it was superior to spontaneous development in capitalist countries.

Insufficient Incentives

Another reason for the failure of the system was the lack of strong incentives to hard and efficient work. In the traditional system the bonuses of managers (and to a lesser extent those of employees) were dependent, as has already been mentioned, on the fulfilment of plan targets. And therefore managers were interested in receiving soft targets and maximum inputs. This was also the reason why they were often not interested in providing truthful information. The linking of the fulfilment of plan targets to bonuses had another effect besides the one mentioned: it encouraged managers to produce not what was demanded in the market, but what was important for the fulfilment of the plan. And because plan targets and market demand – as is clear from the foregoing – often did not coincide, this contributed to shortages. In addition, the mentioned linkage was also one of the main reasons for the shabby quality of goods, lack of interest in innovations and, of course, inefficiencies.

The lack of strong incentives had also to do with the ruling ideology about the more equal distribution of income which the economic policy translated into narrow wage differentials for skill. To make the economy more efficient required allowing relatively wide wage differentials but, of course, nothing like those in capitalist countries. (For more see Chapter 3.)

It has been said that the fulfilment of plan targets was measured by success indicators, usually quantitative indicators, the most important being the gross value of output. This indicator was used though there were objections to it because it lent itself easily to misuse, simply by using more expensive inputs or more inputs, but also because it included semi-finished products and subcontracting services. It is known that enterprises gladly performed services for other enterprises because they could include not only the price of the services rendered, but also a part of the material costs in the gross value of output. And in the course of time cooperation developed between enterprises which, from a macroeconomic point of view, was of little value or maybe even harmful, but it enabled enterprises easily to fulfil the plan targets by performing subcontracting services for one another. It took the authorities a long time to reduce the role of gross value of output since it had the advantage of allowing an easy aggregation of output.

The authorities tried to cope with the misuse of success indicators by enlarging their number and by thus plugging the loopholes. As a result the following logic of success indicators developed: the system could start with a few indicators and at certain periods their number could even be reduced, and after a long while their number could grow again for reasons already mentioned.[6]

Irrational Prices

From what has been said before it is clear that price relativities within individual price circuits (price subsystems) as well as among individual circuits were distorted. Without the possibility of reliable economic calculation, the planning agencies were deprived of a fundamental tool for making rational decisions about alternative uses of resources. Distorted prices hampered the making of rational choices among the alternative investment projects and the use of alternative technology, the making of decisions about what it was advantageous to produce at home and what should be imported, as well as what kind of changes to make in the structure of the economy. The distorted prices also made it difficult to use profit as an objective indicator of performance.

To overcome these difficulties Soviet mathematical economists urged the use of shadow prices, an idea which spread to East European countries. There were attempts to apply them in planning, but because of data problems not much progress was made. (For more see Nove 1980, pp. 182–4; Gregory and Stuart 1989, pp. 137–8.)

Price rigidity contributed to the rise of shortages of producer goods as well as of consumer goods. Shortages of producer goods were the most important reason for their rationing. Consumer goods were not rationed; the authorities preferred to accept queues at the stores, which were quite costly for the economy.[7] (For more, see Chapter 3.)

The separation of individual price subsystems had also contributed to shortages, in that enterprises were able to disregard demand with impunity.

Soft Budget Constraint

The *khozraschet* principle, which was intended to make enterprises self-financed, could not work for several reasons. Enterprises were not economically autonomous units which could freely make decisions about the scope of their activities and the methods of their implementation. The superior authorities determined their activities, in many cases in great detail. They had to obey the orders of the superior authorities with regard to output even if this meant losses. [8] It is clear that such conditions do not create a proper environment for self-financing.

In addition, the authorities did not usually apply sanctions against enterprises which did not perform well. Bankruptcy, which in capitalist countries is the usual fate of enterprises with persistently higher outlays than revenues, did not exist on the books of the socialist countries. The authorities usually bailed out such enterprises by giving them subsidies, making concessions with regard to taxation, allowing new credit, etc. Enterprises worked under conditions which J. Kornai (1992, pp. 142–3) calls a 'soft budget constraint'. Liquidation of non-efficient enterprises was quite rare, primarily for political reasons: the political leaders tried to avoid potential social tension.

The fact that the authorities were willing to bail out enterprises, if they found themselves in a financial bind, undermined various financial incentives and disincentives which were supposed to encourage enterprises to behave rationally.

Investment Decisions

The fact that allocation of investment funds to industrial branches and enterprises did not depend on the amount of profit produced but on the objectives of the plan meant that economic efficiency was often sacrificed in order to achieve objectives which were frequently dictated by non-economic considerations – political and state security reasons, to mention some.

The arrangement that state enterprises were not obliged to repay the allocated funds for investment purposes encouraged enterprises to seek the maximum funds possible for investment. Many high Party functionaries behaved likewise: they used their influence to obtain funds to establish new plants in their constituencies. This was one of the reasons for overinvestment. However, the economic policy of maximum economic growth was the main reason for overinvestment. The approved investment projects usually exceeded the construction capacity, and as a result they could not be finished as planned, though the lead time (the time between the planning of the project and completion) was much longer than in the West. The phenomenon of a growing number of unfinished projects was one of the ills of the traditional system, which the socialist countries did not manage, though they tried, to cure. The high number of unfinished projects had negative consequences for the economy. It caused investment cost overruns which in turn were reflected in inflationary pressures which were compounded by the frequent fact that investment funds spent on wages were not matched by supply increases in consumer goods. Due to the long lead time many projects became obsolete before they could be finished.

Technological Lag

When the communists seized power, the countries under review were much behind Western countries in technology. The same was true of the USSR. From the 1950s to the 1970s they managed to close the gap somewhat. In the 1980s the gap started to grow again. Western countries managed to respond to the challenge of big oil price increases by developing new technologies which were less energy intensive and by conservation. Neither the East European countries nor the Soviet Union managed to achieve as much success as the West. What was worse was that even the reforms of the 1980s in Poland and Hungary could not reverse the negative impact of the traditional economic mechanism on the development of technology. It seems that this was so partly because the reforms were not pervasive enough and partly because not enough time had elapsed since they were introduced.

The traditional economic mechanism did not encourage innovations for several reasons. In a system where enterprise incentives were based on the fulfilment and overfulfilment of plan targets, inventions were regarded almost as a nuisance. Before inventions could be introduced into production, they had to be tested for their suitability for the purpose assumed, and workers had to be trained for their proper use. Usually new inventions did not work flawlessly and therefore time and costs were lost. In addition, new inventions often disrupted the production process to the extent that the fulfilment of the plan targets was endangered and with it the receipt of bonuses. Very often the risk involved in the introduction of innovations was not properly rewarded. On the other hand, failing to introduce innovations was less risky. Enterprises did not have to fear that, if they remained behind in technological progress, they would be unable to sell their products.

In addition, the pricing of new products was not addressed for some time. In the beginning of a new product's life cycle its production costs are much higher than when its production mode is stabilised on the basis of experience gained. Therefore the price must be adjusted to the life cycle, or enterprises must get subsidies for the preparation of the production of new products.

For a long time most research and development institutes were centralised, subordinated to the ministries and separated from enterprises. The departure point for this arrangement was the belief that in a socialist system there was no place for commercial secrecy, and therefore measures should be taken which would stave off duplication. However, this arrangement did not work as expected. If institutes came up with a design of a new machine or a consumer gadget, it was a long time before a prototype of the product was tested, let alone produced for consumption. Had the institutes always known in advance which enterprise would be entrusted with the production of the new products, they could have adjusted the design to the needs of the enterprise, thus avoiding long delays, which made many products obsolete before their completion. The idea of centralising the institutes was also wrong, because the impetus for many innovations emerges in enterprises when they are grappling with production problems. This is not to say that once the research institutes became decentralised everything worked well.[9]

Innovators were held in public esteem; their achievements were publicised. But the pecuniary rewards were modest, and therefore innovation was not as attractive as one would expect. In addition, according to Lavigne (1991, p. 223), at least 50 per cent of the inventions 'never resulted in actual production or building of prototypes'.

The lag in technological progress was primarily in civil production, which had a much lower priority than military production. One of the reasons for this was that in the East, unlike the West where a large spin-off exists from defence innovations into civilian production, the spin-off was small because of a separation between the civilian and the military sectors (cf. Lavigne, 1991, p. 196).

According to Kornai (1992, p. 294) technical progress achieved under traditional socialism was almost exclusively the result of copying innovations carried out in developed capitalist countries. I am not sure whether Kornai's statement is entirely accurate, but there is no doubt that in the 1970s and 1980s there was a widespread notion among East Europeans that all the inventions which brought about new working conditions, life style and entertainment were the work of capitalist countries, a notion which did not endear the socialist system to the public. However, a glance at Kornai's list of technical advancements (pp. 298–300) shows that the credit he gives to the developed capitalist countries belongs in reality to the USA. Very few technical advancements listed were made by other developed capitalist countries, and these were countries which were on a much higher level of technology than the socialist countries.

What also worked against the socialist system was the fact that new inventions were not instantly available in the East and, when they appeared in the market, they were very expensive and in short supply. In as far as these were domestic substitutes, they were also often of poor quality. (For more see Chapter 8.)

Some believe that the growing gap in technology was the most important, and some believe that it was one of the most important reasons, for the collapse. Chase-Dunn for example, belongs to the first group: in his article (1992) he takes the position that the collapse was because 'party cadres no longer believed that catching up with the West in high technology sectors was possible'. The view of a leading member of the CP politburo of one of the countries under review belongs to the second group. He insisted, in a consultation I had with him, that the collapse of socialism was due to three factors: huge military expenses, the gap in technology, and excessive support of developing countries. I am inclined to agree with the second view in the sense that the gap in technology was only one of the most important factors, since I believe that political factors were more important or at least as important as economic.

Foreign Trade

The fact that production enterprises were not allowed to enter into trade relations with foreign firms and that this activity was left to special state enterprises, foreign trade corporations, and that domestic prices were separated from world market prices, had negative effects on the economy. All this will be discussed in Chapter 5.

Monopolisation

Production enterprises in their capacity as suppliers had a strong monopolistic position which negatively affected the working of the economy. There were several factors which brought about monopolisation and most of them were of a systemic nature.

Setting horizontal ties from above was one of the most important factors. Enterprises were not free to buy their material inputs from enterprises of their choice. Suppliers were determined from above. Their position was considerably strengthened by the industrial concentration trend which started in the late 1950s in Czechoslovakia and continued in the 1960s in the other two countries under review. This arrangement, combined with shortages, brought about a sellers' market.

Consumers were free to shop for consumer goods wherever they liked. This was not the case for retailers. They were hampered in their choice of suppliers.

Another important factor was the state monopoly of foreign trade. Production enterprises could import inputs only with the approval of the branch ministry and the foreign trade ministry. The branch ministry usually approved imports of inputs only if they could not be produced at home or if they could be produced at home but with very high costs. All the socialist countries pursued a policy of autarky, and to this end they often resorted to import substitution.

Suppliers could not use their monopolistic position in the classical way, by dictating prices. These were determined by the authorities. Even in cases where enterprises were allowed to set prices for new products, they were under the control of the authorities. They could, however, use their monopoly position to impose low-quality goods on enterprises and consumers.[10]

Cyclical Development

The socialist ideology promised an even development of the economy without the known business cycles of the capitalist economy. A glance at the statistics of economic development shows that the economies of socialist countries were also exposed to fluctuations in economic growth. This was much less true about the Soviet Union than of the countries under review. The fluctuations in socialist countries did not have the same effect as in capitalist countries, and also the method used to cope with these fluctuations was different. The decline in economic activity did not produce increases in unemployment as is the usual case in capitalist countries. Enterprises were not under pressure to adjust their workforce to the amount of economic activity. In any case, there was overemployment in many enterprises, and some increase in overemployment did not bother managers very much, all the more because it was expected that the reduction in economic activity would be temporary.

This is not to say that fluctuations did not have a negative impact on the economy. Of course they had. At the peak of the cycle, when economic growth was the highest, shortages were the most severe. Since, in such a situation, investment projects for heavy industry, as already mentioned, were given priority over those for light industry and the food industry, inflationary pressures could not be avoided. Furthermore, other negative phenomena resulted from the over-investment, as discussed above (see p. 32 of this chapter).

The reasons for fluctuations in economic growth did not become a research topic until the 1960s. It would exceed the scope of this book to discuss in any detail the theories of fluctuations, and therefore i will touch on them only very briefly.[11] Perhaps J. Goldmann, a Czechoslovak economist (1964 and 1964a), was the first to come up with a plausible explanation of what he called a quasi-cycle. According to him, the fluctuations were the result of an economic growth rate beyond what was regarded as optimum in the existing conditions. Such a fast economic growth drive brought about a raw material barrier, namely, the production of the extracting and basic material industries lagged behind that of manufacturing industries. The only remedy for such disproportions was a reduction in economic growth. This, combined with newly completed output facilities, stemming from investments in the previous period, mitigated disproportions. Once the government started a new drive for high growth rates in excess of the optimum level, a cycle was in place again. Goldmann used the term quasi-cycle in order to distinguish the fluctuations in Eastern Europe from those in the West. According to him fluctuations in the West are a necessary product of the working of the capitalist system, whereas in socialism they were the result of a lack of knowledge of socialist laws and shortcomings in their application in planning (1964).

If one accepts Goldmann's explanation, one must draw the conclusion that socialist countries did not internalise the knowledge needed to stave off fluctuations in the economy. One can also argue, and this, in my opinion, is closer to the truth, that the socialist countries stuck to their policies of ambitious economic growth for a long time, disregarding its negative effects, and thus created conditions for fluctuations in economic growth. Needless to say, such policies were the result of the industrialisation drive.

CONCLUDING REMARKS

In sum the traditional system was marked by many shortcomings which turned it into an inefficient system, doomed to fail sooner or later. It was a system which hampered innovations and lacked strong incentives to make workers do hard and quality work, and therefore the goods produced under such a system were on the average of low quality, definitely much lower than in the West, and contributed to shortages. As will be shown in Chapter 8, this system could not ensure a growing standard of living, once the factors of extensive growth had been exhausted. In other words the traditional system, after its political and economic consolidation, worked well, but not well enough to survive long in competition with the West (cf. Berliner, 1992). Needless to say, the traditional system needed an overhaul, if the socialist system was to survive.

Despite the shortcomings of the traditional system, the economies of the countries under review would have been much better off had the system not been combined with an economic policy and with improper labour–management relations which compounded the shortcomings of the system. These are discussed in Chapters 3 and 4.

3 Economic Policy

INTRODUCTION

To understand the collapse of the socialist system, it is not enough to discuss the systemic reasons for its failure; it is also necessary to shed light on the economic policy followed by the CPs. In the literature, the two terms, systemic and economic policy reasons or changes, are sometimes mixed up. Considering the very thin line dividing them and the fact that in some cases the two coalesce, it is no wonder that it is often difficult to distinguish between them. This is so because both were the work of the communist leaders: systemic changes – on a general level – were changes aimed at altering the institutional framework within which economic units as well as the authorities were to work – it could be said that they were economic policy changes on a more general level – whereas economic policy changes were usually, or more precisely should be, changes within the institutional framework and as such could be called economic policy changes in the narrow sense. When talking about economic policy in my book, I always have that policy in the narrow sense in mind.

As already mentioned, it is generally accepted that the economic mechanism was shaped by the industrialisation drive – started first in the Soviet Union and later imposed on East European countries by the USSR – and was meant to serve it. This, of course, does not mean that only one kind of direction and pace of industrialisation or, more generally, development was possible. In the framework of the same economic mechanism, it could have been possible to accommodate quite different options with regard to the direction and pace of development, depending on government priorities or, in other words, on economic policy.

The same is true of social policy, understood very broadly to comprise the right to a job, quite an egalitarian distribution of income, stable and low prices for basic foods, services and shelter, and last but not least social security. In practice the right to a job meant job security: if a worker did not grossly violate the labour code, he did not have to fear losing his job, and if something went wrong he could easily find a new job. All this was true of Czechoslovakia and of the other

39

two countries after 1956. Workers enjoyed a great deal of certainty about the evolution of their real incomes, particularly in Czechoslovakia, and they were also sure that, once they reached the retirement age, a pension would be available. They enjoyed an economic security – to use the term Hewett (1988, p. 39) used for the Soviet Union in a similar case – unparalleled in capitalist countries.

As has already been shown, consumer prices were burdened with a turnover tax. Most services were not subject to this tax. This was an economic policy decision which had nothing to do with the economic mechanism. Had services been exposed to such a tax, the economic mechanism would not have been affected. On the other hand, the application of the tax would probably have had a favourable effect on the expansion of services.

Let me mention another example, which may shed even more light on the difference between the economic mechanism and economic policy. In the traditional system, the authorities allocated a planned wage bill to enterprises. The actual wage bill depended on the fulfilment of plan targets. This arrangement was a systemic one. However, the increase in the wage bill for the overfulfilment of plan targets could be of varying size. And really, the adjustment coefficient changed several times during the existence of the traditional system. This was a matter of economic policy.

There is a tendency to blame the system for all the shortcomings in the working of the economy regardless of their nature. However, if we accept the thesis, which in my opinion is obvious, that, within the same economic mechanism, different economic policies can be followed, then it is important to distinguish between the responsibility of the two factors in the collapse of the socialist system.

Further on in the text I would like to discuss several economic policies which contributed to the dismal performance of the economy, and in the final analysis, to the collapse of the socialist system. I will start with industrialisation policy and then discuss the social policy, understood very broadly. While it is generally accepted that social security has a place in every progressive and humane society, the other three components of the social welfare policy (the right to a job, egalitarian distribution of income and low prices), which were characteristic of the socialist system without being a necessary component of the economic mechanism, can be questioned, mainly the way they were instituted. The economic policies discussed in this chapter were introduced during the traditional system and did not change substantially as a result of economic reforms.

INDUSTRIALISATION POLICY

All three countries, the least Czechoslovakia, needed industrialisation in order to be able to modernise their economy and to improve the well-being of their population. However, the way the industrialisation policy was applied contributed greatly to the failure of the traditional economic mechanism, in that it caused significant shortages and hampered the structural changes needed to satisfy changing demand at home and abroad and to keep up with the technological changes abroad. The industrialisation drive is to blame for the neglect of light industry, infrastructure and services, as well as some important social programmes.

To accelerate industrialisation political and economic leaders pushed for high economic growth rates for a very long time, often regardless of the possibilities of the economy. In their push, stress was placed on the rapid development of heavy industry and the armament industry (henceforth heavy industry is to be understood to include the armament industry), a policy largely motivated by security needs, as they were understood by Stalin and his successors. This policy was backed up ideologically by the so-called law of preferential development of the production of producer goods. According to this law economic growth, in a nutshell, is conditioned by the faster growth of production of producer goods than of consumer goods. This law, which was given the status of a dogma which it was not advisable to question, became an obstacle to balanced economic development. Calls for changes in the structure of the economy in favour of consumer goods industries were muzzled by alluding to the law.[1] Even when scientists started to question timidly the general validity of the law – no doubt, production of producer goods must grow faster than production of consumer goods in some periods – the politicians still stuck to it.

In the course of time, the rapidly growing heavy industry created its own powerful pressure group, whose interests became inseparably intertwined with the survival of heavy industry in a privileged position in the structure of the economy. The power of this group resulted from two factors. It had the support of the workers in heavy industry, a segment of the work force which was regarded as the mainstay of the regime and which shared in the privileges of heavy industry in the form of higher wages, and of the military establishment. In addition, many leaders of the Party came from this sector of the economy and were understandably well disposed to the interests of this group.

It seems that Polish economists, primarily C. Józefiak (1981 and 1984) and A. Lipowski (1986 and 1988), devoted more attention to the pressure groups than economists from the other countries did. Perhaps this was because pressure groups were more powerful in Poland than in other countries. Both authors stressed that the heavy industry pressure group was responsible for the fact that the distribution of investment funds was much influenced by political considerations, and this was necessarily at the expense of objective criteria. According to Lipowski (1986) the pressure groups devalued planning so much that, in the 1970s, planning was of a purely ceremonial nature.

Needless to say, this heavy-industry pressure group was the natural protector of the traditional system in opposing changes in the economic mechanism, mainly those which were related to the market mechanism, for fear that those changes might affect heavy industry unfavourably, and thus the pressure group hampered needed changes in the structure of the economy. It also influenced the distribution of investment funds in favour of heavy industry.

This policy of the fast development of heavy industry led necessarily to high investment ratios. Not only this, but whenever the overheated economy could not handle all investment projects, and this was quite often, heavy industry was little affected, since it got priority in raw materials, machinery and manpower. The preferential treatment of heavy industry at the expense of other industries, including light industry, meant that wages were paid without being matched with a proper flow of consumer goods.

The preferential treatment of heavy industry was also co-responsible for the high material intensity of products and discouraged attempts to find ways to reduce it.

The rapid development of heavy industry, as already mentioned, was also motivated by the arms race with the USA. This race imposed, not only on the former USSR but also on East European countries, a great economic burden in the form of high military expenditures, relatively higher than in the USA, since the USA had a much higher GNP per capita than the Soviets or East Europeans had. There are still no reliable figures on real military expenditures over the period, but it is, no doubt, clear that they swallowed up a high percentage of the GNP[2] and they were made at the cost of other outlays which were important for the standard of living. In addition, the arms race drained the most talented, bright and innovative professionals from the civilian economy. Needless to say, the results of this policy also reduced the effectiveness of the centralised system in that incentives were weakened.

When Reagan came to power in the USA, the arms race intensified. The American president calculated that an increased arms race would economically exhaust the Soviet Union and its East European allies. To cope with this threat the Soviet Union exerted pressure on East European countries to contribute to the intensified arms race in the form of increases in the military budget. In the 1980s the Soviet pressure was no longer as effective as in the past. First, the Soviet grip on East European countries weakened to some extent because of the worsening economic performance of the Soviet Union itself. Second, the countries learned how effectively to resist Soviet demands. A high Hungarian functionary, who must have known about his country's contribution to the arms race, told me that the usual tactic was to promise and then not fulfil. Even so, Hungary's military expenditures were quite high, around 8 per cent. Probably Czechoslovakia and Poland contributed a similar sum.

No wonder that some economists in the past saw the cure for the dismal working of the socialist economy primarily in changes in the economic policy. For example, in Poland, M. Kalecki, the renowned economist, took such a position (see Kowalik, 1987). It seems that his book on economic growth (1963), in which he showed the merits of balanced growth and how it could be achieved, was meant as an argument against obsession with economic growth and as back-up to his views on the role of economic policy.

EMPLOYMENT POLICY

The employment policy that was pursued contributed on the one hand to full employment, but on the other it had a negative impact on economic efficiency and incentives. It also contributed to labour shortages. The reasons for this development will be examined on two levels: first, on a very general level and later, on a microlevel.

With the start of the first five-year plan the Soviet Union followed a policy of employment maximisation which had two objectives: to maximise output as an integral part of the industrialisation drive and to bring about full employment. The stress was on the first objective, but by pursuing it the second was also achieved in the course of time. This employment policy was later embraced by East European countries.

The industrialisation drive brought about a massive influx of workers to industry. Most of them came from agriculture. The liquidation of small-scale businesses, which was an integral part of the liquidation process of the private sector, also provided an important source of labour. Finally, housewives increasingly became an important component of the growing supply of labour. Many of the newly employed could not be instantly put to their most productive use, because they had to be trained even for the simplest work and because the rapid influx of workers created tremendous organisational problems connected with placement in suitable jobs. Apart from the short period in Hungary and Poland – 1956 – when both countries suffered from unemployment, the number of economically active people grew rapidly. In the 1970s, all potential labour was more or less absorbed into the labour force[3] and after some time labour shortages started to be felt. The first country which experienced labour shortages was Czechoslovakia.

In his 1983 work J. Kornai expresses the view that full employment in the traditional economy was not the result of 'specific economic policy measures' but of institutional conditions. 'It is the consequence of the soft budget constraint that demand for resources grows almost insatiably. Demand for resources, including demand for labour, necessarily has to grow as long as it does not hit the supply constraint.' To him labour shortage is 'one of the manifestations of resource shortage' (p. 29). In his 1992 book he repeats that full employment was not the result of conscious economic policy. To him it is 'a by-product or side-effect of the process of forced growth'. In the next paragraph he no longer insists that full employment is entirely the result of institutional conditions. Full employment is not only ensured 'by the principles and practical conventions of employment policy but by the operating mechanism of the classical system, above all the chronic, recurrent shortage of labor' (p. 210).

By forced growth J. Kornai apparently means growth resulting from the industrialisation drive. In my opinion the industrialisation drive played a paramount role in bringing about full employment and, at a certain stage, the development of labour shortages. But to me the industrialisation strategy which was applied, combined with ambitious growth, was the result of economic policy. I have already mentioned above that within the traditional system a different strategy of economic development could have been pursued. It is possible to imagine a strategy which followed a more balanced growth with less ambitious economic growth rates. After all, the growth drive after a while created disequilibria in the economy and, in order to eliminate them, the authorities had to slow down the expansion of the economy. The fluctuations in economic growth which East European countries experienced were the result of this policy of maximum growth (see Goldmann, 1964 and 1964a; Bajt, 1971). Thus the decision to introduce industrialisation with great stress on heavy industry and to pursue maximum economic growth was an economic policy decision and was motivated to a great degree by security considerations.

In addition, without conscious economic policy measures the economies of some countries in certain periods would have had to grapple with unemployment (cf. Granick 1987, p. 69).

The industrialisation strategy had not only an impact on economic policy measures, but also on systemic arrangements, some of wich furthered employment increases and contributed at a certain stage of development to labour shortages. Thus the labour shortages that arose were the result of systemic factors and economic policy, besides the demographic factors, which also played a certain role. In my 1984 book I discussed this problem in great detail. Therefore I will only summarise it here.

Demographic factors were important, mainly in Czechoslovakia and Hungary. In the second half of the 1970s in both countries there was a reversal in the growth of the working-age population (see Chapter 8).

Hoarding of labour by enterprises was perhaps the most powerful factor in bringing about labour shortages. There were several motivations for such behaviour. One was the reaction to the ratchet principle, i.e., to the authorities' tactics in setting plan targets for enterprises. Since not having reliable information about enterprise capacity, the central planners used a simple method: they increased plan targets each year (see Chapter 2). The reaction of enterprises lay in accumulating reserves, including labour, in order to be able to cope with the authorities' taut plans.

In my opinion the institution of taut plans was, on the one hand, of a systemic nature, and on the other hand, a tool of economic policy. It was of a systemic nature when it was used as a tool to counter enterprise interest in soft plans in order to be able not only to fulfil but also to overfulfil assigned plan targets. It was a tool of economic policy when it was to serve the drive for maximum economic growth and thus the industrialisation drive.

The linking of the growth of the wage bill to the fulfilment and overfulfilment of the output target was also often an incentive to hoard labour. Even if the adjustment coefficient was lower than unity, it was often advantageous to overfulfil[4] the output target. Often the availability of labour reserves was decisive as to whether the overfulfilment was possible; hence, a tendency to hoard labour.

The uneven spread of the work load during the year, which was a frequent phenomenon in the traditional system for various reasons, one being the late completion of annual plans, was another reason for hoarding. Enterprises usually tried to fulfil the plan by 'storming' at the end of each month and at the end of the year. Such a work rhythm encouraged enterprises to keep a workforce fairly close to the needs of the period of peak activities.

The assignment of employment limits, which amounts to labour rationing, encouraged labour hoarding too. Enterprises reacted to it as consumers do to the rationing of consumer goods.

Up to now I have mentioned several reasons, predominately systemic, for labour hoarding and thus for labour shortages. The next to be discussed will be the reasons for labour hoarding and labour shortages which were primarily the result of economic policy. One such reason was that, whenever the government set a ceiling for average wage growth, enterprises tried to hire workers who could be paid below average wages in order to have a fund for wage increases for skilled workers. Such hoarding occurred even in Hungary after the introduction of the 1968 economic reform. Another motive was the government policy of obliging enterprises to make available 'brigades', mainly for helping agriculture.

Labour shortages also had their origin in the fact that labour was not fully utilised. All three countries suffered from huge losses in the potential work-time fund. Some estimated the losses in the range of 20–30 per cent. These great losses were caused by deficiencies in planning, in the organisation of the production process, lack of discipline in the workplace and absenteeism. In the next chapter I will try to explain why the authorities were not able to cope with these great losses.

Thus labour shortages were combined with gross underutilisation of the labour force. Labour shortages were felt primarily in services, but also in other sectors of the economy. In Czechoslovakia, for example, new industrial enterprises had difficulty recruiting the necessary workforce, whereas at the same time Czechoslovakia had many obsolete enterprises which employed a large number of workers. True, the planners designed plans for shutting down obsolete enterprises though, compared to what was economically needed, their number was modest, but even this did not materialise. For political reasons they did not want to push the scheduled closure of enterprises too hard. Also lack of proper housing hampered the mobility of workers from one place to another.

In my opinion, labour shortages could have been entirely removed or at least substantially eased had the governments embarked on a fast mechanisation of auxiliary jobs. All three countries had a huge number of people employed in auxiliary jobs, such as in the transport of materials and products within enterprises, and the sorting and shelving of goods. Greater mechanisation, mainly in the handling of materials, could have released large numbers of workers, some of whom could have been used in services where labour shortages were the greatest.[5] The politicians surely knew about such a possibility, but did not have the courage to carry it out. Such an action would have required a shift of investment from other sectors, even from heavy industry, an action which might have been resisted by the heavy industry lobby. What was no less important, an expansion of services would require more subsidies, unless the government was willing to increase prices.

A more reasonable employment policy could have eliminated labour shortages, maintained full employment and brought about a better satisfaction of consumer demand.

Full employment was one of the promises of the socialist programme. Unlike capitalism, socialism committed itself to making the right to a job one of the principal rights and it was incorporated in the constitution of the European socialist countries. This did not happen until employment achieved a level which could be characterised as full employment. Full employment had its advantages but also many disadvantages due to the way it was achieved and maintained. In my opinion, the right to a job should be regarded as one of the elements of human rights because unemployed people are not really fully-fledged citizens. In addition, unemployment is costly to society. It means a loss of output and taxes, increased state expenditures and, on top of this, social and psychological costs which cannot be quantified.

In the socialist countries full employment also had its costs. Combined with labour shortages it became a source of underutilisation of labour, lack of discipline in the workplace and an impediment to the restructuring of the economy.

WAGE POLICY

This subchapter can be started with the statement that socialist countries followed a policy of low wages in relation to per capita national income. This is not to say that this was a deliberate policy; it was rather a result of other policies. One of them was the industrialisation policy combined with the arms race. The industrialisation policy generated an obsession with economic growth, reflected in increasing investment ratios which were to a great degree at the expense of consumption. On top of this, a quite significant proportion of government expenditures was earmarked for the military, which also burdened consumption.

A further reason for low wages was the policy of employment maximisation. This, combined for a long time with rigid job security and the workers' inability to quit jobs according to their choice, undermined labour discipline, hampered labour mobility in accordance with the needs of the economy and thus contributed to the low level of productivity.

The policy of low wages was not only affected by employment policy; it also had an effect on employment. It contributed to an expansion of employment, mainly of women. Many women, who would have preferred not to take a job in order to devote themselves fully to their child or children, were forced to take jobs in order to supplement their family budget.

The policy of low wages which helped the authorities to achieve their goal of mobilising women into jobs turned out to be a two-edged sword. It not only encouraged women to take jobs, but it also exerted pressure on the authorities to create jobs for social reasons.

The policy of low wages had an effect on wage differentials, mainly skill differentials. It is understandable that, if the average level of wages is low and the governments want to improve the well-being of the poorest segments of the population, as was the case in the three countries, wage differentials for skills cannot be very wide. In addition, one of the articles of socialist ideology was a more equal distribution of income. Therefore it could be expected that once communists seized power, there would be a tendency to narrow wage differentials, as the Soviet CP did in the 1920s and after Stalin's death.

In the 1930s Stalin ignored the idea of a more equal distribution of income.[6] He introduced a system of wide wage differentials which favoured in the first place the protectors and defenders of the Stalinist system: state security institutions, the officers of the army and propagandists. With Khruschev's coming to power, this trend was reversed. Khrushchev's successors continued this policy of narrowing wage differentials. This policy was again reversed under Gorbachev (Flakierski, 1993).

After the CPs in East European countries seized power, they embraced the policy of narrow wage differentials, mainly in

Czechoslovakia. (It should be mentioned that World War II and its aftermath had already brought about quite a narrowing of wage differentials compared to the pre-war situation.) Besides ideological reasons there were also political reasons for this. The countries were confronted with the problem of how to distribute the growing industrialisation costs and the armament burden. It was clear that agriculture alone could not foot the bill. To distribute the costs evenly, thus affecting badly paid income groups and blue-collar workers, would have hurt CPs politically. Therefore they tried to solve the problem primarily at the expense of white-collar workers and better-paid groups.

In Czechoslovakia in the period 1948–53 there was a dramatic change in the level of average wages between the material and non-material spheres, due largely to a dramatic change in the income differentials between white- and blue-collar workers. According to Hron (1968) average wages in education and culture in 1948 were 24.7 per cent higher than in the national economy, and in health and welfare the difference was 20.8 percent. In 1953, average wages in education and culture were 11.1 per cent lower and in health and welfare 12.4 per cent lower than in the economy as a whole. A similar change occurred in industry between engineering and technical personnel on the one hand, and manual workers on the other. In 1948, the average wages of the former were 65 per cent higher than those of the latter; in 1953 the figure was 32 per cent (for more, see Adam, 1984).

The situation in Poland was similar. Kalecki's analysis (1964, pp. 91–101) shows that real incomes of manual workers increased in the period 1930–60 by 75 per cent, whereas those of non-manual workers declined by 26 per cent in the same period. It can be assumed that the dramatic change occurred mostly in the period after the seizure of power by the communists.[7]

After 1955 there was a small improvement in wage differentials for skill, but it did not last long. The same was true of Czechoslovakia and Hungary during the economic reforms in the 1960s, but afterwards the narrowing continued. Needless to say, it had negative consequences for hard work, inventiveness and initiative, as well as for the socialist system.

Even in the traditional system the politicians promised to remedy the situation, but not much happened. Blue-collar workers were against changes in wage differentials, and the politicians were afraid to challenge them. There were also practical impediments to a challenge. In profit-making enterprises the actual wage bill was dependent on the fulfilment of plan targets, and the wages of most blue-collar workers were paid on the basis of piece work. This arrangement gave enterprises some flexibility with regard to remuneration and gave workers the possibility of exerting pressure for wage increases. Budget-financed organisations, which comprised mostly white-collar workers, did not have such an advantage. There, the actual wage bill could increase only with the explicit approval of the authorities. To some degree this was also true about the salaries of white-collar workers in profit-making enterprises. Their salaries were determined from above and could be manipulated by reclassification of white collar workers into higher skill groups. But there were narrow limits to such manoeuvring (for more, see Adam, 1984).

As a result of such a policy, even in the 1980s engineers with a university education, not in a managerial position, and junior physicians received wages at the level of average skilled workers. Such narrow wage differentials not only had a negative impact on the economy, but also weakened the position of the CPs. The intelligentsia saw the narrow differentials as evidence of an undervaluation of, and disrespect for, their work and they resented them. On top of this, there was the *nomenclature,* an institution which excluded talented people from positions of responsibility, simply for political reasons. No doubt, wage dispersion policy was one of the factors which contributed to the collapse of the socialist system.

CONSUMER PRICE POLICY

In the previous chapter, the price system was subjected to criticism from a systemic viewpoint. The criticism was directed, *inter alia,* against the rigid stability of consumer prices which was intended as an anti-inflationary provision.The consumer price policy, which turned consumer prices into an instrument of social policy, merits criticism too. Using consumer prices for social purposes was not a necessary component of the rigid price stability. The rigid price system would not have been affected if price relations had been neutral to social problems.

The social function of consumer prices was primarily implemented through the distribution of the turnover tax. One of the principles of distribution was that the resulting consumer prices must benefit low-income groups per capita and thus mitigate the differences arising from employment incomes and the number of children. To this end, lower tax rates were set on the consumer goods which played an important role in the family budget of lower-income groups per capita, primarily important foodstuffs such as bread, milk and meat, but also on utilities.[8] Low tax rates were applied to products important for the promotion of education, culture and propaganda, such as books, admissions to cultural events, etc. On the other hand, goods which were regarded as non-essential were taxed heavily. Especially high tax rates were imposed on tobacco products and alcohol.

As in other policy issues, here too the Soviet practice was imitated. In the Soviet Union, prices of clothing (with the exception of children's clothing) and footwear were on the average burdened by turnover taxes much above average, the reason being a shortage of light industry capacity. East European countries took over this pricing policy, though they were in a different situation from the Soviet Union. It seems that the high taxation on clothing and footwear was also motivated by the desire to levy a higher tax on the agricultural population (Nagy, 1960, p. 60).[9]

Prices of services, with some exceptions, did not contain the turnover tax at all. Rents were set at a level much below depreciation and maintenance costs.

The policy described hurt the economy and turned out to be an impediment to its restructuring. Low prices for foodstuffs (e.g., meat) became one of the reasons for shortages and, in other cases (e.g., bread), for waste.[10] The rigid price stability of many foodstuffs, at a time when agricultural procurement prices were rising in order to ensure higher incomes for collective farmers, led to a gradual decline in the turnover tax rates and finally to negative rates, namely subsidies, which made it difficult to maintain budget equilibrium. Not only this, but low prices for foodstuffs (e.g. meat) benefited higher-income groups in some cases more than the low ones for which they were intended.[11] Low-income groups per capita would have been better served if subsidised prices had been limited to a small number of staples, and pensioners and families with several children, who mostly belong to low per-capita income groups, would have received higher pensions and family allowances, respectively.

Distorted consumer prices led to a distorted structure of consumption; to a bigger consumption of some foodstuffs than would have taken place with rational prices at the existing incomes. An example in point was the high consumption of meat per capita in Poland. In the 1970s the Polish consumption of meat was not much behind that of

West Germany but, in terms of national income per capita, the lag was huge. In addition, the high consumption of meat caused Poland economic problems: it hurt its exports and Poland was forced to import more fodder.

A rational price system would have increased the demand for clothing and footwear and durables at the expense of foodstuffs, including meat. Such a change in structure would have had the advantage that the expansion of production of non-foodstuffs could have probably been combined with higher productivity.

Low prices for some services became an obstacle to the expansion of services since this would have required greater subsidies.

The consumer price policy, which was one of the reasons for the existing distorted price system, was at the same time an obstacle to a major economic reform, in which the market should have played an important role. In order for the market to have even a limited coordinating function rational prices are needed. However, a restructuring of consumer prices encountered political obstacles since it would probably have affected more low-income groups per capita.

SOCIAL SECURITY POLICY

When talking about the advantages of the socialist system communist leaders usually put social security and full employment in first place. Social security was a comprehensive programme which took care of most social problems. It was supposed to take care of the under-privileged, the sick and the aged. With some exaggeration it can be said that the social security programmes took care of people from the cradle to the grave. It should, however, be stressed right away that mostly the programmes were not carried out in the manner they were promised: some components of the programmes were implemented in a way that was contrary to the principles declared, and others could not be developed as promised because of insufficient funding, often due to the low priority attached to them.

Without going into great detail, the social benefits from the social security system could be divided into two groups: transfer payments (pensions, sickness benefits, family allowances, etc.) and services (such as hospital services, rest homes). Transfer payments were linked to employment incomes, whereas services depended on needs.

Old-age Pensions

The communist governments transformed the already existing splintered pension system into a uniform and comprehensive system, which in the course of time covered all the population. Collective farmers were included in the pension scheme later than state and enterprise employees, and it was several years before they were put on the same footing as employees. The pension system was based on the principle of universality and transferability. Everyone who was engaged in a legal economic activity (with the exception of house work) was entitled to a full pension after reaching the number of service years required for eligibility and the retirement age. In Czechoslovakia and Hungary the retirement age for men was set relatively low, 60 years, whereas in Poland it was 65. Women had a lower retirement age; it also depended on the number of children that they had had.

In Poland and Hungary pensions depended on employment income. In Czechoslovakia the pension also depended on the work category in which one was active before retirement. There were three work categories based on working conditions and the risk to health and life. In the third category, where the maximum pension was the highest, miners, some workers in iron foundries, pilots and some other professionals who worked in similar difficult conditions, were included. Most of the intelligentsia was in the first category, where the maximum pensions were the lowest (Adam, 1991, p. 8).

One could argue that the classification according to working conditions was justifiable. But most of the intelligentsia did not think so; they saw it as a further proof of disrespect for their contribution to the performance of the economy and as a reflection of the wage dispersion policy which they resented.

The resentment was all the greater because this rule did not pertain to high CP and government officials nor to important CP activists. Higher pensions for the CP and government elite were given in all three countries.

Due to labour shortages pensioners were allowed to continue working, usually part-time, in some cases full-time, and to collect pensions. The pensioners were used as a reserve workforce: when their services were needed they were used and, if not, their employment involvement was limited. Usually manual-worker retirees had better conditions for employment, since the demand for their services was bigger.

Health Care

All three countries introduced universal and free health care which was financed from government expenditures. Of course, the funds needed to finance health care were taken from the tax on wages and profits, and were available from paying lower wages to employees. Where the wage tax was later abolished, as in Hungary and Poland, the missing funds had to be compensated by smaller increases in wages or increases in prices.

The free health care provided was comprehensive: it included medical treatment, hospital services, dental, prenatal, preventive and emergency care, medication (with some limitations), sanatoria, and stays at health spas, etc.

The introduction of a free health-care system was a noble idea; it gave primarily low-income groups, who in the past had limited access to health care, a feeling of security. It also contributed to the narrowing of differences in the standard of living because in no other field were the differences between the haves and have nots as small as in health care.

Health-care delivery was to be based on need, and for this reason there was supposed to be equal access to health services for all the needy. In practice the principle of equal access was violated by the authorities in two respects. First, the elite had special clinics and hospitals which were equipped with more up-to-date technology and which had access to foreign medication. What was worse was that the poor remuneration of physicians and nurses generated a corruption system in the course of time: health-care providers expected in addition to their salaries tips from their patients for their services.[12] The quality of services depended to a great degree on the amount of tips.

The significance and appreciation of free health care was also devalued to a great extent by the poor funding of health care which was reflected in a neglect of modern medical technology; in the distribution of state expenditures, health care was low on the list.

HOUSING POLICY

If the question is posed about the extent to which housing policy contributed to the collapse of the socialist system, the answer would be that it was a mixed bag with strong negative effects. On the one hand, the communist leaders made sure that the cost of shelter to its users was small, in some cases ridiculously small. This helped low-income groups per capita. On the other hand, construction of housing, mainly in the beginning of communist rule, did not receive the proper priority it deserved.

Setting the rent at a level which was below the depreciation and maintenance costs, combined with the policy – which was followed up to the middle of the 1950s – that construction of housing in urban areas was the exclusive responsibility of the government, created a disincentive for housing construction. The more housing units were constructed, the more state subsidies were needed. Since governments' priority was the expansion of heavy industry, little funds were available for constructing dwellings.

After seizing political power, the communist rulers nationalised (municipalised) apartment houses and tried to solve the housing shortage by redistributing the existing living space according to strict norms. In Hungary, moving the exponents of the old regime from large cities, mainly Budapest, was also motivated by the desire to mitigate the housing shortage.[13]

In the middle of the 1950s, when the housing situation took on a critical dimension and the political situation was tense, the authorities decided to give a great role to cooperative housing and also to private housing in rural areas as a way to accelerate housing construction and to alleviate government financial involvement. For completeness it is important to say that, mainly in Czechoslovakia, cooperative housing was supported by loans at low interest rates and state subsidies. In most cases cooperatives also received land for a nominal price or without charge. Private housing was also supported by the authorities.

With the expansion of cooperative and private housing the role of state housing was reduced substantially. It was to be earmarked for low-income groups and for people who, due to their position, were entitled to a service dwelling.

In spite of all these measures, housing shortages were not eliminated and affected negatively the family lives of those who could not find adequate apartments. In addition, due to various forms of housing construction and financing, housing was available to different people under varied conditions. All who had state apartments enjoyed low rents; this privilege was available not only to low-income groups, but also to many high-income earners. On the other hand, living in cooperative dwellings was much more expensive.

CONCLUDING REMARKS

Two topics have been discussed in this chapter: the industrialisation policy and the social welfare policy (after all, social security policy combined with the consumer price and full employment policy and also wage and housing policy could be labelled as welfare policy). The two had in common that the guiding principles for their implementation were determined by economic policy. As has already been stressed above, *this economic policy was not a necessary result of the economic mechanism; it could have been possible to apply a different economic policy to a great extent without affecting the working of the economic mechanism.* In addition, a better economic policy could have reduced the threat to the regime immensely.

The industrialisation policy could have been a blessing, but the way the policy makers implemented it, namely the excessive stress they put on fast development of heavy industry combined with maximum economic growth, turned out to be a very negative factor. The industrialisation policy led to a neglect of the infrastructure, services and the light and foodprocessing industries, and hampered a restructuring of the economy in accordance with domestic demand and the possibilities of exports. It also affected negatively progress in technology and the well-being of the population.

The socialist ideas of equality, social justice and solidarity with the weak, underprivileged and aged, and the promise of an economy of full employment without cyclical development, had a tremendous power of attraction after the war, mainly in Czechoslovakia. Even in Poland and Hungary, where strong anti-Russian sentiments existed which were translated into strong anti-communist feelings, socialist ideas had a strong appeal. Thus the communist leaders had in their hands a potentially powerful instrument for gaining the support of the people, and they were determined to use it. They also hoped that, by solving problems which the capitalist system could not or did not want to solve, the legitimacy of the system would be attained.

Of course, the effect of the social welfare system depended on the extent to which practice corresponded to the ideas professed. It is known that reality is never a true reflection of ideas. But the welfare system that was implemented suffered from too many shortcomings. Some of them have already been mentioned, and there is no need to repeat them. Some of the shortcomings had a common denominator, the idea that the proclamation of the intention to build socialism created conditions for the rise of the new man, *homo socialisticus*, and that taking measures as if he were already in existence would accelerate the process of his formation. This was the case when low salaries for doctors were set, narrow differentials for skill were introduced and pensions in Czechoslovakia were classified. Not much attention was paid to the fact that the people affected were not and could not be ready for such dramatic changes, and that their self-esteem and social position in society, as well as their interests, were badly affected, and that this must have turned them against the regime or at least discouraged them from supporting it. In addition, the measures mentioned were not really necessary.

What was even worse, the communist leaders did not apply the same rules they applied to the public to themselves and their close supporters. They had access to special hospitals, well-stocked stores, and they were not affected by the above-mentioned categorisation for determining the amount of pensions.

Another important common denominator was that when the two principles, equality and economic efficiency, clashed, the communist leaders did not try hard enough to find a proper balance, which in my opinion should have lain in the principle that equality should be pushed at the expense of economic efficiency only if the issue involved was a fundamental principle and there was no other way to achieve it. Full employment in a socialist regime may be such an example. Of course, its negative effects could have been greatly reduced by proper actions (see Chapter 4). Attaching a social role to consumer prices was a kind of push for equality at the expense of economic efficiency which was not really necessary and useful. Equality could have been better served if the social role of prices had been reduced considerably and priority given to efficiency.

The welfare policy, which was believed to ensure permanent popular support for the socialist system, fulfilled this role until approximately the middle of the 1970s. From then on, its role was gradually eroded. This was not only because of its shortcomings, as mentioned above. There was a gradual build-up of the welfare system in the West, which in some respects was superior to that in the East, and this naturally reduced the power of attraction of the Eastern welfare system. Full employment was not part of the Western welfare system and, when the fortunes of the socialist system were already declining, the West suffered from high rates of unemployment. Nevertheless, the public in socialist countries belittled the fact that full employment existed there, partly due to anti-socialist propaganda[14] and partly because people often appreciate advantages properly only after they have lost them.

4 Labour–Management Relations and Incentives

INTRODUCTION

Labour–management relations as a topic did not receive great attention in the literature about the socialist economic system. However, in my opinion, in order to understand the working of the socialist economic system, primarily of the traditional system and its shortcomings, it is important to become familiar with labour–management relations, as they existed under socialism. As is known, these determine to a great degree the extent to which enterprises can meet their goals. Conflicts between management and labour may have a negative effect on the work ethic of workers, which in turn has an effect on the quality of products and economic efficiency in enterprises.

Management–labour relations were not exactly the same in the three countries. What I discuss here is, rather, a model, to which the Czechoslovak reality was the closest. The differences reflected the pre-war differences in relations.

In this short chapter I am first going to discuss the position of a top manager in the traditional system compared to the position of a top manager in a capitalist corporation, and how the former changed under reforms. I will also discuss how the position of managers influenced the economy. In addition, I will devote attention to the position of workers.

THE POSITION OF A TOP MANAGER UNDER THE TRADITIONAL SYSTEM

East European countries (unlike Western countries, where an authoritarian regime exists in factories) had relaxed relationships in their factories.[1] This may seem surprising, considering the dictatorial nature of the political system. Maybe just because of the nature of the system and the fact that the workers were its mainstay, the workplace was given to them as a place where they could let off steam, as a

58

substitute for criticising the regime. In a Western corporation, mainly in the USA, the top management and, within it, the chief executive as the representative of the owners, has considerable power *vis-à-vis* the employees: the chief executive can fire and hire to a great degree at will, primarily in non-unionised firms.[2] In the USA until recently managers could shut down factories from one day to the next without giving workers advance notice. With some exaggeration it can be said that a top manager resembles in certain respects a commanding officer in a military unit. A capitalist corporation is definitely not a democratic institution, though it must follow the rules and regulations imposed by the executive and legislative branches of the country.

The position of the top manager in the West is this strong because his well-being does not depend on the goodwill of the ordinary employees; if the corporation he manages performs well, his position is safe. Not only this, but he also may be offered a better-paid executive job in a larger, more prestigious corporation. His own interest is also closely linked with the interest of the corporation because his earnings depend mostly on its profitability. The value of the package of stocks which he receives as part of his earnings depends, too, on the performance of the corporation. As a result, the interests of management and employees may be in conflict: employees are interested in higher wages; however, the higher the wages, the lower the profit, if all other conditions remain the same. Thus, wage increases may be in conflict with managers' interests. If this is the case, managers will resist wage increases and, in their fight with trade-unions, they can count on the support of shareholders.

The situation in enterprises of former socialist countries was quite different. To begin with, the position of the top manager was much weaker than in a capitalist corporation. Formally, the top manager was entitled to make all the decisions which were left to an enterprise. After all, the socialist countries accepted the idea of one-man management for enterprises.[3] Since the centre made decisions about what to produce, for whom to produce and, to a great degree, how to produce, the top manager's decision-making was quite limited compared to the power of a top manager in a capitalist corporation. This is not to say that a socialist top manager had no influence on the extent of plan targets and their mix. As has already been noted, the planners did not have enough information about the capacities of individual enterprises to be in a position to set targets without the input of enterprises. In addition, the planners were not able in most cases to set very detailed targets.

The decision-making of top managers was also limited to some extent by the right of control given to the CP organisation in enterprises, which formally meant that the organisation could ask for information about the performance of the enterprise and suggest ways to improve it. It had no right to impose its will on the top manager; it could, however, report its dissatisfaction to higher CP bodies which could, if they saw fit, follow up the complaint with the superiors of the enterprise. Many top managers resented this meddling of the CP organisation in what they regarded as their affairs. The situation was compounded by the fact that the local Party organisation, which steered the enterprise organisation, also had the right of control.

A smart top manager tried to avoid conflicts with the CP organisation. If the advice of the CP turned out to be wrong, he could put the blame on the Party organisation. If the opposite situation occurred, he might be praised for listening to the advice of the 'people'. In the matter of appointments, which fell within the jurisdiction of top managers, the CP organisation had the right of veto.

As shown, managerial authority was restricted not only by the superior bodies, but also by the Party organisation. Later it will be shown that trade-unions also imposed certain restrictions on the authority of a top manager.

The question may be posed: to what extent were the interests of the top manager of a socialist enterprise linked to the interests of the economy and to the interests of the enterprise entrusted to his management? After all, the top manager's function was primarily to protect the interests of the economy, or, more precisely, those of the state, the owner.

The financial situation of a top manager was linked – as already mentioned – to the performance of the enterprise he managed. If the enterprise fulfilled the plan targets, he got bonuses and his earnings increased. Since the bonuses in the case of a top manager were quite high compared to his salary, and the latter was very modest compared to salaries in the West, and not very high compared to average wages in the East, he was, of course, very interested in the good performance of the enterprise like his colleague in the West. Apart from pecuniary interests, there were other considerations which encouraged a top manager to do a good job – increase in social status, a chance to be given a higher assignment, etc.

There were, however, other factors which pushed top managers' interest in a different direction. The success of a socialist manager also depended on the goodwill of the employees and, of course, of the CP enterprise organisation and the trade-union organisation, as already mentioned. If he was not able to establish a proper rapport with the groups mentioned and if, as a result, the relationship was marked by conflicts, he sooner or later failed in his position. The authorities were interested in having peace in enterprises and a top manager who was unable to prevent conflicts was an uncalled-for burden.

The relationship between the top manager and his subordinates depended to a great degree on the extent to which the manager was able to protect the employees' interests *vis-à-vis* the authorities. A good manager, in the eyes of ordinary workers, was one who was able to squeeze from the authorities an easily fulfilable plan with the allocation of sufficient inputs, including labour, and an increase in the wage bill which would guarantee an increase in the real wage without the need of much greater intensity of labour. If the employees felt that their manager was not successful in protecting their interests because he was indifferent or because he wanted to balance the interests of the workers and the economy, or if they suspected that he did not have the needed skills (political and professional) for bargaining with the authorities, his popularity necessarily declined. Even the CP organisation, which was called on to defend general economic interests, did not like a loser, though he might have become one because he had done what the CP asked him to do. After all, the members of the CP organisation committee were workers too, and had the same interests as their colleagues. In addition, the CP organisation was concerned that severe dissatisfaction would arise if the management failed.

THE EFFECTS OF THE WEAK POSITION OF THE MANAGER[4]

From the foregoing it is clear that the top manager, as the representative of the owner, the state, was in no position to defend the interests of the owner properly. He was not even in a position always to defend effectively the interests of the enterprise if these clashed with the interests of the employees. Considering the interest of the top manager, one should not forget that it lay not so much in profit – as is the case with his colleague in the West – as in earnings primarily. Usually the incentive system for top managers under the traditional system was linked to several indicators and profit was directly or indirectly only one of them. Managers were usually interested in an increase in workers' wages because this produced contentment in enterprises, but mainly since this could also be translated into an increase in their salaries through higher bonuses. In addition, they were guided by short-term interests like other employees, mainly in the first phase of socialism, when there was a tendency not to leave managers in their positions for long. Thus, managers were not only pushed by pressure from employees to accept the workers' worries as their own, but their pecuniary interest in earnings increases brought them closer to workers' interests.

The weak position of managers *vis-à-vis* workers was further undermined by the labour code, full employment policy and labour shortages. In a capitalist corporation, mainly in the USA, workers usually cannot afford to defy their superiors (managers or supervisors),[5] since substitute jobs are not readily available. In a socialist enterprise workers had no such fear, as will be shown below.

While a capitalist corporation is marked to a great degree by an adversarial relationship between top management and employees, the relations in a socialist enterprise were by no means antagonistic; they were rather a mixture of different elements – support, identification and sometimes adversariness – which, put together, resulted in the weakness of the managers. Considering these relations from a human-relations viewpoint – in particular the fact that in socialist enterprises the kind of authoritarian regime which is characteristic of capitalist corporations, mainly in the USA, did not exist – one might argue that they were a welcome phenomenon. I would add: provided that they were not at the expense of economic efficiency. And this assumed that workers internalised a type of consciousness which would make them immune to the natural inclination of people to take advantage of what is in their interest, even if it hurts the collective interest. The behaviour of workers did not reach the level of consciousness needed and therefore the prevalent labour–management relations did not promote economic efficiency; on the contrary, they hampered it. The top manager, due to his weakness, had difficulty enforcing discipline (making employees work hard, fully utilising work time, and paying attention to quality), enforcing the rule that wage differentials must reflect performance, and distributing bonuses according to merit. In brief, the weak position of top managers undermined the effectiveness of incentives.

THE POSITION OF WORKERS

It would be wrong to draw the conclusion from the foregoing that individual workers in a socialist enterprise had a powerful position.

Only their position as a collective was strong *vis-à-vis* managers when compared with that of workers in the USA. Otherwise their position exhibited many weaknesses. Up to the middle of the 1960s the freedom of choice of job was limited in two ways. On the one hand, workers could not quit their jobs without the consent of management and trade-unions. There were several exceptions to this rule. One was a move to another city because of a change in family status. Health problems were also a good reason. Finally, a worker could quit, if he was willing to work for some time in an industry where great labour shortages existed because of difficult working conditions there (mining). On the other hand, there was forced placement into jobs in industrial branches for which it was difficult to recruit labour even by incentives. This usually did not mean that authorities allocated a certain job; it meant only that the candidate had to accept a job in the assigned branch of industry.[6]

Forced placement was also applied to businessmen, whose business was shut down, to employees of institutions which were regarded as typically capitalist (brokerage houses, the stock market) and to political opponents, etc. In 1951 Czechoslovakia, which probably had the worst record in forced placement, transferred 77 000 white-collar workers to manual jobs. Needless to say, this was a political move: to get rid of workers who were assumed to be politically unreliable and to create job openings for reliable 'cadres', mainly factory workers. This, combined with the 1948–9 cleansing of the universities of a great number of students[7] because of their class origin or because of their negative attitude to the regime, antagonised a large section of the population against the CP.

In addition, there was an administrative allocation of most university graduates to jobs for a certain period of time (usually three years) (Čech, 1959, pp. 82–7; Olędzki, 1974, pp. 226–7). The rationale for this action was to make sure that all the graduates would have jobs and that the countryside would have physicians, lawyers, teachers. One can argue whether or not this action was a violation of human rights. The next action which is going to be mentioned was certainly in the interest of the application of human rights. I have in mind the placement of disabled people who, without the help of the authorities, had little chance of finding a job and keeping it.

On the other hand, workers had job security. A manager had to have a very good reason for dismissing a worker. Workers could be dismissed only with the approval of the enterprise trade-union organisation. If the dismissal was for political reasons, not a very frequent case, which meant that the Party organisation was involved, the approval by the trade-union was automatic. If the dismissal was for disciplinary reasons, the trade-union usually carried out its own questioning before approval was given. It was, however, reluctant to approve dismissal for economic reasons. And even if the manager had a good cause for dismissal, he had to think twice, since a substitute was often difficult to obtain.

If workers became redundant in one enterprise department because of enterprise reorganisation, they could expect the management to place them in another department, after retraining them, if necessary, in order for them to be able to perform the new job. If the enterprise could not place them in its own departments, it helped the dismissed workers to find new jobs. Because there were labour shortages, this was usually not much of a problem.

Up to the middle of the 1960s unemployment benefits did not exist; this fact had to help demonstrate that socialist countries had full employment. But after the suppression of the uprising in Hungary unemployment benefits were introduced for a short period of time in order to cope with unemployment (Rózsa and Farkasinszky, 1970).

Workers were dependent on their enterprises, mostly on the secretary of the Party organisation, if they wanted a passport to visit their relatives abroad, a loan or an apartment in enterprise housing.

Trade unions existed in all socialist countries. But their main task was not to defend the material interest of workers. When the authorities determined the plan for the standard of living, mainly for the development of wages, the trade-union leadership was consulted. But the trade-unions were in no position to challenge the decision of the CP concerning wages. Once the CP leadership approved the standard of living plan, the trade-union leadership was expected to defend it. And it usually did so because the CP decided who would be in leading positions within the trade union. Not only this, the enterprise Party organisation determined who would be at the head of the enterprise trade union.

Strikes were illegal for fear that they might undermine the stability of the regime. The ideologues argued that workers striking against a workers' government could only harm themselves. Nevertheless there were some strikes in the 1950s, besides the riots in Poland and in the aftermath of the suppression of the Hungarian uprising. In Czechoslovakia the 1953 money reform, which deprived many people of their savings, provoked demonstrations and strikes in some localities and enterprises. Needless to say, the organisers of the strikes were punished.

With the political relaxation the authorities in some countries took the position that strikes, as long as they were approved by the national leadership of the trade unions, were legal. This was not a substantive change in the attitude to strikes; it was rather a clever manoeuvre based on the knowledge that the trade-unions would not dare give permission to strike. Still there were many strikes, mainly in Poland in the 1980s.

It has already been mentioned in the preceding chapter that socialist countries were not able to avoid great losses of work time and that lack of discipline and absenteeism were the main reasons for this phenomenon. Of course, these reasons themselves were triggered by others which can be regarded as the fundamental causes of the negatives mentioned.

After the seizure of political power by the communists, many people were forced to change their jobs and accept a job which they did not like because of its lower social status or level of pay. One could not expect these people to work with enthusiasm. Moreover for many years, up to the second half of the 1950s, real wages were declining and, on top of this, there were consumer goods shortages (in one country more than in the others). The widespread application of piece-rates, as a quasi-socialist payment form, without due regard to the nature of the work to be performed, had a negative effect on quality of products. Low labour discipline also had its origin in the tremendous organisational problems which arose as a result of the huge influx of people into the labour force.

The governments tried to solve these problems with non-economic methods. In 1950 the Polish government enacted a draconian law – in the spirit of Stalin's methods – which envisioned prison sentences and a reduction in wages for absenteeism over a certain number of days (Jędruszczak, 1972, pp. 166–7). A similar law was adopted by Hungary (Schönwald, 1980, pp. 129–31). The Czechoslovak authorities had second thoughts about Stalin's measures. Finally, in 1953 they decided to act, but in the meantime Stalin had died and the bill was abandoned. In the first years after Stalin's death the countries went through an economic followed by a political crisis, a period in which Stalinist methods increasingly lost appeal among the communist elites under the pressure of the crisis.

Had the CPs devoted much more attention to incentives than they did, perhaps the situation could have been improved. However, in the first years of their rule they relied too heavily on some revolutionary fervour. No doubt, primarily in Czechoslovakia, a large proportion of the population welcomed the new regime and was willing to bear some sacrifices for a short time. But when the industrialisation drive brought hard times and far-reaching restrictions on freedoms, the enthusiasm for the new regime started to weaken, even among its followers.

When the political and economic situation was consolidated after the 1956 upheavals, no great change occurred in the behaviour of workers. In the meantime a new factor appeared on the economic scene – labour shortages, resulting mainly from the industrialisation policy combined with the full employment policy. In a situation when it was easy to find a job, many workers abused the system by continuing in the old pattern of behaviour, not utilising the work time fully,[8] not working hard and not paying proper attention to the quality of the work delivered. They found justification for their behaviour in two circumstances: first they believed that their remuneration was below what they deserved; many were undoubtedly correct.[9] (See Chapter 3.) Second, they found justification in the often negligent implementation of the managerial staff's duties: for example, it happened quite frequently that some workers could not work for hours because documents and equipment needed for their work were not prepared on time or because the machines were not properly repaired.

It has already been indicated that the managers' authority was not strong enough to cope with labour discipline violations. Many managers were indifferent considering the potential costs of conflict with workers. The problem was that managers could not fully rely on government help in enforcing labour discipline. The undemocratic nature of the system was an obstacle to it. The Communist leaders were afraid to make unpopular provisions which might improve the situation for fear of antagonising workers who were regarded as the mainstay of the regime. In many cases the managerial indifference resulted from the wrong belief that a conflict-less environment might work to the benefit of all. Finally, the incentives and disincentives introduced to cope with the problems mentioned were not strong enough.

Up to now I have discussed the position of individual workers generally. In reality, the position of white-collar workers (disregarding here white-collar workers in leading positions, mainly in the Party and state apparatus, who enjoyed privileged positions) was much weaker than that of blue-collar workers. The latter, primarily those employed in heavy industry, were regarded as the mainstay of the regime, and they were therefore treated with circumspection and caution. In addition, blue-collar workers could speak their minds (provided what they said was not politically very incorrect) without having to be afraid that something would happen to them, as long as they did not aspire to some white-collar job or a better job in their field. On the other hand, white-collar workers were much more vulnerable: from time to time there were actions aimed at reducing the administrative apparatus, and therefore the threat of dismissal loomed over the heads of some. The weaker political position of white-collar workers was one of the main reasons why they were generally poorly treated when it came to wage adjustments.

In sum it can be said that the individual workers' position in a socialist enterprise compared to the position of workers in a capitalist corporation was a mixed bag. On the one hand, they were dependent on the enterprise (including the Party organisation) in matters in which an American worker is independent, but on the other hand, they had extensive job security which a North American worker can only envy.[10] In my opinion Kornai's (1992) statement that 'all workers in a [socialist] firm are largely at the mercy of their bosses' (p. 222) is not precise, to say the least.

LABOUR–MANAGEMENT RELATIONS UNDER ECONOMIC REFORMS

The reforms of the 1960s in Hungary and Czechoslovakia, which meant an expansion of the decision-making power of enterprises, meant at the same time a substantial strengthening of the position of top managers. They could make many decisions which before were the domain of the superior authorities. (For more see Chapter 7.) The position of top managers also improved because increasingly the nominations to such posts were dependent on the training and experience of the candidates. Top managers, mainly up to the 1960s, were selected primarily on the basis of political criteria: political reliability was given precedence over professional competence. Later, when more stress was put on professional competence, it was still only the people who were included in the nomenclature who could be considered for high positions in the economy, including enterprises. (In the 1980s in Hungary and Poland, with the passage of the years, belonging to the nomenclature was less and less linked to membership in the Party.) As a result of this 'cadre' policy, which was applied throughout the economy, many incompetent people occupied positions of responsibility, and many apt and talented people were pushed aside. This contributed, on the one hand, to the mismanagement of the economy and, on the other, to the dissatisfaction and bitterness of those who were rejected. Political criteria were still a viewpoint in the nomination process with the introduction of economic reforms, but by no means the only one. And this lent top managers greater authority and respect.

The increased role of managers in determining the wage bill and bonus fund, combined with a greater role for profit in determining bonuses, weakened the solidarity between managers and workers mentioned above (see p. 62).

In Hungary a conflict even developed between managers and workers – about the distribution of bonuses – which had an effect on wages.[11]

In 1982 in Poland and 1985 in Hungary self-management was introduced in most enterprises. In those enterprises where it worked the top manager had to share power with the self-management bodies. (For more, see Chapters 7 and 9.)

The enterprise Party organisation (or more precisely its secretary) was still around, but its meddling in enterprise affairs was increasingly reduced. It still remained, however, a nuisance for management just because of its existence in enterprises.

Forced placement in jobs was eliminated. But some traces of it still remained. In Hungary, for example, in the second half of the 1960s it was still possible to place someone into a job if he quit his job twice in one year without proper notice or before the notice expired (Horváth, 1970). Placement of university graduates was also gradually abandoned.

The reforms of the 1960s, mainly the Hungarian, were based on the idea that full employment must be sustained. In Hungary various measures were undertaken to stave off possible unemployment. In Czechoslovakia a law on unemployment benefits was enacted as a cautionary measure (Kudrna, 1967). Fears of unemployment turned out to be unsubstantiated; labour shortages continued to exist. Full employment existed in all three countries until the collapse of the socialist system, though from the middle of the 1980s in Hungary and Poland measures were undertaken to revamp the concept of full employment, to make it compatible with labour market rules. The government was to be responsible for the implementation of full employment, whereas enterprises were supposed to treat employment from the viewpoint of economic efficiency. In Czechoslovakia there was no movement in the direction mentioned.

The behaviour of workers with regard to work ethic did not change much. Various incentives and disincentives were tried to bring about a change, but without noticeable effect. The spread of the private sector in the 1980s in Hungary and Poland did not improve the work ethic in state enterprises. Many people, primarily in Hungary, held two and in some cases three jobs. Of course, they could not work with the same intensity in two or three jobs and therefore they neglected the job which was the most secure and that was the job in the state sector. In one of his works Szelényi mentioned that people went to work in the state jobs as the serfs used to go to work on the land of the feudal lord. It is certainly an exaggerated comparison, but it has a grain of truth in it considering the productivity of work in different jobs.

CONCLUDING REMARKS

From the foregoing it is clear that labour–management relations were not of the kind needed for the promotion of economic efficiency. The management authority was undercut by the economic mechanism which largely relegated managers to the position of executors of the central planners' wishes. On top of this, managers were too dependent on the good will of the territorial and enterprise Party organisation, enterprise trade-union organisation and workers. This in itself made it difficult to enforce the labour discipline required to achieve efficient performance and quality products. In addition the incentive system did not encourage managers to struggle for higher economic efficiency.

Even when the authority of managers was increased as a result of major economic reforms, labour–management relations did not substantially change. The role of the Party and trade-unions, though reduced, was still very important in enterprise activities. The CPs took the position that enterprise management should be under a certain control. In the first years of the regime the control was justified by, among other things, the shortage of experienced managers. Later, when 'redness' was of much less significance in selecting managers, the argument for control was more political. The real reason why the Party did not want to give up control over enterprise economic activity was because this meant giving up power and influence over the economy.

Labour–management relations could not fulfil their function as a promoter of economic efficiency, partly because of the full-employment policy which contributed to labour shortages. Workers were not under pressure to work hard; they knew that even if they lost their jobs others would be available. They were so certain of this that even the lack of unemployment benefits did not frighten them. This is not to say that it was a mistake to pursue a full-employment policy. In my opinion, it was a mistake not to combine the full-employment policy with measures aimed at making sure that full employment would not be misused. First, labour shortages should and could have been avoided, and this would have encouraged many workers to appreciate the jobs they had. It should be borne in mind that labour shortages were combined with overemployment in many enterprises. In addition a great number of workers were engaged in auxiliary jobs which could have been replaced by labour-saving equipment. In other words, labour shortages were not an unavoidable result of the economic mechanism (for more see pp. 46–7). Second, more effective incentives and disincentives were needed to encourage workers to work hard and do quality work.

Last, but not least, it was a mistake not to honour the old socialist credo about industrial democracy after the seizure of political power. It was necessary to give workers a say in the management of enterprises and to require in return a certain amount of responsibility for the performance of enterprises. The powers of the self-management bodies could have been restricted in the beginning, mainly with regard to the determination of wages, and expanded in the course of time on the basis of the experience gained in the meantime. If workers had had the feeling that the nationalised enterprises really belonged to the nation and to them, they would, it could be assumed, have reciprocated with responsible behaviour, particularly if they had also been exposed to the measures mentioned.

The communist leaders in the small countries following the policy of the USSR were not willing to allow any elements of self-management. In Czechoslovakia, the workers' councils, a kind of self-management body, which had existed in nationalised enterprises since 1945 and which were mostly led by communists, were liquidated soon after the communist takeover (Osers, 1977). The later introduction of self-management bodies under pressure from the reformers was already too late. This was partly due to the fact that a large proportion of workers had already become used to a certain style of behaviour.

5 Foreign Economic Relations

INTRODUCTION

Up to now I have discussed only domestic issues. However, the way in which socialist countries participated in the international division of labour contributed significantly to the failure of the socialist system.

In his *Economic Problems of Socialism in the Soviet Union*, Stalin (1952) maintained that the Second World War had brought about the 'disintegration of the single all embracing world market' and the rise of two parallel world markets which confronted each other. The disintegration was – according to Stalin – a further reason for the general crisis of capitalism. This idea of Stalin's was primarily the ideological underpinning of his desire to bring the newly established, so-called peoples' republics into the Soviet economic orbit and use them as a substitute for Western markets, mainly in areas affected by the Western embargo on certain products. To this end, he forced East European countries to scale down dramatically their trade relations with Western countries and orient their economies to Soviet markets.

It was no secret to Stalin and his successors that the Western economies were on a much higher technological level than the socialist camp. They undoubtedly wanted to have access to Western technology, but were not willing to pay the price for it in terms of political concessions. It was also clear to them that the race between the two systems would be decided in the area of productivity growth. The Soviet leaders themselves, alluding to Lenin, repeated countless times that only if the socialist camp was able to achieve higher growth rates of productivity than advanced capitalist countries would it eventually be able to overtake the capitalist countries in terms of per capita production. And growth of productivity depends *ceteris paribus* on technological progress. The Soviets spared no effort to achieve technological progress in armaments and branches connected with them, but they were not sufficiently concerned about industries in the civilian economy which were not directly important for the military, as if the race for productivity growth would be determined in the military sphere. They forgot that neglect of non-military industries and, thus, of

71

consumers, would slow down the growth of the economy and negatively affect their military might in the final analysis.

In the first years of its existence, CMEA (Council for Mutual Economic Assistance), an institution for the organisation of cooperation between socialist countries, was not very active.[1] The Soviets were not interested in its activity; they could achieve their goals more effectively by bilateral dealings with the co-members of the Council. They needed the institution only for political and propaganda reasons. Not until Khrushchev's administration was CMEA activated. But it never became what it could have been and what some countries wanted it to become.

Stalin and his successors were primarily responsible for the poor performance of CMEA. Had the political leaders been properly concerned with this institution, it could have become, even with the existing constraints, a catalyst for economic growth, efficiency and technological progress. It could have been the basis for a huge market where specialisation and cooperation could have benefited all the members of the Council. It could also have helped weaker members to reach a higher level of development. And, finally, pooling ingenuity and talents could have become an important source of innovation stimulation. In reality, the results of CMEA activities turned out to be at best meagre and, in some respects, negative.

There was no lack of ideas on how to improve cooperation between CMEA countries and many resolutions on expanding cooperation were even adopted, culminating in a decision to turn the participating countries into a united market, but they were not put into effect. CMEA could only be a reflection of the economic mechanisms of the member countries. The Soviets as the dominant member of CMEA were not really interested in far-reaching reforms. Gorbachev's attempts to reform the system of cooperation between CMEA countries came too late.

THE WORKING OF CMEA

Planning and Organisation

To understand the mechanism of cooperation it is necessary to start with the planning of foreign trade. The point of departure was imports needed in order to fulfil the plan targets. In contrast to capitalist countries, where exports are regarded as an important source of economic growth, they were viewed in socialist countries almost as a necessary evil in order to be able to pay for imports. This approach to foreign trade was also instrumental in CMEA. In a debate about CMEA one Soviet economist expressed the view that the mutual exchange of products between socialist countries was an exchange of 'leftovers' (*The Current Digests of Foreign Press*, 1988, no. 2, p. 15).[2] Perhaps such a characterisation was a slight hyperbole, but still it expressed to a great extent the essence of the exchange. It is also important to stress that, because each country tried to channel all its resources into the fulfilment of its plan targets, which were constrained by the amount of supply which it was able to mobilise rather than by demand, the cooperation could not fulfil the expectations of its members with regard to economic efficiency. In other words the exchange of commodities was not governed by the principle of comparative advantage.

Foreign trade was a state monopoly. Productive enterprises were not allowed to enter into trade relations with their foreign counterparts. This activity was reserved to special state monopoly enterprises which specialised in imports and exports of certain products or groups of products. There were usually special state monopoly enterprises for exports and imports. Enterprises sold their products earmarked for exports to the proper state monopoly at domestic wholesale prices and the latter sold them in foreign markets at whatever prices it could achieve. If a loss came about, the difference was covered from a special government fund; if a profit was made, it was surrendered to the fund. The same procedure was applied to imports. In many cases, enterprises did not even know how their products fared in foreign markets. In this way enterprises were shielded from the impact of world markets; they worked in sheltered conditions. This had the advantage of protecting the domestic market from imported inflation. On the other hand, enterprises were not under pressure to innovate and to increase productivity.

Negotiations about cooperation among socialist countries were carried on at a state level; bureaucracy had a greater say about interstate trade and cooperation agreements than enterprises, which in the final analysis were obliged to put these agreements into effect.

Price System

As already mentioned, the socialist price system, though the same in all member countries of CMEA in its underlying principles, was nevertheless not suitable for calculations of mutual exchanges, the most important reason being that prices were heavily subsidised and, as a result, countries were reluctant to sell their products at subsidised prices. Therefore they agreed that modified world-market prices would be used. The modification lay in the use of the past five year averages of world market prices for the coming several years, with the reasoning that this would enable the speculative elements to be eliminated from world-market prices and bring them closer to the international market value.[3] In addition, for some products, prices used in East–West trade were also applied intra-CMEA trade (Brabant, 1987).

If we take world-market prices as a basis, then prices paid for commodities below world prices can be regarded as subsidised, and prices above can be regarded as 'overcharged'. One of the two situations, when prices of individual commodities are the object of change, must occur if modified world prices are accepted. As is known, world prices, mainly of fuel and raw materials, fluctuate a lot, and if prices in CMEA changed only once in a long while, a discrepancy between world prices and prices paid in intra-CMEA trade necessarily would develop. In the 1970s and 1980s this referred primarily to prices of oil, when during the 1973 Arab–Israeli war, and later in 1979 in connection with the Iranian revolution, the price of oil increased dramatically. These price increases did not instantly affect the smaller countries of CMEA. Marrese and Vanous (1983) drew the conclusion that the Soviets were extending subsidies to East European countries, which, no doubt, was true; the Soviets could have sold the oil on world markets at much higher prices. The question is only whether the subsidies were intended with a certain objective in mind.

Marrese and Vanous came up with the idea that the subsidies were a compensation for the services East European countries rendered the USSR in international policy and military cooperation. This contention about subsidies and their purpose provoked a debate,[4] in which principally East European economists criticised Marrese and Vanous' stand.

In my opinion, the 1973 and 1979 subsidies were certainly not intended; they were the result of the price system which CMEA countries agreed on at the end of the 1950s and of the price increases by OPEC. It would have been politically unwise for the Soviets to push for an instant change in the price formula. In the minds of most East European people, the belief prevailed that CMEA was a Soviet instrument for the exploitation of East European countries and a sudden increase in oil prices would have caused trouble in the economy and strengthened the belief about exploitation. I agree with Holzman (1987, p. 189) that the Soviets could afford to be generous to East European countries because of windfall profits on oil and gold and increased arms sales, and in this way they could help CMEA countries for a while to cope with their economic troubles.[5] The same view is in essence expressed by Lavigne (1991, p. 252).

In the 1980s, when world prices of oil declined, Soviet prices started to increase due the existing price formula which, according to Lavigne (1991, p. 249), did not change in essence.[6]

From the above it is clear that domestic prices had no connection with the prices at which tradable goods were realised, and this was not only true in trade with the non-socialist countries, but also with socialist countries.

In the 42 years of CMEA existence there were several attempts to reform the price system. At the Budapest conference in 1967 there was an effort made to create a 'socialist' price; its main proponents were the Soviet Union and Bulgaria. Needless to say, both expected some advantages from such a price. However, this was at a time when Czechoslovakia was engaged in a major reform and Hungary was on the brink of an economic reform, when both countries wanted to give a certain role to the market and therefore could not agree with a price system which ignored market forces entirely. Luckily, other members of CMEA supported Hungary and Czechoslovakia, of course for other than systemic reasons, and so the price system mentioned above remained in force (see Zwass, 1989, pp. 47–8).

Hard and Soft Goods

Trade between CMEA countries could be characterised for the most part as an exchange in kind instead of in value. In the trade negotiations, all the partners tried to get what they needed to fulfil their plans and to pay for these products with what they could best afford. The situation was complicated by trade with non-socialist countries, mainly Western countries. There the trade was mostly in dollars and was more demanding on quality and technical parameters. Only a limited portion of the commodities which were 'traded' on CMEA markets could be sold on Western markets at world-market prices. On the other hand, socialist countries needed commodities from Western markets which were not available in the East or were only available in a low quality. As a result of these realities, commodities in intra-CMEA trade were soon classified in two groups: 'hard' and 'soft'. Hard goods were goods which could be easily sold on capitalist markets for hard currency, or goods for which hard currency had to be paid on capitalist markets if they could not be bought in CMEA markets in sufficient amounts. Naturally, every country tried to get the maximum amounts of hard commodities and to deliver the minimum of hard commodities. It was only natural that after some time (1970) trade in dollars developed for hard products beyond planned deliveries and for *ad hoc* deals (see Csaba, 1990, p. 55). Why should countries not be willing to pay more for hard goods which were over the quotas in the agreements adopted with their partners in CMEA, if the alternative was to pay for the same commodities bought in the West in dollars?

Payments

In socialist countries enterprises paid for goods bought by transfers from their account to the account of the supplier. No real money was involved. The accounts of buyers and suppliers were exclusively with the bank branch in their locality. A similar payment system for deliveries was used in trade between CMEA countries; this was a non-cash bilateral clearing system. The payments of one country for the deliveries of another were entries in the accounts of the supplier, and vice versa. In order to have a good survey of the fulfilment of obligations which the countries assumed when they signed trade agreements, each country's central (or foreign trade) bank had a single account for trade with each country of CMEA where credits and debits were entered. The payments between two countries were supposed to be balanced within a year (Rusmich, 1972).

Soon CMEA countries realised that this system hampered the expansion of trade, and therefore it was decided in 1964 to introduce a transferable ruble along with the establishment of an International Bank for Economic Cooperation. The idea behind these provisions was that all deliveries would be calculated in rubles, and surpluses on bilateral accounts could be used for buying goods in whatever country was chosen. In addition, the International Bank had to extend credit to countries with a deficit in the balance of payments. It was assumed that the new measures would be an important step in the introduction of multilateral trade (Brabant, 1980, pp. 201–2). Even the Comprehensive Programme, adopted in 1971, which put greater stress on multilateral trade, did not bring about and could not bring about a substantial change. In a situation when strict central planning prevailed in most countries, it was difficult to satisfy the demand for goods which were not planned (more about this later).

Supranational Authority

The smaller countries of CMEA were formally independent; however, in reality they were obliged to follow for a long time more or less Soviet economic, social and foreign policy. A similar situation existed in CMEA. When the Council was established it was not equipped with supranational powers; it had only advisory and consultative functions and decisions could only be valid if all the countries agreed; yet the USSR had a dominant position in it. During Stalin's life the Soviets did not need and did not want for political reasons an institution with supranational powers. At that time in the West politicians started to discuss the possibility of various kinds of integration. The Soviets regarded these endeavours as an anti-Soviet action and launched an extensive campaign against integration. It was branded as an anti-patriotic and imperialistic movement designed to deprive small nations of their sovereignty. Under such conditions it would have been politically damaging to call for an integration of socialist economies.

In the beginning of the 1960s, when efforts were made to expand the activities of CMEA, Khrushchev came up with a plan to establish a supranational authority. Compared to the period of Stalin's life when the leaders of smaller countries regarded Stalin's hints as orders, the relationship between the Soviet Union and the smaller countries under Khrushchev's leadership was less a relationship between a boss and his subordinates. Some smaller countries dared to voice opposition to changes which they disliked, and Khrushchev's proposal did not gain the backing of all the members and therefore it was dropped (Marer and Montias, 1981, p. 161).

Evening out of Differences

CMEA was made up of countries at different levels of economic development. On the one hand, there were Bulgaria and Rumania, developing countries, and on the other East Germany and Czechoslovakia, developed. The difference becomes even more pronounced if non-European countries are considered (such as Mongolia and Vietnam). Needless to say, specialisation between countries at the same level of economic development is more efficient. In the beginning, technological and scientific cooperation was to mitigate the differences in development. It was accepted as a rule that more developed countries would help the less developed to produce sophisticated products, among other things machines, by giving them the necessary blueprints and documentation without charge. This was an idealistic approach which was contrary to national interests and therefore in practice was of no great help. The documentation which less developed countries received was mostly out of date for the more developed countries.

Only later did Soviet leaders come up with the idea of evening out the differences between countries. However, not much has happened in this regard.

CHANGES IN CMEA

During CMEA's existence several programmes and resolutions were adopted for the sake of expanding, deepening and improving the cooperation between the members of the institution. Here I will mention only the most important ones.

Comprehensive Programme

No doubt, the 1971 Comprehensive Programme for the Extension and Improvement of Collaboration and the Development of Socialist Economic Integration of the CMEA Countries was one of the important programmes. Its importance is clear from the fact that for the first time a document from the CMEA session used the word 'integration' as an objective of cooperation. The programme also called for the adoption of the principle that integration projects could go ahead even if not all the countries agreed and participated. This was an important departure from the previous practice requiring consensus, a situation which enabled one country to scuttle a programme which it did not like.

The Comprehensive Programme called for an improvement in coordination of economic plans, which was already agreed upon in the middle of the 1950s. To this end consultations about coordination of plans were to start three years before the end of the five-year plan. 15- to 20-year forecasts of demand and supply were also agreed in order to put the planning of production, investment, consumption and trade on a more realistic basis. The coordination of planning had to be focused on the joint planning of certain selected branches and products (Brabant 1980, p. 232).

The latter meant a further shift of stress from trade to production, more precisely an extension of specialisation and cooperation, which had been, since the second half of the 1950s, the most important objective of CMEA. Specialisation was to focus on high-quality machinery construction for important industrial branches, nuclear power plants, mining, steel foundries, electronics, etc., and on important products in short supply.

The document also stressed the importance of the continuation of joint investment activity, primarily in extractive branches and energy. In the latter, it meant the construction of a huge pipeline for the transport of oil to Eastern and Western Europe, and, in the second half of the 1970s, a gas pipeline from the South Urals to the western border of the Soviet Union and a high voltage power line from the Ukraine to Hungary (Zwass, 1989, p. 83; Lavigne, 1991, p. 89). The vast majority of the investment projects was on Soviet territory since it was rich in raw materials and energy. The importers (this meant mostly the small countries) had to contribute to the financing of the investment projects in the form of so-called long-term investment credits, and their contribution was repaid in the form of deliveries of raw materials. The more the importers contributed, the greater deliveries they received. However they did not have a claim to a share in the ownership of the newly established plants by their financial contribution. Production capacities created by joint investment projects belonged to the country on whose territory they were located.

The need for investment credits was justified by the capital-intensive character of the projects. Though capital was scarce in the small countries, they (mainly Czechoslovakia and East Germany) entered into joint investment projects with the Soviet Union because they were short of raw materials and fuels and they did not have the hard currency to get them from outside CMEA (Csaba, 1990, pp. 104–6). The deals had a silver lining in that the prices charged for the deliveries of raw materials were below world prices.[7] Besides the multilateral plans of cooperation there were also bilateral plans.

In order to create a more reliable foundation for the joint investment policy, the member countries agreed on so-called Concerted plans for multilateral integration in 1975. New investment projects were to be undertaken in the framework of these plans and the member states were obliged to reserve investment funds for these projects in their plans. The Concerted plans were only an interim provision till long-term target programmes were in place, which came about several years later. The objective of the latter was focused on some long-term selected activities; initially they were supposed to cover 10 years, but later their time horizon was extended to 20 years. The activities covered included the improvement of specialisation in engineering branches, the supply of energy and raw materials, the supply of quality basic food and industrial consumer goods and the introduction of an integrated transportation system (Csaba, 1990, pp. 108–9; Lavigne, 1991, pp. 88–9; Brabant, 1980, pp. 240–1).

An investment bank (called The International Investment Bank) was established in 1971 to serve the intensified joint-investment activity. Before 1971 short-term bilateral credits could be extended within trade operations. The new bank was authorised to extend long- and medium-term credit for investment projects in which more members were interested (Rusmich, 1972).

Judging on the basis of its outline, the Comprehensive Programme aimed at introducing a certain degree of monetisation into the organisation. Quasi exchange rates of currencies of CMEA countries, which also set the exchange rate *vis-à-vis* the transferable ruble, were established and a methodology for evaluating joint investments was set (Csaba, 1990, p. 32). It was hoped, as already mentioned, that, with the establishment of the Investment Bank, the role of the transferable ruble would increase. However, the notion that the transferable ruble would pave the way to multilateral payments did not materialise. It was used rather as a unit of settlement (Kornai, 1992, p. 359).

Programme for Scientific and Technological Progress

Another important programme was the Programme for Scientific and Technological Progress until 2000, which was approved in 1985 at a meeting in Moscow, already under the Gorbachev administration. It was an extension of a programme which was approved in 1984, at a time when the USSR was still under the leadership of K. Chernenko. The programme was largely the result of Soviet recognition of the urgent need of a turnaround in the growing gap in technological progress *vis-à-vis* the West, which also found its way into the objectives of the Soviet 12th five-year plan.

The long-term programme designated five priority areas for scientific and technological cooperation: computerisation with the purpose of establishing modern communication and information systems; atomic energy; automation; discovery of new cost-saving materials; and biotechnology. The five areas of cooperation included 93 sub-areas of cooperation. It was not expected that small European countries, far less non-European CMEA member countries, would take part in all the programmes. The latter were promised aid which would contribute to their growth. The Soviets promised that their research institutes would be at the head of the effort for implementing of the programmes and appealed to the small countries to do the same (Csaba, 1990, p. 334; Zwass, 1989, pp. 164–5).

According to the long-term programme, enterprises and associations of individual countries were supposed to play a crucial role in the implementation of the new tasks. In the past cooperation was determined by bureaucrats, this time enterprises were to be allowed to enter into direct cooperation with their partners in other countries. This provision was welcomed mainly by countries which had fought for the reform of CMEA for some time, such as Hungary, Poland and also Czechoslovakia. The reaction of the Czechoslovak deputy prime minister, responsible for CMEA, is a testimony to it:

The analysis of the unsatisfactory state of direct cooperation in production with other members of CMEA shows that a big obstacle was the centre's excessive meticulousness and its mediating role with regard to such activity on the level of enterprises. The whole system of issuing licences for foreign business activity, the limited number of enterprises which were allowed to enter into direct relations and the low efficiency of such cooperation, deterred international cooperation (*HN*, 1986, no. 23).

The direct links were not supposed to be limited to scientific and technological cooperation. However, to judge from the Czechoslovak regulations, the direct inter-enterprise links were of quite a limited nature. In the case of scientific and technological cooperation, enterprises were allowed direct links – with few exceptions – only within the framework of achieved bilateral or multilateral agreements. Direct links in trade relations were not allowed to expand beyond enterprises which had in any case the permission to enter into trade relations with enterprises in other countries. In the case of coordination of economic plans enterprises could participate in the bilateral negotiations (Supplement to *NH*, 1992, no. 38). Some countries (Rumania, East Germany) did not even go so far (Csaba, 1990, p. 357).

According to Zwass (1990, p. 161) Gorbachev explained to the prime ministers of CMEA member states the objective of the long-term programme in this way: 'The Comprehensive programme just adopted was designed to make the community independent of Western technology and also to make it invulnerable to pressure and blackmail from the forces of imperialism.' Assuming that Zwass' information about Gorbachev's statement was correct, one can pose the question : could the CMEA countries have got on without imports of technology from the West? Did the CMEA have the scientific and technical expertise and organisational sophistication to be able to produce the necessary technology and to diffuse it?

It is generally known that the European CMEA member countries were behind the West in their level of technology and therefore they imported a considerable amount of modern technology from the West. If the West had not imposed export restrictions on strategy goods as they were set by the COCOM (Coordinating Committee for Multi-lateral Export Controls) list, an institution established by American initiative in 1949, the imports of technology from the West would have been even larger.

There are disagreements about the extent of the technological gap, which to a certain degree depended on the methodology used to calculate the role of technology in the pace of economic growth. It can also be stated with some degree of certainty that the gap in technology was primarily in industrial consumer goods and was the smallest in military equipment. It is known that the Soviets, and the same is true of the small countries, were much behind in the use of personal computers (Lavigne, 1991, pp. 195–201). The gap in technology was in indirect relationship to the importance which the Soviets attached to individual areas.

The Soviets applied the same differentiated approach to technology in cooperation with CMEA countries. In this respect the experience of a Hungarian high official is very interesting. He approached his counterpart in the Soviet government with a concern about the lack of modern technology. When he explained to the Soviet official what he actually had in mind, the latter promised that Soviet technicians would do their best to develop the machine the Hungarians needed, and, in fact, they did so in a relatively short time. The Soviet official shrugged his shoulders when the dialogue turned to the development of gadgets for consumers. This apparently was not a top priority for the Soviets.

According to Sobell, whom Lavigne quotes (1991, p. 224), in 1980 90 per cent of equipment in CMEA intra-trade consisted of traditional products with low R and D content. The figure seems very high, and it is not clear whether the author considered it to be more or less typical of the whole period or only of 1980. There is no doubt that cooperation between the member countries did not exhaust the potential for joint technological advancement. The approved long-term programme did not bring about a noticeable change in this regard. This was not surprising under conditions when many problems, affecting the working of CMEA, were not solved and the differences in the economic mechanism among member countries were quite large and, in the course of time, increased. Poland and Hungary increasingly expanded the role of the market in the coordination of the economy. On the other hand, other small countries stuck more or less to the old system. Even the Soviet 1987 reform could not change much in the general picture. Perhaps another reason for the meagre results of the long-term programme was that the member countries' trust in the effectiveness of CMEA had diminished considerably, after many disappointments with the various programmes. If the Soviet Union had manifested greater interest in joint efforts to advance technology in the 1960s, perhaps even in the first half of the 1970s, when it was still believed that CMEA could be turned into an effective instrument of technological progress, the Programme could have been more successful. (See also Chapter 2.)

Of course, there was indigenous technological progress in the Soviet Union as well as in the countries under review; it was, however, not sufficient considering that economic growth was increasingly dependent on such progress as the extensive growth factors had been more and more exhausted. Under such conditions Gorbachev's objective to make CMEA independent of Western technology was not very realistic. Maybe he did not even mean it seriously; it was, rather, a pep-talk.

When in Poland and Hungary the communist rule was broken it was clear that this would have a significant change in CMEA. In 1990-1 the Soviets pushed through a shift to dollar-accounted trade and world-market prices, an idea which had already been urged by Hungary. Trade in dollars was not entirely a new idea; it started to be practised in the 1970s. As already mentioned, it was usually applied for deliveries of 'hard' goods above the agreed quotas and in *ad hoc* deals. This time it was to affect all trade, and meant an improvement in the terms of trade for the Soviets and, naturally, a worsening for the smaller countries of CMEA. The Soviets did not feel that they should subsidise countries which no longer regarded themselves as allies of the USSR (Köves, 1992, p. 63).

The change to a dollar trade and genuine world-market prices accelerated the process of disintegration of CMEA, which was dying out anyhow as a result of the collapse of the socialist system in the member countries. Very soon the parties agreed to liquidate CMEA, which happened in 1991.

FOREIGN TRADE

Before the Second World War the smaller countries of CMEA had minimal trade relations with the Soviet Union. Even trade between smaller countries was not very extensive. Only after World War II did mutual trade relations start to expand. After the seizure of power by the communists, this trend intensified dramatically. In 1948 Czechoslovak trade with the USSR amounted to 16.1 per cent, and with the later CMEA countries to 32.5 per cent. At the same time trade with advanced capitalist countries was 45.5 per cent of the total trade. In 1952 there was a clear reversal: trade with the USSR jumped to 34.8 per cent and with CMEA countries as a whole to 71.4 per cent. On the other hand, trade with advanced capitalist countries suffered a dramatic decline: it plummeted to 20.5 per cent (*Historická statistická ročenka*, 1985, p. 320). A similar situation occurred in Poland and Hungary.

In 1967 the percentage of trade with the Soviet Union was almost the same in all three countries, around 35 per cent. However, the three countries already differed in trade with capitalist countries: Czechoslovakia's was the lowest- 18.9 per cent whereas Hungary's was 24.1 per cent and Poland's 27.5 per cent (*Economic Developments in countries of Eastern Europe*, 1970, pp. 546–9).[8] This trend continued in the years following.

In 1973 Czechoslovak imports from Western Europe increased to 20.5 per cent, Hungarian to 25.1 per cent and Polish to 35.1per cent. In 1975 Polish imports increased to 39.6 per cent. The three most important commodity groups in imports were machinery, manufactures and chemicals. In 1975 in Poland the first two groups made up 73.4 per cent of all imports. It is clear that all three countries, but Poland in particular, tried to modernise their productive apparatus (Wolf, 1977, pp. 1048 and 1050).

In the 1980s Czechoslovakia, unlike the other two countries, increased its trade with CMEA countries because of a substantial increase in trade with the USSR. In 1985 total trade with CMEA countries increased to 74 per cent and trade with the USSR to 44.8 per cent. On the other hand trade with capitalist countries declined substantially. In 1985 it made up only 15.5 per cent (*SR*, 1987, p. 445). (See Chapter 8 for the reasons.)

In the 1980s the Polish and Hungarian trade with advanced capitalist countries was more than double that of Czechoslovakia. In 1985 Hungarian imports from capitalist countries made up 38.5 per cent of total imports and exports 30.8 per cent of total exports. In the same year the Polish figures were 34.9 per cent and 34.7 per cent respectively (*SE* 1986, p. 208; and *RS* 1988, p. 356).

Trade with advanced capitalist countries was of course expanded at the expense of trade with CMEA. In the 1980s Polish and Hungarian trade with CMEA countries was almost 20 per cent lower than Czechoslovak trade with the same countries. Trade with the Soviet Union did not suffer as much as trade with other members of CMEA.

From the foregoing it is clear that in the 1980s Poland and Hungary were well integrated into world trade which was dominated by the developed capitalist countries. This had no doubt an advantage; it enabled the two countries to take advantage of Western technological progress to some degree. It should not, however, be forgotten that access to Western technology was limited by the regulations of COCOM (see p. 82). The mentioned expansion of trade was often combined with a deficit in the balance of trade but, even when the two countries managed to achieve a surplus, the surplus was not sufficient to service the debt. In both cases it meant that foreign indebtedness increased.[9] Furthermore, the two countries were much more exposed than Czechoslovakia to Western business cycles, which had of course a negative impact on the economic development of Poland and Hungary.

As will be shown in Chapter 8, Czechoslovakia curbed its trade relations with Western countries for economic and political reasons.

CONCLUDING REMARKS

In its more than 40 years of existence, CMEA went through many changes which were intended to make it an instrument of economic integration. It would be wrong not to see that it achieved some positive results, but it is also true that it remained far behind its objectives. There were several factors which hindered the realisation of these objectives. I disregard here the initial period when, on the Soviet side, there was no interest in establishing a genuine multilateral economic cooperation.

The cooperation of CMEA countries necessarily reflected the internal systemic arrangement of individual countries. The economic relations among the socialist countries could not deviate much from the principles on which the working of domestic economies was based. Detailed planning from the centre in CMEA countries set the framework within which the cooperation could move; such a system did not allow market relations among them – anyway the leaders were against them for political and ideological reasons. After all, the countries were pursuing a socialist cooperation. Even in the 1960s when major reforms in Hungary and Czechoslovakia came about (reforms in which the market mechanism played a role) no great changes in the CMEA working could occur because the USSR was not interested. When under Gorbachev the Soviets were prepared to overhaul CMEA, it was already too late. Most of the smaller countries, which in the meantime had started to abandon socialism, were no longer interested in CMEA.

The process of cooperation was determined on the state level. Not only did the governments of individual countries agree on the modes of cooperation, but state officials were instrumental in the implementation of the programmes approved. The concretisation of the programmes and their implementation became too politicised and bureaucratised, and what was achieved did not further economic efficiency and technological progress significantly.

In specialisation and cooperation, two of the most important objectives of CMEA, only very meagre results were achieved, since progress depended primarily on the agreement of officials and technicians, and in their decision-making political, technical and engineering considerations played a paramount function. Prices and costs which should have been decisive were reduced to a subordinated function. One of the important reasons for this was the absence of a logical connection between the distorted domestic prices and the modified world prices at which trade took place (cf. Nove, 1980, p. 274). In such a situation it was very difficult to make the reliable economic calculations needed for a rational allocation of resources and specialisation.

Specialisation was hampered by the frequent resistance of enterprises to projects which entailed giving up a production line in which they already had experience, or accepting a new production line which required substantial training of workers. Another contributing factor was the lack of a long-term guaranteed market in other countries for the products resulting from specialisation. Finally, there was no mechanism for joint risk taking (Marer and Montias, 1981, p. 157).

Great differences in the level of economic development of the member countries of CMEA was a further obstacle to specialisation. Usually specialisation between countries at the same level of development can be more effective than between countries marked by great differences in the level of economic development, especially if all the countries have the ambition to produce machinery, as was the case with European members of CMEA.

Nationalistic attitudes influenced negatively the process of specialisation and the process of integration. This was primarily true until 1971 when the adoption of new programmes depended on the unanimous approval of all members of CMEA. Nationalistic attitudes led some countries to produce products for which they did not have the best preconditions in terms of costs, but did so for prestigious reasons. A good example was the production of automobiles.[10]

Another objective of CMEA, to bring about multilateral trade relations, an important precondition for integration, did not materialise. There were mainly two reasons for this. All output was planned, and there was usually a shortage of idle capacities which made it very difficult to produce goods, not included in the plan, but instead resulting from a new demand from foreign customers. In other words it was difficult to satisfy demand which went beyond the contingents agreed between individual countries (cf. Marer and Montias, 1981, p. 156–7). The second reason for the lack of multilateral relations was connected with the first in that there was a large lack of convertibility of commodities. The socialist countries were quite inflexible when adjustment of production to demand was needed. The lack of convertibility of commodities was the main reason that the convertibility of currency, even within the CMEA, could not really materialise.

Of course, in the final analysis all the programmes resulted in an expansion of trade, mainly between the USSR and other member countries. Trade with the former Soviet Union was a blessing, but also a curse. It was an advantage to have access to a huge market which was not very demanding about quality. However, this very circumstance had another, negative side: enterprises exporting to the USSR were not under sufficient pressure to do their best in terms of technical parameters and quality. Trade with the Soviet Union and the intra-East European trade did not work as a stimulus to technological progress and higher productivity in the way that trade between open economies does. On the contrary, the past intra-socialist trade is one of the main reasons why the smaller countries, as well as the Commonwealth of Independent States, have a hard time nowadays competing in Western markets.

In the more than 40 years of CMEA's existence various programmes which aimed at bringing the economies of the member countries closer to integration remained far from their goals. This necessarily resulted in a loosening of ties within CMEA and the search for more trade with Western economies. Such a development was characteristic mainly of Poland and Hungary (Šafaříková, 1989).

In brief, the centralised system had influenced adversely the socialist countries' external economic relations, and these in turn aggravated the working of the traditional system. Even the reforms in some countries could not change substantially the underlying principles of the working of CMEA. Perhaps the greatest shortcoming of CMEA was that it did not become an instrument of rapid technological progress.

6 Political and Ideological Factors

INTRODUCTION

The socialist system cannot be understood unless we know its political structure. Since this book is intended to focus primarily on the economic causes of the breakdown of socialism, I only want to show some of the political aspects which were responsible for the failure of the socialist system. To this end it is important to discuss the political system briefly. But before doing so I would like to mention the views of Marx on this topic.

In the *Manifesto of the Communist Party* (Marx–Engels Reader, 1978), which was first published in 1848, Marx and Engels assumed that in the fight with the bourgeoisie the proletariat might use force in order to establish itself as a ruling class. The purpose of this seizure of power was to bring about revolutionary changes in production relations. The seized political power would enable the proletariat 'to centralise all instruments of production in the hands of the State' (p. 490).

The authors also make it clear why they believe that the proletariat has a historical mission to destroy capitalism. To them the proletariat is the only revolutionary class. All other classes will disappear in the wake of modern industry. Shopkeepers, artisans, and peasants fight the bourgeoisie in order to maintain their existence as part of the bourgeoisie; thus they want to reverse development (Marx apparently assumed that they are doomed to proletarianisation) and therefore they should be regarded as reactionaries. Only proletarians, who do not own the means of production, can become masters of production by abolishing 'their own previous mode of appropriation . . . and every other previous mode of appropriation'. In contrast to other movements, which were movements of minorities, the proletariat is an 'immense majority, in the interests of the immense majority' (p. 482).

To Marx the rule of the proletariat is supposed to be temporary only. Once the old capitalist order is swept away, the 'public power will lose its political character' and with the disappearance of the old conditions the proletariat 'has swept away the conditions for the existence of class antagonisms and of classes generally, and will thereby have abolished its own supremacy as a class' (pp. 490–1).

In his *Anti-Dühring*, Engels (1969) echoed a similar sentiment to that of Marx, with the difference that he talked about the role of the state. According to him, with the disappearance of classes, 'State interference in social relations becomes, in one domain after another, superfluous, and then withers away of itself; the government of persons is replaced by the administration of things, and by the conduct of processes of production. The state is not "abolished". It *withers away*' (p. 333).

In the *Manifesto of the Communist Party* the term 'dictatorship of the proletariat' was not used. However, in his *Critique of the Gotha Program*, which was written 27 years later, Marx wrote 'Between capitalist and communist society lies the period of the revolutionary transformation of one into the other. There corresponds to this also a political transition period in which the state can be nothing but *the revolutionary dictatorship of the proletariat.*' (Marx–Engels Reader, 1978, p. 538).

Since Marx was not specific about what he meant by the dictatorship of the proletariat, politicians and scholars have tried to interpret his view, mostly in a way that fitted in with their own ideas.

In his *State and Revolution,* Lenin (1967, vol. 2, p. 334) argued that, in the transitional period from capitalism, dictatorship was needed, 'for the *resistance* of the capitalist exploiters cannot be *broken* by anyone else or in any other way'. In other words, he had in mind a genuine dictatorship of the proletariat and believed that it was in line with Marx's and Engels' ideas. He also argued that democracy in capitalist countries was 'democracy for the minority, only for the property classes, only for the rich' (p. 333).

In 1918, after the Bolsheviks seized power, K. Kautsky (1964), one of the leading Marxists in Europe, published a pamphlet on the topic of dictatorship of the proletariat. It was on the one hand a plea for democracy and thus a censure of the methods used by the Bolsheviks in their fight for power. On the other, it was an attempt to show that Marx, when talking about dictatorship, did not really have in mind a system contrary to democracy. This view he tried to back up with Marx's evaluation of the French Commune, which was the result of a general suffrage, and concluded 'The dictatorship of the proletariat was for him a condition which necessarily arose in a real democracy, because of the overwhelming numbers of the proletariat' (p. 45). As is known, Marx believed that the socialist revolution would first triumph in highly developed countries, where the industrial proletariat was growing fast and probably assumed on the basis of his theory of concentration that the proletariat would achieve a majority.

Regardless of what Marx had in mind, his suggested idea of the dictatorship of the proletariat was welcome to the Bolsheviks in Russia, where a long tradition of authoritarianism existed which also affected their thinking. Marx gave them the ideological tool for doing what they had an inclination to do anyhow.

All those who had in mind a genuine dictatorship of the proletariat did not mean that the proletariat itself would exercise the dictatorship. A class cannot govern, it can only rule, as Kautsky mentioned (p. 45). It was assumed that the dictatorship would be organised by a political party, as vanguard of the proletariat. As will be shown later, the political power in the Soviet Union was not concentrated in the hands of the Communist Party (henceforth CP or simply the Party); the latter served only as a well-thought-out instrument for the dictatorship of a small group of people.

For some time the socialist countries openly admitted that their system was a dictatorship of the proletariat. At the end of the 1950s Khrushchev came up with the idea that the Soviet Union was no longer a dictatorship of the proletariat: the dictatorship had fulfilled its functions, particularly in liquidating the capitalist system, and the state was gradually becoming a state of all the people. Later this idea was elaborated on and included in the new 1961 Party programme. According to The New Program of the Communist Party of the Soviet Union (*Essential* . . ., 1965) the dictatorship of the proletariat fulfilled its mission by insuring the victory of socialism and was no longer necessary, and therefore 'the organs of state power will gradually be transformed into organs of public self-government.' (p. 451). After 1965 the socialist countries no longer talked about their system as a dictatorship of the proletariat, though the new CP programme did not bring great changes to the structure of their Party and the political system.

THE ONE-PARTY STATE

The political system in the former socialist countries can be characterised briefly as a one-party system and thus a one-party state. In all these countries the political power was concentrated in the hands of the CP. True, the CP had a different name in some countries, [1] but this was done for political reasons. Regardless of the name all the parties behaved more or less the same way until the start of the reforms.

In some countries other parties existed besides the CP, for example, in Czechoslovakia and Poland. The existence of non-communist political parties did not turn the political system into a genuine multi-party system. The other parties were subordinated to the CP, were forced to recognise its leading role and accept socialism as their programme. They had a dual task: on the one hand, to act as veil to cover up the real face of the CP and thus lend some legitimacy to the socialist system and, on the other hand, to act as a mass organisation, namely, to be a transformation belt between the Party and the people who were associated with these non-communist parties. True, the latter usually had some representatives in the government, but these were picked by the CPs rather than by the non-communist parties themselves. In brief, they could not be real participants in the exercise of political power. [2]

CPs controlled all facets of political, social and economic life. This control was exercised indirectly, with the help of governments appointed by the CPs. In order to maintain tight control the governments imposed far-reaching limitations on human rights, such as freedom of expression, association, travel etc. And a powerful secret police, aided by a large net of informers, saw to it that the CP's rule was not violated. In addition, a well-organised army in every socialist country, in alliance with the Soviet army, had to make sure that external intervention would not take place.

This tight control was possible because the CP itself was hierarchically organised and authoritarian. The underlying principle of the organisation of the CP was the so-called democratic centralism. According to it, all the CPs' governing bodies were supposed to be elected democratically. The centralism was to mean that subordinated bodies in the hierarchy should obey the decisions of superior bodies. This principle, which seems logical and sound at first glance, was an important component of the party organisation concept. Its background and purpose can be found in Lenin's *One Step Forward and Two Back* (1967). When Lenin still headed the Bolshevik Party (as the CP was called up to 1922) the principle of democratic centralism was respected to a great degree. Once Stalin took over the leadership of the CP, internal democracy was gradually destroyed and democratic centralism was used as an instrument to bring about a dictatorship of one person. All the political power was concentrated in the hands of the Secretary General of the Party (or First Secretary as he was called in some periods and some countries), which in practice meant that Stalin, who was the Secretary General, was a dictator up to his death in 1953. Unlike Hitler, who called himself and was called the leader (Führer) and who made it clear that all the power, which his subordinates used, came from him, Stalin tried to maintain the ideological cover that he was the first among equals. With Stalin's death the role of the Secretary General was diminished (in different countries to different degrees) in favour of the Politburo, the collective organ, which was chaired by the Secretary General. The governing bodies, which according to the constitution were above the Politburo, that is the Congress and the Central Committee (CC), were usually relegated to being rubber stamps. The Politburo used two instruments primarily to make the CC a submissive body. First, the discussions in the sessions of the CC were organised in advance. The discussants were picked in advance and were told what to say, or else what they intended to say was checked. Voluntary discussants had to show their contribution in writing in advance and if it did not 'fit in' they were told that there would not be time for their contribution and that it would be added to the minutes of the session.

Second, the Politburo presented only the proposals of the majority for approval by the CC. The Politburo members were not allowed to defend their minority view in the session of the CC. Not only this, members of the CC usually did not know what the minority view in the Politburo was.

In addition, members of the CC did not dare criticise the Politburo for fear of retribution. Only if there was a rift in the Politburo could the CC become active.

The Congress, which was formally the highest governing body of the Party and elected the CC, was also manipulated by the Politburo. The latter, with the help of the party apparatus, saw to it that only 'reliable' (meaning faithful to the leadership) members of the CP were delegated to the Congress. The members of the CC were in fact selected by the Politburo and rubber stamped by the Congress.

This system, which was established in the USSR, was embraced at the end of the 1940s, after the CPs seized power, in all East European countries. After the twentieth Congress of the Soviet CP in 1956, at which Stalin was subjected to sharp criticism, the internal working of the Party was to some extent democratised. The Politburo became largely a collective body and the role of the CC was increased somewhat. This trend to democratisation within the Party was strengthened by the reforms of the 1960s and even more by the reforms of the 1980s.

Formal pressure groups, or even organisations which might develop into pressure groups, were not allowed. This does not mean that no pressure group existed, in reality there were some and very powerful, but they could not signal their existence by public presentations of their interests. It has already been mentioned that the managers of heavy industry were a powerful pressure group. One should also regard the local party organisations, which intervened with ministries in favour of the interests of enterprises located in their territory, as some kind of pressure groups. The objection by the CPs to formal pressure groups was motivated by the fear that they might develop into centres of opposition to the CP and thus erode the leading role of the Party.

In all the socialist countries there were so-called mass organisations, such as women and youth organisations whose purpose was to serve as a transmission belt between the CP and the masses. Mass organisations were fully subordinated to the political leadership of the Party. Trade Unions were also treated as a mass organisation, and their main task was to mobilise workers for the fulfilment of the economic plan. Protection of workers' interests was a secondary task.

I agree with A. Meyer (1965) who believed that the structure and functioning of the Soviet CP was very similar to that of giant corporations. 'It has [the Soviet CP] in common with them a thoroughly authoritarian political structure, in which the elite is independent of control by the lower-ranking members of the organisation, even though all or most giant bureaucracies in the modern world insist that their rank-and-file constituents participate in the organisation's public life' writes Meyer (quoted according to White, Gardner and Schöpflin, 1987, p. 21).

The political power of the CP was so all-embracing not only because the government, including local authorities, was appointed by the governing bodies of the CP, but also because the CP controlled the economy as caretaker of the nationalised and collectivised means of production.

At the head of a huge bureaucracy the communist leaders determined the structure and direction of the economy and the economic mechanism. In the final analysis they determined the main objectives of the five-year and annual plans, the expected pace of economic growth, the distribution of income, the rate of accumulation, etc. They thus determined which social goals would get priority and which would be put aside.

They controlled not only the macroeconomic sphere, but also the microeconomic sphere, on the one hand through top managers whose nomination depended on the approval of the CP, and on the other hand through territorial CP organisations and CP organisations at the work place. The tight CP control over the economy seemed to the leaders to be not only convenient, but also advantageous. It made it possible for them to dispose of resources almost according to their will, constrained, of course, by economic realities. Control over the economy, combined with the enforced absence of any kind of public control, at least in the form of a liberal press, gave the leaders almost a feeling of omnipotence. And this really hid many dangers for the economy, and also for the leaders themselves in the final analysis. In such an environment, where reliable signals about the performance of the economy did not function well and a self-correcting mechanism like the market did not exist, enormous mistakes could easily be made and, once made, they were very difficult to correct. Since all the levers of control over the economy were in the hands of the CP, the public credited the CP with all the successes, but also blamed it for the failures. Because there were more of the latter, mainly in the 1980s, the CP lost credibility.

During the economic reforms there was some attempt to put a part of the responsibility for the well-being of workers on enterprises. For example, in the Hungarian economic reform of 1968, but even more in the reform of 1987, enterprises were given quite a lot of input into the decisions about the evolution of wages and the distribution of the gross profit. Of course, the main reason for the changes in the regulation of wages had to do with the desire to give enterprises greater autonomy in the hope that this would generate economic efficiency. No doubt, this change was also aimed at making enterprises responsible in the eyes of workers, or at least co-responsible for their material well-being. Needless to say, this attempt was not successful.

LEGITIMACY OF THE REGIME

The one-party system was not the result of the free will of the people: in some countries, such as in the USSR, China, Vietnam and Cuba, it was the result of a civil war and in the countries under review it was imposed by the USSR. The CPs did not seek genuine popular approval of their rule, even after consolidating their power. Any parliamentary elections they held were a farce; every constituency had only one candidate who was formally selected by the National Front (which grouped all political parties and mass organisations and was dominated by the CP), but was in reality more or less the choice of the CP. To the extent that other political parties existed and had representation in the government, they could not contest their strength in parliamentary elections on a separate slate. The CPs saw to it that their candidates received at least 95 per cent of the poular vote. To achieve this figure the Party apparatus used pressure, intimidation and propaganda and it probably rigged the results in some cases.

The Hungarian CP was the only one of those under review that tried (in 1985), when the regime still seemed to be stable, to depart from traditional elections. It did not allow a multi-party system, but it allowed the public to nominate more than one candidate for each election constituency. However, to make sure that the top leadership was elected, the CP ran a country slate which made the election of its candidates a sure thing. This experiment was quite successful: none of the active high functionaries was defeated, more communists were elected than in previous elections and many independent candidates were elected (see Pozsgay, 1989, pp. 75–9). There was no further occasion to expand the experiment because in 1989 the socialist system collapsed. Considering that the elections took place at a time when the economic situation was bad, one may speculate that in the 1960s, when the reforms started, the CPs in both Czechoslovakia and Hungary, but mainly in the former, had a good chance to gain legitimacy through free elections, particularly if they took lessons from the West about campaign techniques aimed at influencing the voters.

True, not only supporters of the regime, but also a large proportion of the population did not care about legitimacy as long as the regime was able to ensure a decent standard of living. People accepted the argument of the communist leaders that their legitimacy lay in solving problems which the capitalist system was not able to, such as full employment, a more equal distribution of income, an extensive social net etc. Once the regime found itself in an economic and political crisis, the situation changed and, legitimacy became an issue. The opposition could and did use lack of legitimacy as an important instrument in its fight against the regime. And it turned out to be a powerful instrument.

POLITICAL FACTIONS

The so-called democratic centralism, the basic organisational structure of the CP, did not allow any formal factions[3] in the Party in order to prevent the creation of oppositional political parties. This was, no doubt, important in the initial period of building the socialist system. But later it turned out to be a tremendous shortcoming of the system. True, factions came into being in Poland as well as in Hungary in the second half of the 1980s, but they could not establish themselves as quasi political parties. Anyhow, it was too late, because the countries were already in the grip of a deep economic and political crisis.

Allowing factions might have prevented the socialist system from making many wrong decisions which hurt the economy. Because the factions would have had to contend for the support of members of the Party or voters, the economy would have been pushed more in the direction of being consumption oriented. The factions would have also prevented gross violations of human rights. The system would have received a democratic appearance.

What is more important is that factions might perhaps have rescued the system. In a capitalist system, the fact that an unlimited number of political parties can contest political power is an important protection of the system. If the public is dissatisfied with the ruling party, it can get rid of it in the next election by voting for a rival party. The latter may not be much different in its world view than the ruling party of the day was; however, the public finds some satisfaction in feeling able to punish those who caused its frustration. Usually all the important parties profess an ideology of free enterprise, though in details they differ. Thus the system is safe, even if the country is exposed to a deep recession.

The media which are mostly in the hands of big corporations make sure that the capitalist ideology is the ruling ideology. Usually the owners (big corporations) do not interfere in the daily activities of the media: editors, anchormen and reporters have a considerable amount of freedom of expression. Broadcasting networks, daily papers, magazines and journals differ in their positions on vital problems of the economy, political and social life. This plurality of views gives the impression that it reflects the thinking of the people. However, the opposite is true; people mostly accept what the media tell them is right. Unfortunately, most people are not politically educated enough to understand what is really going on in the economy, and therefore they can be easily manipulated if the proper language and reasoning, close to their values, is used.

The impression that the media serve the people is strengthened by the fact that there are no legal restrictions in advanced capitalist countries on what can be published. Anti-capitalist daily papers and magazines can be freely published. This is so in theory; in practice it is difficult to take advantage of such a possibility. To publish a daily paper costs a lot of money, and big corporations would be unlikely to finance such a venture. In addition, such a paper would surely not get business advertisements. And even if there are several anti-capitalist papers, how big can their influence be in competition with the powerful media supporting the capitalist system?

It was mentioned that the media personnel have freedom of expression. It is necessary to add that they know very well that their freedom of expression has certain limits with regard to criticism of the capitalist system. If they cross this red line frequently, their jobs will be in serious danger.

The existence of factions in the Party which could have become political parties might perhaps have allowed the political tensions of an economic crisis to be defused by the transfer of power from one faction to another. Such an outcome could have had a chance if the factions had come into being when the Party's standing was relatively strong, and if, in the course of time, the new structure had become entrenched and certain temporary restrictions on freedom of creation of political parties had been imposed. In addition, what was needed was a media with pluralistic views, but which supported a restructured socialist system. Of course, without restructuring the economy in the direction of a market economy, even with some limitations, the chances for the survival of such a system in the long run were small. Limitations should also have been set for the private sector. The constitution could have contained a limit on the number of people who could be employed by a private company.

Needless to say, small countries alone could hardly sustain such a system. Multinational corporations would regard it as a threat to their interests and would try to undermine it and, considering their economic power and solidarity, they would be bound to succeed.

CHANGES IN THE PARTY AND STATE APPARATUS

Changes within the Party and state apparatus, primarily the former, were an important factor in the collapse of the socialist system. After World War II the Party and state apparatus was mostly headed by people who were ideologically committed to the ideas of socialism and communism. In Czechoslovakia these were people whose faith in the ideals of the CP was hardened in the struggle of the Party for its goals and in opposition to the governments of the day between the two wars. Their commitment to socialism was strengthened because socialism as an applied system had its origin in the Soviet Union, which had freed their country from German Nazism. In addition, these people still remembered the Great Depression and its tragic effect on employment and the standard of living. Between the two world wars in Poland, where the CP was mostly illegal and in Hungary where it was always illegal, many of the leading functionaries of the Party apparatus came from people who worked in the illegal Party, in other words, people who were emotionally and ideologically linked to the CP. In all three countries factory workers were promoted to important functions in the Party, the state and the economy in the hope that their elevation to positions of responsibility would be reciprocated by faithfulness to the Party line. In most cases this happened.

In the 1960s and 1970s the Party and state apparatus structure started to change. Particularly in Poland and Hungary this process was considerably accelerated in the 1980s. The new people recruited for the apparatus were different from the old generation. They were better educated, many of them had a university education. In his paper F. Gazsó (1993) indicates figures for Hungary which confirm this. In 1981, 50.5 per cent of the CP elite (politburo members, central committee members, secretaries and department heads of CC) had a university background; in 1989 this number had increased to 75. 2 per cent. A similar development occurred among the state and economic elite, with the difference that there the percentage of people with a university education was much higher. What is also of importance is that in the 1980s in the state and managerial apparatus there was a 70 per cent turnover of cadres against 9. 3 per cent in 1970s. In addition, in the 1980s many technocrats got in positions in the state and managerial apparatus which (positions) were before reserved for members of the party apparatus. Probably a similar situation occurred in Poland.

In Czechoslovakia, the politicians stuck more to the old 'cadre' policy, but even here the percentage of people with a university education in the Party apparatus, let alone the state apparatus and economic management, grew fast.

This change in 'cadre' policy was the result of several factors. It was a response to the increasing sophistication of the economy and the need for greater expertise to handle economic problems. Educated people were also needed in order to cope with the non-economic problems faced by the CPs. Last but not least, communist leaders wanted to believe that people educated under the socialist system would be at least loyal to the system.

Most of these newcomers to positions of responsibility in the 1980s were not very emotionally connected with the Party; they were not part of the experience that the older generation had gone through. They were less ideologically oriented, more critical and independent in their thinking, and pragmatic. They were no longer as committed to the ideals of the CP and socialism as their predecessors had been. They were in a sense the product of the changes which had occurred in society: the revolutionary fervour, which dominated a proportion of the population, had evaporated long before, because this normally survives the revolution only for a short time and because great disappointment set in due to unfulfilled expectations.

Many of the newcomers were cynics who were willing to feign certain stands in order to acquire positions of power. Political power was more important to them than the ideals of socialism. They were willing to work in the Party and state apparatus because they were interested in having political power and influence and because these positions were better paid. Because of their superior knowledge such people can be good servants of a cause, even better in some cases than the previous ones, as long as the regime functions well. Once a political and economic crisis starts to develop and doubts arise about the stability and survivability of the regime, their loyalty to the cause, which was insignificant in any case, diminishes quickly, and they turn into real bureaucrats who are willing to serve any regime. At any rate such people would not stick their necks out for the regime; on the contrary, they might even accelerate its demise if their interests were served by doing so. [4] It is no accident that many members of the former nomenclature, including members of the state and Party apparatus, used their positions of power for various acts of legal or illegal privatisation which enriched them. In her book J. Staniszkis (1991) mentions a whole series of methods used in Poland for this purpose. She maintains that nomenclature companies control 10–20 per cent of state assets (p. 68). A similar situation occurred in Hungary.

When the economic situation began to worsen in the second half of the 1980s and when various attempts, undertaken to salvage the situation, turned out to be unsuccessful, a political crisis started to develop in Hungary (Poland was affected by it even earlier) which afflicted the CP itself. The cohesion of the CPs started to loosen and the ability to control events slowly slipped from their hands.

THE EROSION OF THE IDEOLOGY

The 'Marxist' ideology was the glue which held together the CPs, which played the leading role in the countries. The quotation marks around 'Marxism' are to indicate that what was put forward as Marxism by the regime was in reality a twisted and distorted Marxism: elements of Marxism which fitted in with the Stalinist system were taken over; on the other hand, other elements, for example those that had to do with humanism and self-fulfilment, were dropped. Marxism, even in its twisted form, was still a powerful force which united believers in socialism. [5] In Czechoslovakia, ideas associated with Marxism and socialism – like full employment, development of the economy without recessions, more equal distribution of income and an extensive social safety net – were mostly accepted with satisfaction and in many circles with enthusiasm. In 1946, the Czechoslovak CP got more than 40 per cent of the popular vote in free elections. It is necessary to state that the CP did not lose its support when it seized power in February 1948 through pressure, intimidation and propaganda. The masses were willing to believe that this was necessary in order to build a more just system.

In Poland and Hungary, where the Communists had little backing before the war, the new regime was also able to attract support. Brzezinski (1989, p. 108) writes that both countries had

> large numbers of rural poor, as well as some highly radicalised industrial workers, who were willing and even eager to identify with the new regime. For them, the onset of the Communist rule opened the doors to rapid advancement through greater educational opportunities, as well as in the new institutions of power, notably the police and the military . . . The new order also mobilized in the early years the support of many of the young, drawn by the vision of a new age, by grandiose urban and industrial projects, and by humanitarian goals of social reform.

The ideology used by the CPs was not made up solely of ideas about how future society and the economy should be organised, how the diseases of capitalism would be cured and thus how socialism would differ from capitalism. It also included a code of behaviour to which great importance was attributed in the struggle to build socialism. The most important elements of this code were: discipline, the obeying of the orders of higher decision-making bodies in the hierarchy without hesitancy, a willingness to sacrifice one's own interests for the sake of the collective, and vigilance against the real and potential enemies of socialism (see Kornai, 1992 p. 57). The principle of discipline is applied in every hierarchical society, including a democracy. But it played a specially important role in the organisational structure of the CP as well as in the structure of the economic mechanism. Without discipline the traditional economic mechanism could not have worked. If several enterprises did not fulfil the assigned output targets, other enterprises could not either, and a chain reaction might arise with shortages as a consequence. If discipline is increasingly ignored, the regime must necessarily be weakened.

Of course, socialist countries relied not only on ideology to ensure that discipline would be followed: they backed up ideology with a stick and carrot approach. Under Stalin's rule there was more stick than carrot: violations of discipline were treated with a heavy hand, often with prison. Later the stick was less oppressive and was replaced with more of a carrot.

The ideology was also backed up by propaganda which, mainly in the first years of the new regime, was coarse and clumsy. The propagandists had little experience in knowing how to make their explanations of government policies believable and how to explain the contradictions between the ideology and reality. They believed that, if they denied the self evident, spread half-truths and repeated them frequently, people would be willing to accept them. They believed Goebbels, the propaganda minister of the German Nazi government, who maintained that if you repeat a lie many times, people will believe it. In brief, the propaganda was not very convincing and often had the opposite effect to what was desired. It negatively affected in particular the attitude of the intelligentsia to the socialist regime.

The propagandists had a hard time defending government policies, mainly those at the beginning of the 1950s, which caused great hardship to the population. The burden which the first medium-term plans imposed on the working people did not square with the CPs' claim that their policies were dictated by the interests of the working people. The communist leaders tried to blame the shortages and the decline in the standard of living on 'plotters and traitors'. Show trials at the end of the 1940s and the beginning of the 1950s, a product of Stalin's method of scaring off potential opposition, were used by the propagandists as proof that the decline in the standard of living was really the work of traitors and agents of the West (cf. Fejtő, 1974, pp. 14–25).

The propaganda about the USSR was especially awkward and crude, and frequently insulted national feelings. The attempts to portray the USSR as the best country in all respects including the standard of living, a kind of role model for other countries, were the best proof that propagandists did not understand how mass psychology works. In the beginning many people believed in the lie, mainly those who favoured the regime or those who lacked information to the contrary. There were also people who had doubts about the truthfulness of the propaganda about the USSR, but did not object to it, believing that it served a good cause. Despite the Iron Curtain the truth slowly worked its way through and the propaganda about the USSR had the opposite effect: people ceased to believe positive reports about the USSR even if they were true.

The effect of the propaganda was also diminished by the communist leaders' preaching water and drinking wine, to use a Hungarian proverb. In capitalist countries people accept as natural that the elite lives in abundance and luxury. They believe in 'filter-down economics', understood in a non-pejorative manner. In the socialist countries egalitarianism hit deep roots, and the public expected the communist leaders and their subordinates to endure at least some of the hardship as they did. They resented the fact that there were special stores for the elite, stocked with goods which were not available in ordinary shops. They believed, rightly, that if the wives (or husbands) of the members of the elite had to line up for consumer goods in times of shortages and spend several hours in queues during the week, the elite would have a better understanding of the importance of a smooth supply of consumer goods. Special hospitals for the elite, where better service and foreign drugs were available, were also resented. It is also known that in Czechoslovakia members of the central Party apparatus used to get untaxed and therefore illegal supplementary payments. There were various other privileges which the elite enjoyed. They had easier access to housing, travel etc. For completeness, it should be said that their legal incomes were quite modest compared to the incomes of the elites in capitalist countries. What is also important is that they could make decisions about the use of capital assets, but they could not own them or bequeath them to their children.

The gross violation of human rights, which was typical of the first decade of the communist regime, also made the work of propagandists more difficult, mainly among the intelligentsia. The communist leaders tried to scare off real and potential opposition to their regime. To this end they made judges sentence people to arduous physical labour and even resorted to judicial killing on trumped-up charges. They also used less harsh methods. Some of the methods had the character of 'overkill' (e.g., the expulsion of certain types of students from universities in Czechoslovakia (see p. 63) or the deportation of the 'exponents of the capitalist regime' from Budapest (see p. 55) and resulted from paranoia.

In the course of 40 years the socialist ideology changed very much and its influence fluctuated, but in the long run it diminished greatly so that in the second half of the 1980s it was discredited to such an extent that in the power struggle between the CP and its opposition it ceased to be an important factor. It would exceed the scope of this study to engage in a detailed analysis of the changes in the ideology and in the propaganda used to back it up; therefore I will mention only some of the important changes.

After Stalin's death in 1953 the countries under review gradually started to use more subtle methods in propaganda. This change in propaganda helped for a while because it was coupled with changes in economic policy. The hardships of the first middle-term plans were eased by slowing down the investment drive and paying greater attention to consumption.

The Twentieth Congress of the Soviet CP in 1956, in which Khrushchev revealed Stalin's gross abuses of power and crimes, became an important milestone in the erosion of the ruling ideology. Many assertions about the superiority of the socialist system turned out to be lies. Many dogmas which were presented to the people as undisputable truths (among them that economic growth is possible only if production of producer goods grows faster than production of consumer goods, a principle which was supposed to back up the industrialisation drive) collapsed and undermined the system. In Hungary, the verbal attack on the CP started with attacking and ridiculing the Stalinist dogmas, and this in turn helped to mobilise people for the 1956 uprising in Hungary.

In the middle of the 1960s political relaxation, which had already started with, *inter alia*, the idea of the CPs that the dictatorship of the proletariat came to an end, was accelerated by the economic reforms in Czechoslovakia and Hungary. Writers, playwrights, artists and social scientists should be given some credit for the political relaxation. In particular writers fought for the expansion of human rights, freedom of expression and for non-interference by the government in artistic creation. They were in a sense the spokesmen of the opposition.

The political relaxation was manifested in the greater role of parliament in legislative activity, more independence for the judicial system, a greater consideration to human rights and a greater role to the trade unions: all this under the catch phrase 'socialist democracy'. In Czechoslovakia, where the political relaxation went beyond Hungary's, the Action Programme of the CP (*Rok . . .*, 1969, pp. 112–18) redefined the leading role of the Party in the sense that it wanted to be an initiator of changes and a creator of consensus by persuasion and example. It also promised to make sure that human rights were respected and to give interest groups the right to organise themselves.

The political relaxation on the one hand strengthened the regime, mainly in Czechoslovakia, but on the other hand it slowly opened the door to ideologies which opposed socialism. Nevertheless in Hungary and Poland (with the exception of the period of martial law) political relaxation continued to expand so that in the second half of the 1980s gross violation of human rights was the exception. In Czechoslovakia, after the Soviet-led invasion, a period of human rights repression followed.

In the beginning of the 1950s the communist ideologues professed the idea that socialism was different from capitalism in almost all aspects, and therefore everything should be eliminated which was a reminder of capitalism. The market was regarded as an integral part of capitalism and its elimination from parts of the economy where it still survived (as in agriculture) was assumed to be only a matter of time. The economic reforms brought about a change in viewing the market. The old view that the market was an integral part of capitalism was untenable when the reforms used the market, though in the 1960s only as a supplementary coordinating mechanism to planning. Therefore the idea that the market was neutral from a systemic viewpoint, that it could be used by both systems, socialist and capitalist, found its way into the ideology.

In the second half of the 1950s Khrushchev challenged the West to a peaceful competition between socialism and capitalism. This idea was also included in the Soviet CP's programme (*Essential . . .*, 1965, p. 418). The challenge to a competition opened the door to comparisons of the economic performance of the two systems. In the beginning, when the Soviet economy and the economies of the smaller countries were growing faster than the economies of the West, the comparisons worked in favour of socialist countries, all the more because they had control over what kind of comparisons were published. Even during the economic reform of the 1960s in Czechoslovakia, when censorship was almost removed, the comparisons hurt the socialist system though socialist ideology had still a sway over a great proportion of the intelligentsia. In the 1980s the comparisons undermined the credibility of the socialist system and served as proof of its inferiority.

In the second half of the 1980s, the socialist ideology increasingly lost ground to capitalist ideology. This was especially true when the CPs in Poland and Hungary started to embrace the idea of market socialism under pressure from radical reformers. In wide circles of social scientists the market was becoming more and more accepted as the only efficient economic coordinating mechanism and the privatisation of state-owned enterprises was seen as a precondition for the working of the market.[6]

This new thinking was to a great degree reflected in the Hungarian study *Turning Point and Reform* (1987), which was worked out by a relatively large collective of researchers. The study called for a radical economic and political reform. In the economic sphere the writers of the study demanded monetary policy to be made a paramount instrument for managing the economy. Planning was supposed to be reduced to a tool in the services of monetary policy and the market mechanism had to become the coordinating mechanism of the economy. The study urged the opening of the door to all forms of ownership (for more, see Adam, 1993, pp. 136–7).

Calls for the introduction of a market were also heard in Poland, as the debate on the columns of *Życie Gospodarcze* in 1988 showed. The debate was initiated by an editor of the weekly, M. Mieszczankowski (1988), who argued that capitalist relations cannot be transplanted into a socialist economy. The debate lasted more than a year and all the participants in it favoured the expansion of the role of market forces in the economy.

In the course of time, the socialist ideology abandoned more and more the components which made it different from capitalism.[7] A contributing factor to this, besides the factors already mentioned, was also the fact that planners in socialist countries relied on trends in economic development in capitalist countries when designing long-term plans. With this the planners admitted indirectly that socialism was in some respects similar to capitalism.

The advantages which the socialist system offered were shrinking; even full employment, which was regarded by socialist countries as their greatest achievement, was de-emphasised, that is, it became only the concern of the government. On the other hand, the advantages of capitalism – steady availability of consumer goods in great variety, democracy, human rights, no restriction on travel, etc. – were very much emphasised in the anti-socialist propaganda. In a situation in which socialism was portrayed by the anti-socialist propaganda more as capitalism without the advantages of capitalism and in which, on top of that, promises were made that once a genuine market economy was established – and its establishment was presented as a not very painful operation – prosperity would be within reach, it was no wonder that people opted for capitalism.

It is interesting that some of the propagandists themselves became victims of this propaganda. In 1987 I had a consultation with a well-known political scientist who seriously argued that in five years his country would be independent and as prosperous as Switzerland. His assertion about independence was really prophetic, but his assertion about the economy belonged to the sphere of utopia.

In talking about the erosion of the socialist ideology the picture would not be complete if no mention were made of the anti-socialist propaganda. The socialist system was brought down primarily by internal forces; however the West, mainly through its propaganda, also played an important role. The USA built up powerful propaganda machinery in Munich which beamed anti-socialist propaganda incessantly into Soviet and East European households. Radio Free Europe and Radio Liberty performed a good job in undermining the credibility of the socialist system. Their propaganda was subtle and administered within news, reports and plays. The broadcasters, writers and researchers working there had a very good knowledge of what was going on in socialist countries and what were the problems on people's minds. The broadcasts focused, to put it generally, on three groups of topics. They dealt with the acute problems which annoyed people and linked them indirectly to the shortcomings of the system. They discussed events and problems which were interesting news for East European listeners because the socialist media did not report them. As is known the socialist media were selective in their reporting; the censoring authorities decided what the media should and should not report. And finally, the broadcasts reported on events in the world, mainly in the West, with the understandable aim of showing how people in the West lived prosperously and enjoyed the advantages of democracy and human rights. In his book Z. Brzezinski (1989) stressed the importance of human rights in the fight against communism. He writes, 'Human rights is the single most magnetic political idea of the contemporary time. Its evocation by the West has already placed all the Communist regimes on the defensive' (p. 256). The impact of the human-rights weapon was enhanced by the 1975 Helsinki accord in which the West recognised the *status quo* of a divided Europe and in return the Soviet Union and East European countries vowed to respect human rights.[8]

The West waged an ideological struggle not only with the help of the media, but also by using much more subtle methods which were primarily directed to winning over leading social scientists to a market economy and democracy. The award of scholarships for the purpose of enabling the East European awardees to conduct research at universities or in research institutes and invitations to conferences were perhaps the most effective. There were many applicants who wanted to see the West and to work there. And this was the best way to expose them to the doctrines of free enterprise. It is not clear whether these actions were initiated by government agencies or came about through the initiative of universities and research institutes themselves, or through the initiative of individuals. At any rate it seems that they had the blessing of the authorities.

East European countries had an increasingly hard time countering the anti-socialist propaganda. With the continuing erosion of the authority of socialist ideology in the 1980s, the Western propaganda managed to influence more and more the thinking of the East European public.[9]

POLITICAL DEVELOPMENTS

The scope of the study allows me to focus on only the most important political events in the last forty years of the socialist regime and their impact on the socialist system. In my opinion these were: the twentieth Congress of the Soviet CP, the Hungarian uprising and the riots in Poland in 1956, the invasion of Czechoslovakia in 1968 and the rise of Solidarity in the 1980s.

All over the countries under review in the first decade of the new regime even ordinary supporters of the CPs felt that gross violations of human rights were occurring and that the promises about the well-being of the population were disregarded. The twentieth Congress of the Soviet CP confirmed this and condemned the policy. And this opened the gates to previously held-back indignation and rage, which became an important driving force in resistance to the regime (for more, see Fejtő, 1974, pp. 64–8). In Poland this took the form of riots in Poznan, whereas in Hungary it led to an uprising. In Poland the authorities managed to stave off the spread of riots by promising to change the system. And indeed a new leadership, headed by W. Gomulka, came to power with the promise of far-reaching changes in the management of the economy and in the political system. In Hungary the Russian tanks brought the uprising to an end. Though in Hungary the uprising was suppressed with tanks, the new Hungarian leadership, headed by J. Kádár, managed after some time to bring about political stability. However, the use of violence to suppress the uprising left a deep scar on the psyche of most Hungarians and its influence was not negligible when the socialist system found itself in crisis. In Poland, though the friction was solved peacefully, full stability was never reached. The reasons for this different development will become clear in the text which follows.

In Hungary, J. Kádár managed to achieve the unthinkable: he became the most popular leader in the socialist countries, mainly in the 1970s. This he achieved despite the fact that in the 1956 uprising he stood on the side of the Soviet suppressors and became the leader of the CP and the country through their will. He managed to assemble around him a CP leadership which took a centrist position, and focused his efforts on a reconciliation with his countrymen. He gained the trust of the people by coining the slogan 'who is not against us, is with us', followed up by various liberal measures, such as allowing people who left the country in 1956 to return home for good or for a visit and raising the Iron Curtain to some extent for travel abroad. Collectivisation of agriculture was reintroduced, but in a way which did not antagonise the peasants to a great extent and which in the long run turned out to be the path to relative prosperity. The Hungarians reacted positively to his reconciliation efforts and came increasingly to accept Kádár's regime as the best possible under the existing geopolitical conditions. What also contributed to Kádár's popularity was that in his conduct of affairs he paid attention to the most fundamental principles of socialism; otherwise he exhibited an increasing understanding for pragmatism. Under his leadership Marxist ideology, purified of its dogmatic elements with the passage of time, became less and less important as time went on and had increasingly to compete with ideologies hostile to Marxism.[10]

In Poland Gomulka and his associates, who came to power after the 1956 riots against the regime and were welcomed with great hopes, soon lost their popularity because they gradually turned their backs on the policies and ideas which they had promised to nurture, and increasingly embraced a conservative–communist agenda. Their turn-around was also reflected in the dismissal from positions of responsibility of people who had helped Gomulka to power in 1956 (cf. Bielasiak, 1983, pp. 13–15). The best evidence of their moral decline was that the Polish Communist leaders, along with the East German leaders, pushed the most for the 1968 intervention in Czechoslovakia. In order to take the wind out of the sails of one Party faction which used anti-Semitism as ammunition in its fight with the Communist leadership, Gomulka himself started an anti-Semitic campaign which led to the mass dismissal of Jews from universities, research institutes and other institutions and their migration to other countries (see Fejtő, 1974, pp. 295–9). Gomulka's intolerant attitude to cultural performances which did not square with his ideas brought about student demonstrations. On top of all this, the Polish economy was in poor shape. The effort to bring about a minor reform, which would improve the working of the economy, failed. An integral part of this reform was to be a large increase in prices, which provoked demonstrations and clashes with the police and exacted a toll of 70 deaths among the demonstrators. The demonstrations and their consequences led to the ousting of Gomulka. The new CP leadership tried to regain the trust of the population by attempting at the same time to boost the growth of the economy and increase the standard of living. Its success was brief.

In the 1960s the CPs in Czechoslovakia and Hungary managed to renew the credibility of the system through economic reforms. In Czechoslovakia, it was a short-lived event. Because the Soviets and some of their allies regarded the Czechoslovak economic reform as too radical and some political changes as a threat to the leading role of the CP, they occupied Czechoslovakia.[11] This brought the reforms to an end and had a far-reaching negative effect on the further fortunes of socialism. The reform was a good opportunity to give socialism a new direction: on the one hand, by allowing the market to play an important role in coordinating economic activities by limiting planning to a macroeconomic role, and on the other, by giving socialism a human and democratic face. At that time the socialist ideology still held sway over a great number of intellectuals and ordinary people. The modifications in the ideology did not bother the believers in socialism; on the contrary, they welcomed them. They saw the changes as a sign that the leaders were freeing themselves of dreams and illusions and coming closer to reality on the one hand, and, on the other, were willing to apply less authoritarian methods and coercion. Most intellectuals resented the talks about communism; they regarded communism as a utopia or at best something which might or might not be in the very remote future. They wanted the authorities to make good on the slogan 'socialism with a human face'.

This great opportunity for reforms was missed. Not only this, but the use of force against a member of the socialist camp, Czechoslovakia, only because it wanted to reform the system and make it more efficient and human, sent negative signals abroad and within the camp. It alienated many friends of socialism in the socialist camp and abroad. It signalled that there were limits to reforms, and that those limits were determined by the USSR in the first place. Reforms which exceeded these limits might be a source of internal instability and a threat to the limited national sovereignty, and therefore should be shunned. It also signalled that in a conflict with the USSR the small countries were on their own: they could not expect help from the West.

The large dismantlement of the economic reform in Czechoslovakia which followed the invasion and huge purge in the ranks of reformists, undermined the credibility of the CP. Attempts to put the blame for the invasion on foreign and domestic enemies had little success.[12] The Czechoslovak CP had to buy tranquillity by increasing the standard of living for some time and by resorting to more suppressive measures against the real and assumed opposition.

In 1980 the Polish government for the third time tried to reduce market disequilibrium by bringing in huge price increases. This time the government encountered opposition which had learned from the previous clashes. The workers of the Gdansk shipyard where the opposition was initially concentrated did not go into the streets to demonstrate and riot, but stayed inactive in the shipyard, declaring they would not return to work as long as their demands were not met. The strike spread and the Polish leadership was forced to negotiate with a new trade union in the making, which soon was known by the name of Solidarity. The demands for economic reform did not exceed the framework of socialism; they were similar to what O. Lange and W. Brus had called for. Solidarity was recognised as a trade union, a phenomenon unprecedented in the socialist camp. In addition, the government promised to consult the unions in matters of economic reform and the standard of living.

In 1980 the unheard-of happened in Poland: workers who were regarded as the pillar of the communist regime turned against it and demanded, *inter alia,* the recognition of a new trade union which they had created. In other words, they expressed non-confidence in the official trade unions, which turned out to be powerless when it came to defending the material interests of the workers. The CP leaders who determined the leadership of the trade unions did not care enough to listen to the interests of the workers and in this way discredited the trade union leadership (cf. Korbonski, 1989).

This new development was, of course, primarily the result of the government's insensitive wage and price policy applied throughout the 1960s and 1970s, and the government's violent reaction to the protests of the workers in 1970. A great proportion of the workers had never embraced the regime; the Communists' anti-religious stand and the fact that the supervisor and guarantor of the regime were in essence the Russians who, in the past, together with Germany and Austria, had brought Polish independence to an end, were anathema to them.

The successful negotiation with the government swelled the ranks of Solidarity to nine million (it managed to gain the support not only of the non-Communist intelligentsia, but also of many members of the CP) and increased its popularity tremendously among the public. In cooperation with the intelligentsia it managed to forge a powerful opposition to the regime. Aware of its power, many in Solidarity were no longer satisfied with its position as a trade union and wanted to challenge the authority of the CP.

The political aspirations of Solidarity very soon had an international effect. Needless to say, the Soviet Union watched with great displeasure Solidarity's rise as an independent trade union, fearing that such a development might spread to other CMEA countries and undermine the leading role of the CP, the guarantor of Soviet interests in the socialist camp. Therefore it exerted pressure on the Polish CP, by economic means among others, to restrain Solidarity; thus a clash between the government and Solidarity was inevitable. And indeed, in December 1981, as mentioned, martial law was declared, Solidarity was outlawed and its leaders arrested, an event which shocked Poland and the world and was condemned by the international community (Rakowski, 1991, pp. 15–41). (For more, see Chapters 7 and 8.)

CONCLUDING REMARKS

The greatest weakness of the socialist system was that it was a system which did not originate in the will of the people, and the communist elites did not even seriously try to make the system legitimate. They did not want to take any risks, perhaps because they underestimated the importance of legitimacy. Russian authoritarian traditions had, no doubt, an impact on the thinking of the Soviet CP and therefore also on the behaviour of the CPs in the small countries, all the more because most of the latter had no democratic traditions. Perhaps they also believed that they did not have a chance in democratic elections. In really free, non-manipulated elections the CPs had no chance. But in manipulated elections like the 1985 Hungarian elections, and the same is true of the 1990 elections in the USSR, their chances were not so bad.

Gross suppression of human rights and injustices committed against many people, though mostly in the first decade of the Communist rule, also worked against the regime. Usually people have a tendency to forget and forgive injustices if they get a redress or even if they feel that the injustices can never be redressed. For more than three decades the socialist system seemed to be eternal. Once the system started to crumble, people began to recall the injustices they had suffered, partly because they expected some compensation.

The structural changes in the Party and state apparatus, which brought about the rise of a bureaucracy which was little committed to socialism, was one of the reasons for the collapse of the system. The same is true of politicians to a great degree. The behaviour of bureaucrats and politicians was in a sense normal: they were not immune to anti-socialist propaganda and were influenced by changes in society. Last but not least, they pursued their own interests primarily.

Another shortcoming of the system was that it started out with a dogmatic ideology which could not withstand the pressure of economic realities. As a result the ideology often changed and in the long run was discredited. In the critical period for the socialist system the remains of the original socialist ideology, though more human and realistic, could no longer play an important role.

The heavy-handed and clumsy propaganda made matters worse. The slavish imitation of the Soviet Union and the uncritical treatment of its activities, phenomena not seen in Poland and Hungary since the second half of the 1960s, were received with displeasure and were subject to many jokes which hurt the system.

The four above-mentioned events (see pp. 108–12) undermined the credibility of the system inside the countries under review and outside. Disregarding the Soviet factor, the survivability of the socialist system depended primarily on internal forces, but moral support of some of the Western leftist forces was also of importance. The latter was no negligible shield against anti-socialist propaganda in the West and had a slight positive effect on the public perception of socialism inside the small countries. After World War II a large number of people in the West supported socialist changes in the East. Each of the political events mentioned reduced the support for socialism in the West so that, when socialism collapsed, there were few mourners. The support was also lacking because East European socialism hurt the cause of socialism all over the world.

Part III
Economic Reforms and the Collapse

7 Economic Reforms

INTRODUCTION

It has already been indicated that the socialist economic system was doomed to failure unless far-reaching changes in its working were carried out. And therefore it is no wonder that the politicians agreed to changes, first to 'perfections' of the management system and only later to major economic reforms. In some countries and some periods, the CP leaders did not want to admit publicly that the traditional system needed an overhaul. They were afraid that such an admission would undermine the effectiveness of the ideology and the credibility of the Party. The minor changes in the system of management in the former Czechoslovakia in 1958 could be characterised as a typical 'perfection'.

In my opinion, economic reforms should be understood as changes which exceed the framework of the traditional economic mechanism, but which do not negate the socialist economic system. In the traditional system, which was based on almost complete collective ownership, the planners made not only macroeconomic, but also microeconomic decisions. Enterprises were assigned compulsory output targets whose fulfilment was measured by gross indicators. The market played only a limited role in this system. It was a system with a closed economy. As will be shown, the economic reforms of the 1960s (the Czechoslovak of 1966 and the Hungarian of 1968) eliminated to a considerable extent the characteristic features of the traditional system. They did not, however, touch ownership relations to any extent. In the 1980s, when more far-reaching reforms were carried out primarily in Hungary and Poland, changes in ownership relations were also included. Economic reforms can thus be understood as changes which exceed the framework of the traditional economic mechanism, whether or not they affect ownership relations too. In this sense my definition of economic reform seems to be no different from that of J. Kornai (1992, pp. 388–9) who discusses reforms rather than economic reforms. In his criteria for reform (which is a broader term than economic reform) he naturally also includes a radical change in the political structure (in the undivided power of the CP). If the monopoly power of the CP is broken it is the end of the socialist system according to him. In other words he does not believe that a reformed socialist system based on a pluralistic political structure can exist. I do not share this view.

The CPs agreed to changes in the economic mechanism because the working of the economy exhibited serious signs of crisis or actually was in crisis, reflected in a slow-down in economic growth and/or a declining (or stagnating) standard of living and/or shortages – mostly in a combination of all the phenomena mentioned. In most cases the CP leaders consented to changes under pressure from below: this was the case in Czechoslovakia in 1965[1] and in all the three countries under review in the 1980s. The 1968 Hungarian reform was a reform from above, because the Hungarian leaders, still in trauma due to the 1956 suppressed uprising, realised that it was necessary to react quickly to the signs of the worsening performance of the economy and thus stave off the danger of a larger economic crisis which might provoke a political crisis.

Such pragmatic thinkers as the Hungarian communist leaders in the 1960s were an exception. As already mentioned, communist leaders in general were afraid of the ideological and political consequences of economic reforms. This is nothing unusual; ruling elites in capitalist countries do not behave very differently. For example, they are faced nowadays with high unemployment rates increasing at each business cycle, but they are reluctant to interfere with the system, even though, in my opinion, it is urgent for them to do so. They rely on the market to solve the problem eventually, an expectation which is not very promising. Communists have always believed in social engineering, and the socialist system was the product of such an idea. Therefore it would be nothing unusual, if they had made some substantial changes and then substantiated them by 'reaching a new stage of economic development', a phrase which they used quite frequently.

The problem was that reforms had to be directed towards widening the scope of the market, combined with changes in ownership of the means of production, and these changes moved the countries in the direction of the capitalist system, an action which was not acceptable to the majority of communist leaders, who mainly in the 1960s and the 1970s believed that socialism must be different from capitalism in almost all important institutional aspects.

REFORMS AND THE COLLAPSE OF THE SOCIALIST SYSTEM

Despite reforms – or because of reforms, as some would say – the socialist system collapsed. Some believed that the system was irreformable, and therefore the collapse was inevitable. However, nobody denies that the demise of the socialist system could have dragged on for many years to come. If not for the changes initiated by Gorbachev and his associates, the socialist system could still be around.

The irreformability of the system has been explained in different ways. One explanation, which had many followers before the collapse of the socialist system, was that the CP would never agree to the kind of economic reforms needed in order to make the system more efficient. The supporters of this view believed that the communist elites were determined not to give up the amount of power needed to make enterprises autonomous units. They did not have objections to the involvement of the central bodies of the CP as to the county, district and local organs of the CP. The lower bodies were the real meddlers in the affairs of enterprises, very often in petty matters. When making decisions about managerial appointments or even policy decisions, top managers had always to contemplate what would be the reaction of the local Party bodies. Many managers resented the Party's meddling in enterprise affairs. Needless to say, the local Party's bodies were reluctant to give up their role which lent them power and influence.

The followers of such a view were not against socialism; they were willing to accept market socialism with a certain limited role for the CP.[2]

At the other end of the spectrum, there were economists who believed that only a capitalist system could be an efficient system, and all efforts to reform the socialist system were futile. A good representative of such views is J. Kornai, who in his 1986 study had already characterised reformers such as Lange, Brus, Šik, Liberman etc. as naive, because, in his opinion, they wanted to make the impossible workable, to combine 'indirect bureaucratic control' with the market. He also expressed doubts whether under the political system existing at that time it was possible to restrict the bureaucracy to the set rules of the reform (1986, p. 1734). In his book *Road to a Free Economy* (1990) where he could more freely express his views, he indirectly made it clear that only the market based on private ownership can work efficiently.

Perhaps, if J. Kornai had written his verdict about socialism several years later when the Chinese boom was in full swing, he would have been more careful in his pronouncements. China has shown that even under a communist authoritarian system it is possible to introduce market relations with considerable success.[3] Everyone who is familiar with the economic development in China admits that it has made considerable progress. To a lesser degree this is also true of Vietnam.

It seems that Z. Brzezinski (1989) was also of the view that the socialist system was irreformable when he stated, as already mentioned in Chapter 1, that economic reforms must destabilise the system politically. In other words, the avoidance of political destabilisation requires the shunning of economic reforms. Judging from his statement, one can speculate that had Brzezinski published his book several years later, he would have argued that economic reforms were one of the most important reasons for the collapse of the socialist system.

Kornai, as already indicated, believes that the reforms could not succeed because planning and the market are incompatible. He believes that market forces cannot be made an effective coordinating system if planning is allowed to play an important role in the coordination of economic activities. There were also economists who believed the traditional system should not be reformed because planning could not work effectively if combined with the market mechanism.

There are economists who believe that the reforms had gradually undermined the socialist economic system, and that, with the rise of the recession, the system necessarily came to an end. But they do not profess the idea that the system was irreformable; they take the position that the collapse was rather the unintended result of economic and political changes. Ellman and Kontorovich (1992) seem to belong to this group. They write about the Soviet collapse: 'A major contribution to the economic collapse . . . was made by the unintended consequences of the systemic changes and economic policies pursued by the Gorbachev leadership. Gorbachev was quite successful in dismantling the old system, but failed to create a viable new one.' Gorbachev contributed to the collapse by weakening or removing 'three crucial load-bearing "bricks" from the building they tried to rebuild. These "bricks" were: the central bureaucratic apparatus; the official ideology; and the active role of the party in the economy' (p. 31). They also mention a series of reform measures which contributed to the collapse. *An expansion of enterprise independence is mentioned too; not only this, but it is listed in another place as one of the main contributors to the collapse* (p. 7).

REFORMS OF THE 1960s AND THE COLLAPSE

I do not share the view that reforms brought about the collapse of the socialist system, though there is no doubt that economic reforms posed a danger to the socialist system, more so if they were combined with political reforms. This was also the reason why the communist leaders in Hungary and Czechoslovakia were against a major political reform. In an authoritarian regime, as the socialist system was, a major political reform, if it is not carried out at a suitable time – when the regime still enjoys some of the public's trust – and with great caution, may soon turn against the regime. To stave off such a possibility in a socialist country, the political reform must be gradual and combined with a major economic reform which, in the minds of the people, would have a good chance to succeed. All this is valid generally without taking into consideration Brezhnev's doctrine;[4] as long as the Soviets were determined to apply it, no major political reform was possible. As is known, socialism came to an end in the smaller countries when the Soviets dropped Brezhnev's doctrine.

Nor do I share the view that the socialist system was irreformable. In my opinion, the reforms did not succeed first because they were not given enough time for their development and second they *did not and could not go far enough* as long as there was still relatively strong support for socialism. It is possible to argue that, considering the socialist camp as a whole, this was true for the second half of the 1960s and the first half of the 1970s. (Of course, if individual countries are examined separately, one can come to different results with regard to the proper time for reforms.) At that time the economy, as well as the standard of living, was growing relatively fast. This was the golden age of socialism. What is also important is that the socialist ideology still held sway over a large proportion of the intelligentsia. People still believed that socialism was a viable system.

Only Czechoslovak and Hungarian communist leaders took advantage of the favourable conditions for reforms, but these did not go far enough. What was worse was that the Czechoslovak reform was reversed as a result of the Soviet-led invasion, and, from the begining of the 1970s until the end of the 1970s, no reform activity took place in any country of the Soviet bloc. Even in Hungary the reform came to a halt. Precious time needed for the development of the reforms was lost.

It would be no exaggeration to state that in the 1960s most European CMEA countries (in one country more and in others less) came to the conclusion (many of them with regret) that the traditional system had not succeeded and that steering the economy in great detail from one centre had failed to make enterprises strive for economic efficiency; on the contrary, it encouraged waste, discouraged innovations and produced shortages. In the 1960s only in Hungary and Czechoslovakia did a situation develop which allowed a far-reaching reform. No doubt, other countries of the socialist camp, including the Soviet Union, also wanted to make planning more effective and enterprise activities more efficient and oriented to the needs of consumers, but were not willing to go beyond the centralised framework. They were not willing voluntarily to make economic reforms which might weaken the leading role of the Party and thus their own power. As a result, the 1965 Soviet reform was confined – to put it with some simplification – to improvement in methods of planning, reduction in the number of indicators and a new incentive system. (For more about this, including the reasons for different approaches to reforms, see Adam, 1989.)

In Czechoslovakia and Hungary the view prevailed that a remedy for the problems could only be found in a system in which planning is supplemented by the market mechanism, thus creating an environment in which enterprises would have to produce what the market required. In such an arrangement there can be, of course, no place for binding targets and allocation of inputs from the centre. This does not mean that the reformers wanted to expose enterprises to spontaneous market forces. At that stage, what most reformers wanted was a market regulated by the plan; they believed that society should determine its priorities in a planned way and that the market could be useful if it was regulated from the viewpoint of socialist principles (full employment, reasonable price stability, more equal distribution of income), all the more because some problems could not be solved by the market alone. The plan was not supposed to be simply the model of the future market (Kouba, 1968, pp. 222–31).

The plan was thus to remain the main coordinating mechanism; what was to change was the way the plan was drafted and primarily how the objectives of the plan were to be achieved. In the new system of management, enterprises were to be autonomous units for the most part, pursuing their own interests. The objectives of the plans were not to be imposed on enterprises; the central planners were supposed to create an environment equipped with incentives and disincentives, in which the objectives of the plan – of course, substantially reduced compared to the past since much of the supply could be left entirely to market forces – would be followed willingly because they were in the interest of enterprises. It was expected that enterprises would behave rationally because their possible expansion and the well-being of their employees would depend on how much they were able to realise from selling their products on the market. And therefore enterprises could be free to determine (with some exceptions) what and how to produce and where to buy inputs.

The reforms were to bring a redivision of decision-making between the centre and enterprises by allocating to each the sphere of decision-making which was close to its interests and which it knew best, namely the macrosphere to the centre and the microsphere to enterprises. Such a solution had to allow the benefits of both central planning, confined primarily to the macrosphere, and the market mechanism, applied to the decision-making of enterprises, to be combined.

The reforms of the 1960s brought about radical changes in planning. The annual plan did not cease to be compiled, but was no longer broken down into compulsory targets for enterprises. It was rather information for enterprises about intended government activities, resulting from the five-year plans. Enterprises had to work out their own annual and five-year plans; these had to reflect their own interests. The coordination of the government and enterprise plans was to be achieved by regulators. Not only was the system of assigned targets eliminated, but also a market for producer goods was introduced, though with many exclusions. These two important changes meant that the reformed system went beyond the framework of the traditional system.

The reforms made price determination more flexible and more market-sensitive. The number of prices directly determined by the price authorities was reduced substantially. The less important producer and consumer goods were sold at free prices, whose expansion was assumed with the entrenchment of the reform. There was some reduction in the huge number of turnover tax rates, as a step in restoring the linkage between different price subsystems, an important precondition for the working of the market.[5]

The authorities no longer assigned a wage bill to enterprises; enterprises had to earn it by their own economic activities. In order not to lose control over wage evolution and to protect the economy against inflation, the authorities determined terms under which wage growth was linked to performance. In both Czechoslovakia and Hungary taxes, though in different ways, were also used to control wage growth. It is not clear to what extent the change in wage regulation was also motivated by the desire to make a change in how employees viewed the responsibility for wage increases. Under capitalism employees in private enterprises blame the companies if they have wage grievances. It seems that the authorities wanted to achieve a similar situation to some extent.

The reforms increased the role of enterprises in decision-making about investment. The central authorities reserved their right to make decisions about major investment projects in the material sphere which had a great impact on the structure of the economy and technology and, of course, about the infrastructure. Other projects were left to the decisions of enterprises, which were supposed to finance them from their own resources and bank credit. However, taxes on enterprises were intentionally so high that enterprises were usually dependent on credit. And the banks, in making decisions about extension of credit, followed two criteria: the potential efficiency of the project and the extent to which it fitted in with the economic plan. In such a way the control of the authorities over investment was sustained.

The reforms also brought about a weakening of the state monopoly in foreign trade; a few enterprises in both countries were given licences to enter directly into trade relations with foreign countries. In addition, foreign trade corporations, which had a trade monopoly up to the reforms, became financially more independent.

The reforms also made some progress in linking domestic prices with world market prices. In Hungary, world market prices were converted into domestic prices for exporters as well as for importers by a multiplier which was calculated as a ratio of average domestic cost of exports and the receipts in dollars (or in rubles in trade with CMEA countries). Since the multiplier was based on average and not marginal costs, this meant that enterprises with higher than average costs were still dependent on subsidies in order to be able to continue exporting. In Czechoslovakia, a uniform adjustment coefficient to the exchange rate, larger for dollar trade than for ruble trade, was applied. In both countries imports were licensed. (For more about the reforms see Šik, 1967, and 1990, pp. 89–143; and Nyers, 1988, pp. 50–110. The former was the architect of the Czechoslovak and the latter of the Hungarian reform.)

The question can be posed: what was the impact of the changes mentioned in Hungary and Czechoslovakia? I agree with Brus and Laski (1989) who argue that in evaluating reforms it is easier to examine the changes in 'the conditions of economic activity and the behavioural pattern of economic actors' (p. 63) than in the overall performance of the economy or its welfare effects.

In evaluating the reforms it is necessary, in my opinion, to deal separately with the economic reforms of the 1960s and the 1980s. Only such an approach can show how the reforms developed and their tendencies. Focusing primarily on the reforms of the 1960s and disregarding the reforms of the 1980s gives a distorted picture of the reforms. It is even worse when the macroecononmic performance for the whole period from the start of the reforms in the second half of the 1960s to the collapse of the socialist system is used for the evaluation of the reforms. It should not be forgotten that in the 1970s the reforms were at a halt and that the change in economic performance in the 1980s in Poland and Hungary was much influenced by external factors and huge indebtedness.

The reformed economic mechanism, no doubt, was progress compared to the traditional system. However, it was far from what was needed in order to bring about a turnaround in the working of the economy. It was an illusion to expect that one reform could do the job. This was impossible for economic and political reasons. The present transformation difficulties in the post-socialist countries show that considerable systemic changes cannot be absorbed in a short period of time. More about this later. First, I wish to discuss the shortcomings and inconsistencies of the reforms.

The autonomy given to enterprises was limited. The authorities could still interfere and did indirectly, directly[6] and excessively, in enterprise affairs. Some direct interference was written into the reform blueprint. In addition, the branch ministries could use their right to nominate enterprise directors to exercise pressure on enterprises in the direction needed. Enterprises were dependent on the goodwill of the branch ministry in many respects, e.g. if they wanted to change the group production mix. In Hungary the authorities also used some very subtle methods, such as consultations in the presence of officials from the National Bank, to influence enterprises. And the fact that top managers felt that the reform was not irreversible made them even more vulnerable to pressure from above.

It was unrealistic to expect that enterprises could become self-financing units maximising profits, as the architects of the economic blueprint expected. For enterprises to become self-financed, they must have a considerable say in all the decisions affecting cost of production. And for profit to become a guide to decision making and an incentive, as was envisaged, there is a need for an environment in which increases in profit can mostly be achieved by better performance, which in turn requires rational prices and the elimination of monopolisation to a great extent. None of these preconditions existed.

In the 1950s and the 1960s the economies of the three countries underwent a process of industrial concentration. The motivation for this was the desire to simplify the administration of industry. It was believed that, with a lower number of enterprises, the hierarchical build-up would become more manageable. Some groups hoped that such a concentration would make economic reform superfluous. Some industrial concentration was justified by technological requirements, but most of it was an impediment to the development of competition since it intensified the monopolisation of the economy. The reforms brought changes to the concentration at the edges only.

One of the promised principles of the reforms was that the economic regulators would be applied uniformly as much as possible. This was important in order to put an end to a practice which allowed the authorities to withdraw funds from thriving enterprises for the purpose of bailing out poorly working enterprises. Needless to say, such a practice was an impediment to increases in economic efficiency and a damper on the desire to make enterprises profit maximisers. Both Czechoslovakia and Hungary promised to abandon this disincentive to financial economy, for which J. Kornai coined the term 'soft budget constraint'; but not much was done to honour this promise. Implementation of such a promise would have required liquidating obsolete and restructuring inefficient enterprises and to do so on a large scale would have produced unemployment, at least temporarily, and dissatisfaction in the workers' ranks, a situation which the political leaders wanted to avoid for political reasons.

The inability of the authorities to apply the regulators uniformly opened the door very soon for a new kind of bargaining: in the traditional system enterprises bargained with branch ministries over plan targets, while in the reformed system the object of bargaining became regulators, subsidies and everything which might affect the performance of enterprises.

The economic reforms of the 1960s limited the role of the market to the microeconomic sphere, but even there it was in rather a supplementary role. In the Hungarian concept of the reform, its role was to objectivise plans, to be a check on their practicality, to help to satisfy consumer demand (Hetényi, 1969, p. 41; and Nyers, 1966, p. 58). Planning and the regulation system based on it had to determine the limits and the terms of the operation of the market.

In addition, the role of the market was limited to commodities; the introduction of capital and labour markets was not in the blueprint. At that time it was believed that the market could work without a capital market. In addition, a capital market was regarded as a capitalist institution, irreconcilable with the principles of socialism, mainly the principle of income distribution according to labour. The lack of a capital market forced enterprises to use their profit within their enterprises, even if there was a possibly better use for it outside the establishment, or as a deposit in the bank, and it was thus an impediment to an increase in economic efficiency. Not only that, but the lack of a capital market meant the continuation of the use of quasi-administrative methods in a very important segment of the economy. Brus and Laski believe that the exclusion of the capital market from the Hungarian reform was to blame in the first place for the failure of the reform to 'subject the economy to a market coordination' (1989, p. 85).

Though in practice market forces had some impact on the distribution of labour, the reforms were not intended to and did not introduce measures which would bring about a genuine labour market. In the 1960s, it was unthinkable to introduce measures which might undermine the principle of full employment, which was regarded as an inalienable right.[7]

At that time there was no noticeable challenge to the collective ownership of the means of production, and the communist leaders did not feel that anything had to be done; they acted according to the well-known popular saying 'if it's not broken, don't fix it'. However, the reforms encouraged the rise of a limited number of private businesses. (For more, see Chapter 9.)

The development of the economic mechanism was hampered by the duality of regulations in foreign trade and their impact on the regulation of production. R. Nyers (1983) writes:

> While in the CMEA it is essentially the state organs that do business, on the world market it is enterprises. Trade in the CMEA is settled bilaterally: on the world market it is settled multilaterally. Finally, within the CMEA, trade is transacted at contractual prices agreed by states, while with the West at market prices ... It is not easy to bridge over the resulting difficulties; the dualism weakens the possibility of a consistent application of reform principles.'

The economic reform was not combined with a reform of the political system. In Czechoslovakia there were proposals in this direction, but they were rejected by the Party establishment. In Hungary the politicians, conscious of the Soviet attitude to political reforms, were very careful not to give the impression that they intended to make any big changes in the political system which might lead to a weakening of the leading role of the CP. However, in both countries the reforms brought about a considerable political relaxation, an extension of freedom of expression (primarily in Czechoslovakia) and an expansion of human rights. But there were no changes aiming towards liquidation of the one-party state and its replacement by a multi-party system. Perhaps in Czechoslovakia some moves in this direction would have been made if the Soviet-led invasion had not put an end to the Prague Spring. But I doubt whether the Czechoslovak CP would have agreed to a pluralistic system; it could have used the Soviet threat as an excuse for maintaining a modified and more relaxed one-party system.

Interference by the Party apparatus in the affairs of enterprises, though reduced, was not abandoned. Mainly in Hungary, the CP leadership did not want to antagonise the local Party apparatus.

To understand the economic development in the 1960s, it is also necessary to consider the *economic policy* of the countries, which I have discussed in Chapter 3. Here I would only like to mention that the reforms did not put an end to the ambitious economic growth policy in which the stress was placed on heavy industry with all its consequences.

In Czechoslovakia the reform was, as has already been mentioned, short-lived due to the Soviet-led invasion. In Hungary the development of the reform came to a halt in 1972 and even some recentralisation occurred.The short-term nature of the reform and the acceleration of economic growth in all European CMEA countries in the second half of the 1960s make it very difficult to draw reliable conclusions about the effect of the reform on economic performance. Since in Czechoslovakia and Hungary the rates of economic growth during the reforms or closely following increased, it seems that the reforms had some positive effect (see *SE*, 1990, p. 2; *Historická statistická ročenka ČSSR*, 1985, p. 89).

It is possible to agree with Brus and Laski (1989) that the reforms (it is not clear whether they also include the changes in the 1980s) did not bring about a breakthrough. However, I do not agree with them that the reforms of 1968 brought no qualitative change to the operation of the economic mechanism (p. 66). There is no doubt that the 1968 economic reform took the Hungarian economic mechanism beyond the framework of the traditional system. I agree with T. Bauer (1983) who maintained that changes made in the economic mechanism – such as the abolition of plan targets, the establishment of a market for producer goods and that enterprises' submission of their plans was only for consultation – 'makes the system different from the traditional Soviet-type planning' and, I will add, *qualitatively* different.

As has already been mentioned above, the 1968 Hungarian reform was marked by many shortcomings, and the role it allowed the market to play was quite limited; therefore I would not call the economic mechanism, which resulted from the 1968 reform, market socialism. The architects of the reform did not want market socialism and it was not market socialism. For this reason Kornai (1992) is not correct if he characterises the Hungarian reform from 1968 to 1989 as a type of market socialism (p. 479). He contradicts his own definition of market socialism. To him market socialism is 'for the market to become the basic coordinator of the socialist economy, or at least equal in rank with the bureaucratic mechanism, augmenting central planning, while public ownership remains the dominant property form' (p. 474). The 1968 reform did not enhance the role of the market – nor did it intend – to the point that it became equal with planning, let alone a basic coordinator.[8] Therefore it would be wrong even to use the term 'plan cum market' for the characterisation of the Hungarian reform of 1968 without making clear that the market was in a subordinated role.

Brus and Laski (1989, p. 105) defined market socialism more precisely when maintaining that a reform 'which includes a capital market along with the product and labour markets, [they call] *market socialism proper*'. However, their definition is not complete since they do not mention anything about ownership.

To me market socialism is a system in which the market is of more importance than planning and in which the dominant role of state ownership is maintained; therefore I would reserve this name for the system which started to develop in Hungary and Poland after 1987 and which will be discussed below. No objection can be raised at the new economic mechanism in Hungary, arising from the 1968 reform, being called indirect, as Antal did in his 1985 book. In his 1986 article Kornai also used the term 'indirect' too to characterise the 1968 reform, but complemented it with the words 'bureaucratic control'. To him then the difference between the system after 1968 and the traditional system was that the former was an indirect bureaucratic one, whereas the traditional was a direct bureaucratic system.

Perhaps both reforms, the Hungarian and the Czechoslovak, could have gone further if not for domestic and international political reasons. Many of the politicians, the CP and the government bureaucracy were against reforms. The same is true of managers. All were afraid that reforms would affect their interests. Even workers did not favour reforms; they were afraid that the reforms would generate unemployment. For this reason alone, the leadership of the Hungarian Party was careful not to push too far and thus antagonise large segments of the population. This was also the reason why the reforms did not bring about a restructuring of the government administration and the Party bureaucracy.[9] In Czechoslovakia, the CP leadership only reluctantly approved the economic reform. Only after Dubček, who was elected to the post of first secretary of the CP in January 1968, did the scope of the reform extend and its implementation accelerate. However, he too could not ignore the domestic situation.

This was only part of the problem. The reformists themselves were uncertain of how best to combine planning and market without undermining the leading role of planning. This uncertainty stemmed mainly from perplexity about what the market could do and what should be done in order to make it function well. The relatively long isolation of both countries, particularly of Czechoslovakia, was not helpful. On top of this, the existing ideology was an impediment to radical reforms.

The domestic difficulties could probably have been gradually overcome if there had been no intervention from outside. *However, far-reaching reforms, which can only be the result of trial and error, require time. And the reforms were not given the time needed for evolution.*

REFORMS OF THE 1980s AND THE COLLAPSE

When discussing the economic reforms of the 1960s, my focus was on Hungary and Czechoslovakia, whereas in researching the 1980s, the focus is going to be on Hungary, which continued its reform, and Poland. The conditions in the 1980s were quite different in many respects from those pertaining to the second half of the 1960s and the first half of the 1970s. Both countries groaned under the burden of their huge international debt. The borrowing abroad did not have much to do with the economic mechanism, though the unproductive use of the loans certainly had. Both countries engaged in borrowing for economic reasons. They did not have, or at least not to the same extent, the kind of worries Czechoslovakia had of becoming indebted to the West. They did not fear that the West might use its loans to enforce systemic concessions. On the other hand, the West was not reluctant to lend funds, particularly to Poland and Hungary, where an opening in the Iron Curtain seemed to be the easiest. In a recent book, edited by I. Bodzabán and A. Szalay (1994), a former CIA agent explains that the purpose of loans to Hungary was to cause its economy to break down under the burden of huge credits. It is difficult to verify the statement of the agent, but, considering the American interest in bringing down the socialist system, it seems plausible.

In Poland and Hungary, especially the former, the economic situation worsened in the 1980s (for more, see Chapter 8). In addition, the West went through a deep recession in the beginning of the 1980s which had its impact on CMEA countries too, mainly on those which were in intensive trade relations with the West, such as Hungary and Poland.

In both Poland and Hungary, mainly the former, the standard of living was developing unfavourably as a result of the worsening economic situation. In Poland this brought Solidarity into being. At the end of 1981, as noted, Solidarity was outlawed, but in spite of that its influence had increased after several years. Growing opposition to the regime, led by Solidarity, was combined with fading belief in the reformability of the economic system. (For more about Solidarity, see Chapter 6.) In Hungary the opposition to the regime grew more slowly and was headed mostly by the CP intelligentsia.

In discussing the reforms of the 1980s one must distinguish those of the first half of the 1980s from those of the second half of the 1980s which culminated in the collapse of the socialist system. In the first half of the 1980s, the 1982 Polish reform and the reforms of 1981 and 1985 in Hungary were not reforms which intended to establish market socialism in the sense explained above. The objective of the reforms was to strengthen the autonomy of enterprises, thus giving a greater role to the market, and to create legal conditions for the expansion of the private sector. In order to strengthen the autonomy of enterprises, the rules which governed property rights were changed. The management of enterprises was given the right to exercise property rights with some restrictions, yet enterprise assets remained the property of the state. Top managers and their deputies had to share their expanded rights with the self-management bodies established in most enterprises. Self-management bodies received quite far-reaching decision-making powers with regard to basic policy problems of enterprises. This was more true of Poland than of Hungary. This does not mean that the founders of enterprises gave up all control over them. The founders had the right to veto top managers elected by the self-management bodies.[10] In addition, the founders in Hungary had the right to evaluate the work of the manager when making decisions about his bonuses. (For more about self-management, see Chapter 9.)

The excessive interference of the authorities with enterprises, which the introduction of self-management had to cope with, was reduced but not eliminated. Enterprises were still dependent on the goodwill of the authorities (for subsidies and tax breaks) and thus gave the authorities a good opportunity to influence enterprise activities in the direction desired.

Though the role of the market was increased in the first half of the 1980s, it still remained a market for products; the policy makers did not intend to introduce a capital market. There was some movement in the direction of a labour market in Hungary in an effort to increase the economic efficiency of enterprises. To this end full employment was supposed to become the concern of the government, whereas enterprises had to handle employment from the viewpoint of efficiency (Havasi, 1984).

The reforms in both countries buttressed the private sector (see Chapter 9). However, they did not challenge the state sector and did not come up with suggestions for its privatisation. In Poland in 1981, even the reform proposals of institutions and collectives did not call for privatisation. This is not to say that all economists were against privatisation; no doubt, many were in favour. However, despite a more relaxed political situation, no public call for privatisation was voiced. After all, Solidarity committed itself in the Protocol of Understanding, concluded with the government, to a socialist system based on collective ownership, and it took a similar position at its first congress (*Glos Vybrzeza*, 1981, 1 September ; *Program . . .*, 1981).

In the second half of the 1980s the situation changed dramatically and this change had to do with many factors. The hopes in both countries that the economic situation would improve did not materialise. In Poland the 1987–8 attempt to bring about market equilibrium failed. In Hungary the foreign debt, which was high anyhow in 1985–7, doubled (see Chapter 8). The advent of Gorbachev to power and his commitment to a radical economic reform strengthened the hands of the radical reformers in both countries, and they used the new opportunity for new demands, in which the authorities reluctantly acquiesced .

In both countries in 1987–8 new reform measures were undertaken – which could be characterised as the first stage of market socialism – in the hope that these might bring about an improvement in the performance of the economy and pacify the growing opposition. In

Hungary these were brought about by the government Action Programme and Party resolution, and in Poland these new measures were known as the second stage of the economic reform.

In September 1987 the government Action Programme adopted by the Hungarian parliament (*Nsz*, 19 September 1987) and based on CC resolution (*Nsz*, 4 July 1987) promised to improve the planning system and stressed the increased importance of medium- and long-term plans. It also promised to build up the regulated market and to create conditions for a freer flow of capital. A part of the programme was the further freeing of industrial prices, the overhaul of the tax system, the reduction of the budget deficit and the application of strict monetary policy. What was of special interest was that the government vowed to reduce redundant labour from the economy and not to bail out enterprises with government funds. There is no doubt that the Action Programme was much influenced by the study *Turning Point and Reform* (see Chapter 6).

Two months later, in its November 1987 resolution (*Nsz,* 13 November), the CP made a big jump in its approach to the restructuring of the economic mechanism. Perhaps a quotation from the resolution will show the change best. It reads

> the socialist economy is such a planned economy, in which societal ownership of means of production plays the decisive role and which gives room to other forms of ownership and which is based on the regularities (*törvényszerűség*) of commodity production and applies market relations.

True, planning was still in the centre, but the market was no longer qualified by the usual adjective 'regulated', from which one can conclude that the CP leaders were reconciled with the idea of market socialism. What is also of importance is that the resolution promised that the government, parliament and interest groups could independently pursue their activities, a promise which at best meant that the Party would exercise its leading role in more subtle ways.

In April 1987 the Polish government published very detailed Theses of the second stage of reform (supplement to *Rzeczpospolita*, 17 April 1987) which were based on a Party decision. Soon the Theses were discussed by the *sejm* (Polish parliament) and approved (*TL*, 27 September 1987). The programme as laid out was intended within three or four years to pull Poland out of the economic crisis in which it found itself. To this end the renewal of market equilibrium was regarded as the first goal. Of course, the increase in economic efficiency was also set as an important goal. For this purpose the programme envisaged an increase in the autonomy of enterprises combined with some changes in the economic mechanism. In the sphere of annual planning, financial planning was supposed to be developed gradually at the expense of physical planning. Greater room for the working of the market was to be created also by gradually achieving equilibrium prices. The programme also promised to ease further entry into the private sector, which was to be concentrated primarily in retail trade and services.

The programme discussed cannot in itself be unambiguously regarded as a concept of market socialism. However, the changes suggested in the report of the politburo to the CC (*TL*, 18 November 1987) were of such a nature that if the socialist system had not collapsed before they were implemented they could have led to market socialism. The report criticised the practice of putting planning and market against each other. In certain areas long-term planning should dominate, whereas in others it should be the market mechanism. The criterion for the application of one of the two coordinating mechanisms in individual areas should be economic efficiency. From the foregoing the conclusion could be drawn that the two coordinating mechanisms were set on the same footing.

The report also suggested the need for changes in thinking about ownership relations. It continued to insist that collective ownership of the means of production was the foundation of socialism, but at the same time it claimed that the economic reform should create an atmosphere that allows different forms of ownership to exist side by side. It also promised that the main criterion in restructuring ownership relations would be the extent to which the restructuring contributes to the development of productive forces and the satisfaction of the needs of working people.

Let us examine to what extent the programmes were implemented. Both countries, primarily Hungary, took quite a stride. The role of the market was substantially expanded and conditions created for its application to capital and labour. In Hungary the monobanking system had already been liquidated in 1987; the National Bank was limited to the functions of a central bank in the West, and some of its departments were converted into commercial banks. Some banks started to sell bonds. The tax system was overhauled, and a value added tax was introduced in 1988. All these actions were implemented in Poland later. The private sector was also allowed to expand.

All these actions came too late really to lead to the rise of a fully-fledged market socialism. The economic situation and, with it, the political situation continued to worsen, and the regime plunged into a deep crisis. Sensing that the regime was no longer protected by the Soviets, that Gorbachev was no longer committed to Brezhnev's doctrine, the opposition in Hungary and Poland was no longer interested in reforms which would salvage the socialist system; what it wanted was to bring down the regime. Its job was made easier because the crisis affected the CPs themselves in that they started to disintegrate rapidly. The Communist ideology had lost its hold over the supporters of the CP even earlier. In addition, the opposition had the support of the West.

CONCLUDING REMARKS

Though they did not bring a turnaround in the economy, the economic reforms of the 1960s in Czechoslovakia and Hungary had a positive effect on the economies of both countries and brought about political relaxation. Unfortunately for the socialist system, the Czechoslovak reform was brought to an end by military intervention and the Hungarian was stalled by internal and external pressures. When the economic reform started again in Hungary and was taken up by Poland in the beginning of the 1980s, the economic and political environment was worse for orderly economic reforms. This is in particular true of the second half of the 1980s. Though under pressure from the opposition, the CP leaders were willing to engage in reforms, but at the same time they were gradually losing control over the economy because of the nature of the reforms themselves, but mainly because a process of disintegration in the CPs themselves started. Due to the interruption in the 1960s reforms, precious time was lost, which negatively affected the further development of the reforms.

The introduction of market socialism had its beginnings when the socialist system came close to an end in Hungary and Poland and therefore it could not stand the test of time. To make a judgement about market socialism, to what extent it is a viable system, it would have been necessary to have such a system fully established and to let it function for some time. Of course, the establishment of market socialism could not be a matter of one or two years. In the history of mankind it would have been something new, never before experienced, and therefore the introduction of market socialism had to be the result of the method of trial and error.

Kornai always took the position that market socialism was doomed to failure. He writes in his 1993 article (p. 47):

> For example, compare East Germany, Czechoslovakia, and Romania – countries whose political leaders stubbornly resisted all market-socialist reform – with Yugoslavia, Hungary and Poland, and the Soviet Union, which took the market-socialist road for varying periods. The macroeconomic situation on the eve of the postsocialist transition is clearly worse in the second group than in the first: the budget deficit is greater, inflation is faster (or the combination of shortage and inflation more acute), and debt is higher. The market-socialist experiments led to a situation in which the leadership lost control.

I assume that J. Kornai's verdict refers to market socialism, though he uses the term market-socialist reform in the quoted sentences, because several paragraphs below he writes: 'The main proposition in this study is that *the blueprint of market socialism is doomed to failure*' (p. 47).

With the exception of Yugoslavia, Poland and Hungary took only the first steps towards market socialism, and therefore it was too early to make a judgement about it. Kornai would certainly object if I were to say that the deep recession which affected post-socialist countries in transition to a market economy is proof that a market economy is not good for the countries. Furthermore, to make a judgement about why countries which resisted economic reforms fared better with regard to macroeconomic equilibrium would require a deep analysis of the countries' economic policies besides their economic mechanism. In addition, in talking about macroeconomic equilibrium Kornai forgets to consider equilibrium between aggregate demand and aggregate supply. Everyone knows that Hungary's record for this indicator was the best and Rumania's the worst.

Besides the argument that countries which did not experiment with market socialism fared better than those which did, Kornai presents further arguments which are supposed to back up his proposition. It would exceed the scope of this study to engage in a detailed analysis of his arguments, and therefore only some will be touched on briefly. He combines market socialism with communist monopoly rule, which is in accordance with his definition (see p. 129). But market socialism does not necessarily need to be linked to one-party rule. When it started in Poland and Hungary the one-party rule was much undermined, and if the socialist system had survived, the communists would have probably shared power.

His further argument is '*there is no real decentralization without private ownership*' (p. 52). No doubt private ownership can ensure more decentralisation than state ownership. But private ownership is not necessarily superior to state ownership with regard to performance. (Before proceeding let me make clear that state ownership needs to be changed from what it was under the traditional system, where the state bureaucrats micromanaged state enterprises. It is imaginable that enterprises remain in the hands of the state, but the management of enterprises is privatised in different ways or made public.[11] Such an arrangement can eliminate the deficiencies which the traditional system generated.) As is known, ownership alone does not determine economic efficiency. The *Economic Survey of Europe* (1992), discussing the experience of market economies, writes that 'the superiority of private enterprise depends critically on the degree of competition prevailing in the market, the incentive structures in alternative organizational forms, and the coherence of regulatory policies'. When all this is in place, still 'the key factor determining the efficiency of an enterprise is not whether it is publicly or privately owned, but how it is managed' (pp. 196–7).

The statement that ownership alone does not determine economic efficiency is indirectly backed up by experience with privatisation as evaluated in three articles and reported by the *Economic Survey of Europe* (1992, p. 196):

divestment of state-owned assets in market economies has not unambiguously led to lower product prices, improved allocative efficiency, ameliorated internal efficiency in privatized enterprises, brought about people's capitalism, or generated better service or quality of delivery. Moreover, public enterprises were often divested well below their 'market value' thus generating sizable short-term capital gains at the expense of the state – ultimately the taxpayer at large.

I agree, however, with Kornai that market socialism was doomed to failure, but not for the reasons he mentioned. In my opinion, such a system in small countries had no chance of survival because multinational corporations and financial markets, which manifested their economic power and solidarity more than once, will not put up with market socialism, seeing in it a danger to their interests.

8 Development of the Economies

INTRODUCTION

There is no doubt that the worsening economic situation in the 1980s was one of the decisive factors which brought down the socialist system. From the beginning of the socialist system up to the second half of the 1970s, the three countries could boast quite good results in economic growth rates, though they were marked by a falling tendency. There was even a time when they could bask in the propagated myth that the socialist system ensures higher rates of growth than the capitalist system. They were able to back up this myth at least with regard to most capitalist countries.

In the second half of the 1970s the situation changed forever. In the beginning of the 1960s, most socialist countries went through a decline; in Czechoslovakia there was even an absolute decline, but soon the economies recovered. This was not the case after the second half of the 1970s; the relatively high rates of the past did not return. It is possible to argue that the three countries, one more than the others, found themselves in an economic crisis.

In this chapter I will try to analyse the reasons for the decline in economic growth rates and for the plunge of the economy into stagnation. I will also discuss briefly the evolution of the standard of living.

COMMON REASONS

There were several reasons for the decline in economic growth rates which were common to all three countries. One of them was that the sources of extensive economic growth were increasingly exhausted. Labour shortages were compounded by declining growth rates in the working-age population, a phenomenon which was strongest in Hungary. In the 1960s the average growth rate of the working-age population was 0.5 per cent, in the 1970s 0.2 per cent and in the 1980s it turned into a negative rate, −0.5 per cent (*SE*, 1986, p. 51 and 1990, p. 47).

Of course, labour shortages could have been overcome had the governments managed substantially to improve labour utilisation and make significant progress in solving structural deficiencies in the economy. Investment in labour-saving devices in sorting, shelving and transporting goods, where a great number of workers were employed, could have considerably alleviated labour shortages (for more, see Chapter 3). Industrial production, mainly heavy industry, was overgrown. Services and the infrastructure were neglected. In agriculture productivity grew at such a slow pace that an excessive proportion of the work force was tied up in it. The governments were aware of these problems, but did not devote proper attention to them.

The investment rate, which in the 1970s grew faster in some countries than was envisaged in the plan, in the 1980s substantially declined (see Table 8.1). The lower investment rate had to bring down the rate of economic growth for the sake of coping with disequilibria, but at the same time it slowed down capital replacement which is a precondition for technological progress.

Increasing shortages of raw materials and energy were another important factor. The extraction of raw materials and fuels in the USSR, which supplied the other countries of CMEA, was shifting more and more to the Eastern regions with unpleasant climatic conditions and often difficult access to deposits; therefore productivity in the extracting industry was declining, and cost per unit of production, also due to high transportation costs, was increasing. Expectations of more economical use of raw materials remained mostly behind planned targets. Though the material intensity of products was much higher than in advanced industrial countries, the three countries did not manage to reduce it at the same pace as it was being reduced in Western countries, one reason being that the former lagged behind the West in the development of high technology industries which are less material intensive (see Drucker, 1986).

The three countries were, in addition, affected, though with some delay due to the pricing formula in CMEA, by the explosive increases in oil prices which resulted in worsening terms of trade, except for Poland. Demand for oil and its derivatives was growing, and the Soviets were not willing to go beyond the agreed quotas or substantially increase quotas when new trade contracts were concluded.

The slump in the West, accompanied by protectionist tendencies, made the competition for Western markets more difficult for CMEA

Table 8.1 Some indicators of performance (annual growth rates in per cent)

	1971–5	1976–80	1981–5	1986–9	1981	1982	1983	1984	1985	1986	1987	1988	1989
Poland													
GDP*	11.6	0	0	2.6	–10	–4.8	5.6	5.6	3.7	4.2	1.9	4.1	0.2
Industrial production, gross	10.2	3.8	0.1	3	–13.2	–1.5	6.6	5.6	4.1	4.4	3.4	5.3	–0.5
Agricult. production, gross	3.6	–1.5	2.3	1.3	3.8	–2.8	3.3	5.7	0.7	5	–2.3	1.2	1.5
Economically active	1.8	0.9	–0.2	0	0.5	–2.4	–0.3	0.3	0.8	0.3	–0.3	–0.7	0.6
Investment in the economy	17.5	–2.6	–2.3	2.4	–22.3	–12.1	9.4	11.4	6	5.1	4.2	5.4	–2.4
Consumer prices	2.5	6.7	31.5	52.6	21.2	100.8	22.1	15	15.1	17.7	25.2	60.2	251.1
Real wages	7.2	1.1	–4.3	4.2	2.2	–25	1.2	0.5	3.8	2.7	–3.5	14.4	8.3
Former Czechoslovakia													
National income distributed	5.7	3.7	0	3.1	–3.4	–1.6	0.6	1.2	3.1	4.9	2.8	1.9	3.1
Industrial production, gross	6.7	4.7	2.6	2.1	2	0.9	2.9	3.8	3.6	3.5	2.5	1.6	0.8
Agricult. production, gross	2.2	1.8	1.8	1.5	–1.7	4.2	3.2	4.7	–1.5	0.8	2.3	0.7	2.2
Economically active	0.5	0.8	0.7	0.7	0.7	0.4	0.4	0.9	1	1.3	0.6	0.6	0.3
Investment in the economy	8.2	3.5	–1.1	2.8	–4.5	–2.5	0.6	–3.9	4.6	1.4	4.3	4	1.6
Cost of living of employees	0.1	2.1	1.7	0.6	0.9	4.5	0.8	1.7	0.8	0.8	0		1.6
Real wages	3.5	0.7	0	1.4	0.8	–2.4	0.8	0.8	0	0.8	2.4	1.6	0.8
Hungary													
GDP	6.3	3.2	1.8	1.1	3	2.9	0.7	2.8	0	1.4	4	0	0.3
Industrial production, gross	6.3	3.4	1.1	1.3	2.9	2.4	0.9	2.7	0.7	1.9	3.8	0.2	–0.6
Agricult. production, gross	4.6	2.4	0.7	0.9	1.9	7.6	–2.7	2.7	–5.8	2.8	–2.2	4.7	–1.3
Economically active	1.9	0.3	–0.5	–0.3	–0.6	0.4	–0.6	–0.5	–0.4	–0.2	0.3	–0.6	0.7
Investment in the economy	7	2.4	–2.8	1.5	–5.2	–2.2	–3	–2.8	–2.3	2.3	7.6	–7.7	4.4
Consumer prices	2.8	6.3	6.7	11.6	4.4	6.7	7.3	8.4	6.8	5.3	8.6	15.9	17.1
Real wages	3.3	0.8	–0.8	–0.6	1.2	–0.1	–3.3	–2.5	1.3	2.1	–0.4	–5.1	0.9

* Data for 1971–80 and 1976–80 refer to national income distributed.

Sources: For Poland, *RS* 1992, pp. XVI–XXXII.
For Czechoslovakia, *RS* 1987, pp. 20–9 and *SR* 1992, pp. 30–9.
For Hungary, *SE* 1990, pp. 2–4, 9 and 14.

products. On the other hand, Western corporations tried hard to increase their exports to Eastern Europe. Western banks were more than willing to finance the trade deficits which arose; they tried to recycle the petrodollars, and they also regarded loans to East European countries as safe investments, believing that, if something went wrong in the borrower countries, the Soviets would bail them out (Fekete, 1983). (See also p. 85.) In addition, the developing countries had increasingly become competitors of East European countries in Western markets.

The taking-up of loans from the West in the first half of the 1970s, mainly by Poland and Hungary, had to be serviced, and this necessarily contributed to balance of payment deficits.

The reaction to external factors was slow; they were to some extent under-estimated, perhaps because the effects of the explosive price increases were for some time cushioned by the price policies in CMEA and, when measures were taken, they were quite half-hearted; the countries were somehow reluctant to face reality (Urban and Lér, 1982 and 1986; Höhmann,1985).

Some Soviet ideologues were delighted that the oil price explosion caused serious difficulties in Western economies and at the same time produced windfall profits for the Soviets. Retrospectively, it is possible to say that oil price increases in the final analysis affected the Soviet bloc more than developed capitalist countries. The latter managed to overcome the resulting recession, albeit with some bruises, due to new technologies and oil conservation, but for the socialist camp this was the beginning of an economic crisis which contributed largely to the collapse of the socialist system. Instead of using the windfall profits for modernising the civilian economy and helping East European countries, the Soviets squandered them for military purposes to a great extent. The oil price crisis accelerated the gap in technology between the West and the East.

The worsening economic situation was reflected in a gradual decline or stagnation in the standard of living, mainly in real wages. (It is, however, important to stress that decline in real wages in Poland and Hungary was minimal compared to what happened in the transitional period to a market economy.) What was annoying was that the gap in the standard of living between the socialist countries and Western countries was increasing.

People appreciated the fact that many services were available without charge, such as education and health care, or at a low charge, such as housing. But there were many complaints about the delivery of services, especially in health care. People disliked the idea that the elites had access to better care than the rest of the population; health services were supposed to be delivered according to need and not according to position. The authorities tried to deliver health care at minimum costs, and this was reflected on the one hand in insufficient funding of new technology and, on the other, in the relatively low remuneration of health-care workers, mainly physicians. Poor funding caused health care in East European countries to lag increasingly behind the West in medical technology and the newest medications. Patients in need of foreign medicine had to fight hard to get it from the authorities, or beg from relatives or friends abroad. The system of tipping physicians (see Chapter 3) introduced a two-tiered care system: a better one for those who could afford to and were willing to bribe the physicians, and a worse one for those who could not afford to or were not willing to support the corrupt system. It was mainly surgeons who expected big tips. The gratuities undermined discipline in hospitals; a corrupt doctor did not dare enforce discipline at his workplace.

Shortage of housing was another factor which frustrated many people, mainly the young who wanted to enter into marriage and people whose marriage broke up.[1] In the beginning of the socialist system housing was treated as a social service which must be provided from state funds and at low rents. Yet housing was low on the list of government priorities. As mentioned before, only in the second half of the 1950s were cooperative housing and private housing (for the countryside) encouraged and financially supported. However, the expansion of different forms of ownership improved the housing situation, without solving it. Seekers of housing still had to wait years for housing. In addition, the introduction of new forms of housing construction created a situation in which differentiation of rents was accidental to a great degree and had little to do with social justice. (For more, see Adam, 1991.)

The standard of living was also negatively affected by the delayed and insufficient supply of modern products in general, but especially of electronic products. The high prices of the products was another factor. It was mainly the young people who wanted to enjoy the fruits of modern technology and did not want to be behind their peers in the West. They had no understanding, and rightly, for an economic policy of the government which hampered the satisfaction of their demand.

What was also of importance was that all these electronic products were invented in the West. This in itself increased the prestige of the West, mainly in the eyes of youngsters, and decreased respect for the

East. The superiority of the West in producing new electronic products was linked to capitalism and the lag behind the West in this activity to socialism. If one adds to this that Western contemporary music and dance, which became part of the lifestyle of most youngsters in the West, had a powerful resonance in the East (because the entertainment mentioned reflected their feelings too or because it came from the West), then there were additional reasons for most young people to adore the West and with it capitalism, and to despise the East and with it socialism.

A shortage of automobiles and their relatively high prices was another issue which angered people. They resented the fact that they could not get a car instantly even if they had the cash, and had to wait 3 to 4 years for delivery.

People wanted to travel and see the world like their peers in Western countries. The shortage of cars was not the only obstacle. Travel restrictions, mainly in Czechoslovakia, which were imposed for political reasons and/or non-availability of foreign currency, were an even greater hindrance. The political elite was reluctant to allow freedom of travel for fear that the visitors to foreign countries would be overwhelmed by the abundance of consumer goods and 'poisoned' by anti-socialist thought in the West. No doubt, travel abroad, which in the 1980s increased considerably even in Czechoslovakia, was an important factor in the rise of a credibility gap between the population and the regime. Typical East European tourists, supplied with suitcases of canned food instead of hard currency, dependent on relatives or friends for accommodation if they did not have a car with a primitive trailer – as was mostly the case– and short of money to buy some of the goods not available at home as gifts for their families, felt humiliated and angry at the regime. In addition, because of the humiliation and because tourists' judgement about countries they visit is very much influenced by superficial impressions, tourists had a tendency to see Western countries only in rosy colours and did not fail to share their impressions back home with friends and those who were regarded as trustworthy. Needless to say, the negative impact of travel abroad from the regime's viewpoint was largely of its own making because it did not pay proper attention to consumer demand. In addition, it was foolish not to recognise that the 'poison' could not be kept out in the existing advanced state of communications.

It was the political elite's great mistake to disregard the fact that people wanted to enjoy themselves and to take full advantage of all possible pleasures. They wanted to use their incomes according to their priorities and not according to the priorities of the planners, and were tired of constant shortages.

POLAND

In the 1960s the Polish economy grew quite fast, but suffered from large disproportions and therefore the authorities decided to introduce a minor reform, with the primary objective of improving the incentive system. An integral part of this reform was supposed to be a huge, upward adjustment of prices by the end of 1970, with the purpose of improving market equilibrium and price relativities. This intention of the government triggered riots which were suppressed by brutal force.[2]

To placate the public, W. Gomulka, the leader of the Party, was ousted. The new leader, E. Gierek, rescinded price increases and promised a new strategy of economic development. The new strategy, which lay in restructuring and modernising industry with up-to-date technology bought in the West with Western credits, and in simultaneously improving the standard of living of the population, turned out to be a huge failure. The imported technology was excessive and could not be effectively absorbed, and the expectations that loans would be paid back by commodities from the modernised enterprises did not materialise. Poland was not able to produce many products which could be competitive on Western markets, and the slump in the West reduced its chances even more.

To reconcile the workers Poland resorted to a policy of high wages. In the period of 1971–5 real wages increased on the average by 7.2 per cent annually (see Table 8.1). These huge increases in wages, which were not matched by increases in consumer goods, were inflationary.

Poland did not react quickly to the price changes in foreign markets. Instead of investment, which was very dependent on imports, being scaled down, it continued to grow and with it foreign debts piled up. As a result servicing costs and the balance of payment deficit increased. In 1973 foreign debts amounted to $3 billion and their servicing to 17 per cent of exports, still a bearable burden; in 1974 the debts amounted to $15.3 billion and their servicing required 55 per cent of exports, and in 1980 the debts jumped to $24.1 billion and their servicing came to 101 per cent of exports. Of course, the growing debt was also caused by high interest rates. In order to be able to meet its interest obligations Poland had to take up new loans.[3] All this happened at a time when the terms of trade were not really deteriorating. In 1979, a year when the terms of trade did deteriorate slightly, they were the same as in 1970 (Mieszczankowski, 1984; Jędrychowski, 1982, pp. 99, 152–4).

The investment drive was one of the main causes of inflation. It was focused on huge new projects in metallurgy and engineering at the expense of the modernisation of existing factories. Because of overinvestment new productive capacities were put on stream with great delays while wages – not matched by consumer goods – were paid to workers. Market disequilibrium was compounded by the worsening situation in agriculture. A change in agricultural policy[4] combined with poor weather brought down agricultural growth rates in 1975–6 after an impressive growth in 1972–4 (Mieszczankowski, 1984; Kisiel, 1984).

Considering the situation in which Poland found itself, the five year plan, approved in 1975 for 1976–80, was still an ambitious one (Mosóczy, 1979, p. 136). Not until 1976 were the Polish leaders finally prepared to act; the so-called economic manoeuvre stipulated a substantial decrease in investment and a shift of resources to consumer-goods industries in order to arrest the rapidly developing market disequilibrium, which was also worsened by the failed attempt to increase the prices of foodstuffs. (The Polish leaders again tried to restore market equilibrium by attempting to increase prices substantially. As soon as the government saw that the workers were determined to riot to thwart such attempts, price increases were rescinded.) Furthermore, the document called for a reversal in the balance of trade situation in order to arrest the increasing indebtedness. Even before this, some changes in the system of management, which in substance meant greater interference with enterprises, had been carried out.

Again the leaders mismanaged their own decision: investment was reduced but, at the same time, the construction of the second stage of the huge metallurgical combine in Katowice was started. In addition, imports were slashed in an arbitrary way, which aggravated the developing shortages (Kisiel 1984; Fallenbuchl 1986, p. 371).

As a result of the rise of Solidarity (see Chapter 6) and its political ambitions, the Polish CP found itself between a rock and a hard place. Solidarity tried to achieve its objectives by strikes and pressure for higher wages, activities which contributed to a decline in output and an intensification of market disequilibrium. The decline in coal production in particular, combined with a reduction in material imports from the West, had a multiplying, negative effect on total production. GDP continued to decline, this time dramatically – in 1981, by 10 per cent and in 1982, by 4.8 per cent (see Table 8.1).

On the other hand, the Soviets used the carrot and stick method to make the Polish leaders act against Solidarity. In 1980 the Soviets offered help in the form of more oil which the Poles could use as payments for purchases in the West. But when the Soviets saw that despite their pressure Solidarity was becoming stronger, they made it clear that they would not hesitate to invade Poland and in addition tightened the economic screws. At the trade negotiations for 1992 the Soviets offered to deliver to Poland 4.1 million tons of oil against the Polish request for 13.1 million tons (Jaruzelski, 1992, pp. 34 and 249).[5]

The outlawing of Solidarity in December 1981 (see Chapter 6) was done primarily for political reasons and to forestall a Soviet invasion.[6] But economic considerations also played an important role, as M. Rakowski mentioned in his book (1991, p. 34). Martial law enabled the Polish leaders to renew, at least for a while, the semblance of market equilibrium by huge price increases. The existing widespread shortages threatened to bring the economy to the point of collapse.

The three year plan for 1983–5 was fulfilled in many of its important aspects. National income distributed increased by 15 per cent against the planned 10–12 per cent, but was still far from the pre-crisis level of 1978. In the following years the economy continued to grow so that in 1989 the national income distributed was only 6.5 per cent below the level of 1978 (See *RS*, 1988, p. XXXIII; and *MRS*, 1992, p. 344). According to G. Kolodko's (1992, p. 18) computations the growth of net national income was positive for the period 1980–9, though the increment was quite small, only 0.3 per cent.

However, many problems which had plagued the economy before 1986 were not removed or solved. Economic equilibrium was not achieved. Inflation was still in double figures (in 1986 it even increased to 18 per cent from 15 per cent in 1985; this was, however, not so bad compared to what happened in 1990, when consumer prices increased by 586 per cent); it was fuelled by the budget deficit, primarily as a result of growing subsidies and the inability of the government to bring wage growth under control. (What was also worrying was that wage growth was marked with growing inequities in the distribution of income.) Exports to non-socialist countries were not increasing and foreign indebtedness continued to grow and therefore imports from those countries were again slashed, to the extent that they had an unfavourable effect on further development of the economy. In restructuring the economy little progress was achieved (*Report* . . ., 1987).

As noted above, in 1987 the Polish central authorities announced the second stage of the economic reform. An integral component of the reform was to be a radical price reform including huge increases in the retail prices of food, coal and energy in order to bring about market equilibrium and rational price relativities. It seems that the IMF and World Bank pushed in this direction.

Aware of the bad experience with price reforms, the Polish government this time approached the preparation for the reform cautiously. It asked the population to approve the reform in a referendum. It hoped that, if the reform was approved, an explosion of discontent could be avoided. In order to sweeten the pill of price reform it promised compensation for wage earners and pensioners and for the depreciation of the purchasing power of savings (within three years) (*TL*, 1 November 1987). Many Polish economists were against the reform, realising that under the existing conditions it could not solve the problems it was intended to solve. In addition, they argued that in foodstuffs demand and supply were in balance. Solidarity, which was underground, but still had considerable influence on the public, was not interested in supporting government efforts. As could be expected, the public rejected the price reform. As a result the Polish leaders carried out a smaller price reform in 1988, but without achieving their goal. On the contrary, consumer prices increased by 60 per cent in 1988, whereas wages rose by 81 per cent, which meant an increase in real wages of 14 per cent and an increase in market disequilibrium (see Table 8.1).

Despite efforts to improve the working of the economy by further reform, the situation did not improve. The attempt to silence Solidarity did not succeed; the defeated referendum only increased the disillusionment with the regime and the distrust of the ruling elite, and increased the popularity of Solidarity. In 1988 a wave of strikes broke out, supported by Solidarity. The central authorities were indirectly forced to look for a way out in a dialogue with Solidarity. This time they did not have to be afraid of Soviet intervention. Gorbachev's leadership had dropped Brezhnev's doctrine. And so in April 1989 government and Solidarity representatives agreed in roundtable negotiations to restructure the political as well as the economic system. As to the latter, the representatives agreed to introduce market relations and competition, allow free development of ownership structures including privatisation, develop self-management, and limit central planning to the formulation of government policy – to mention only the most important principles. In the sphere of economic policy, it was concluded that the budget deficit should be reduced by slashing subsidies and selling apartments, shops, productive facilities, etc. In order to protect the consumers from inflation, a 80 per cent wage indexation was promised. The preservation of the principle of full employment was pledged (ZG, 1989, no. 16; TL, 7 April 1989).

The June 1989 parliamentary elections brought about a shattering defeat for the Party, and the Solidarity leaders managed to manoeuvre it out of political power.

The fluctuations in economic growth were reflected in the evolution of the standard of living. Of the three countries under review Poland had the worst record until 1971–5, when real wages grew quite fast (see Table 8.1). In the period 1976–80 there was a considerable decline in the growth rates of real wages, though on the whole they were still positive. The increase in prices during martial law brought about a dramatic decline in real wages; they dropped by 25 per cent, approximately to the level of 1972–3. In other words, the increases in real wages, which the workers pushed through when the government wanted to appease them, were to a great degree lost. The government used martial law, when the public was quite intimidated, to reduce the standard of living. No doubt, the performance of the Polish economy could not sustain the existing level of real wages. However, most workers had no great understanding for the government problems (and rightly) and blamed the system and the government for the dismal performance of the economy and low real wages. When in 1988 the government was most anxious to hold the line on real wages, they surged by 14 per cent ; they remained, however, 10 per cent below the 1981 level, the martial-law year (RS, 1983, p. XXXV; 1992, p. XXIX).

Private consumption per capita was much less affected by the price increases during martial law; it declined by only 12.3 per cent. The main reason for this difference was that nominal transfer payments grew much faster than nominal wages and salaries (see RS, 1987, p. 93). Interestingly enough, in 1988 when real wages increased substantially, private consumption per capita increased only moderately.

An important indicator of consumption is the consumption of meat, all the more because the Poles attached high priority to it and therefore were willing to forgo other purchases in order to maintain the level of meat consumption. Their habits were encouraged by the historically relatively low prices of meat. And therefore consumption of meat in Poland was higher than in other countries at the same level of economic development. In 1970 consumption of meat and meat products reached the level of 53 kg per capita. In 1975, when real wages were relatively high, it increased to 70.3 kg . In 1982, it plummeted to 58.5; since then it has continued to grow slowly: in 1988 it reached 67.8 kg (*MRS*, 1989, pp. XLVIII–XLIX).

On the whole, the 1980s were characterised by a decline in the standard of living, which was much more far-reaching than in Czechoslovakia or even in Hungary. The situation in Poland was compounded by shortages and by the rationing of some products. People were forced to spend a lot of time, including work time, in queues. Needless to say, people were tired and angry. Their anger was enhanced by what they heard about the standard of living and supply of goods in capitalist countries and by what they themselves had experienced or what they believed were the experiences of others abroad.

CZECHOSLOVAKIA

Of the three countries under review Czechoslovakia was the most developed before World War II. It belonged to the developed countries of Europe; it was not far behind Austria in terms of GNP. In the 1960s, it started to fall behind Austria in the pace of growth and, in the second half of the 1970s, the rate of economic growth started to decline.[7] According to Komárek (1989), in the period 1979–88 the growth rate of national income distributed was only 1.5 per cent on the average; if this figure is deflated, the growth rate was below zero. In 1980–2 economic growth slightly declined (0.8 per cent on the average) and in 1983–4 Czechoslovakia, like Poland and Hungary, experienced a recovery. (In Poland the recovery was the strongest and in Hungary the weakest, see Table 8.1.) The recovery in Czechoslovakia was, on the one hand, the normal result of the cyclical development of the economy which was influenced by the business cycle in the West and, on the other, was due to the increased deliveries of fuels and materials from the Soviet Union. Some conservation also helped. But soon the economy started to decelerate again (Dyba, 1989).

Taking the period 1978–89 as a whole it is possible to argue that economic stagnation was caused by internal and external factors, among them labour shortages, shortages of raw materials and fuels, an inability to restructure the economy, the increasing gap in the technology level compared to the West, and, of course, the explosive oil-price increases. Furthermore, labour productivity and capital productivity were declining.

Labour shortages, which were felt in all three countries, were the most acute in Czechoslovakia. Already in 1975 the economic participation rate in Czechoslovakia had achieved a very high level (83.2 per cent) and no further major increases were possible. The increment in the working-age population, which in the second half of the 1970s was only 0.6 per cent on the average, declined in the 1980s to 0.4 per cent (*SR*, 1992, pp. 30–1). The situation was compounded by the demand for labour in the service sector which was undermanned. The authorities hoped that the needed labour for new capacities could be gained from enterprises scheduled for closure. However, closure plans materialised to only a small degree.

The shortage of materials and fuels was caused by the irrational and ineffective structure of the economy, marked by the hypertrophic role of heavy industry, which was one of the main reasons for the Czechoslovak distinction of having a much higher consumption of energy and steel per unit of production than most advanced industrial countries. According to computations, made by the Czechoslovak Prognostic Institute, the consumption of steel for $1 million of GDP in the middle of the 1980s was 2.6 times higher in Czechoslovakia than in the developed capitalist countries. As to comparative energy consumption, the situation was much better, but it still was 46 per cent higher in Czechoslovakia than in capitalist countries. The conservation effort in Czechoslovakia remained behind that of capitalist countries. The latter managed to reduce the steel intensity of production in the period 1971–85 almost twice as much as Czechoslovakia. In a comparison of energy conservation Czechoslovakia remained only 20 per cent behind (Vintrová, 1989).

The situation was compounded by foreign trade developments. The terms of trade continued to worsen as a result of the oil price shock, whose consequences were not fully felt until 1980 (compared to 1970, the terms of trade worsened by 10.6 per cent in 1975 and in 1984 the figure was 50 per cent, and improved only slightly in the next three years). The deficit in the balance of trade even with socialist countries was persistent enough for some time for debts to pile up (*SR*, 1988, p. 452).

The difficulties in foreign trade had their origins in the traditional system of management and in economic policy. The rigid shielding of enterprises from foreign competition worked against innovation. If enterprises know that they will get a price equal to domestic price regardless of prices on foreign markets for their commodities sold abroad by state foreign trade corporations – and this was the real situation – there is no incentive to try very hard to reduce costs. In addition, the planners did not take export needs and possibilities sufficiently into account in distributing investment.

Czechoslovakia was not successful in its effort to narrow its gap in technology with advanced industrial countries; on the contrary, the gap was increasing because, as already mentioned, that country, like the other two, was slow in its reaction to the explosive price increases in oil and less effective with regard to progress in technology. No doubt, the existing economic mechanism did not exert sufficient pressure on enterprises to innovate. Technological progress was also hampered by the slashing of imports from the West, where Czechoslovakia could get the machinery needed for modernisation (Altmann, 1987). Imports were reduced because the number of competitive products which could find a market in the West was declining, and, for political reasons, Czechoslovakia did not want to increase its indebtedness; on the contrary, it tried to reduce it. It was on the whole much smaller than in the neighbouring socialist countries at the end of the 1980s it was US$ 8 billion (see Kouba, 1991). As a result, Czechoslovak trade with the USSR and other CMEA countries increased, at a time when the other two countries were reducing it. (For more, see Chapter 5.)

Czechoslovakia was only able to sell its products on Western markets at lower prices than Western countries did. A striking example is a comparison of export prices for one kilogramme of machinery. In 1970 the price achieved by Czechoslovakia was 58.7 per cent of that realised by Austria, whereas in 1985 it had declined to 25.8 per cent (Dyba, 1989). This difference reflected not only the lower quality of Czechoslovak products, but also discrimination against East European products generally. Western buyers used the weak bargaining power of East European exporters to their own advantage.

The central planners tried to remedy the situation both by an 'intensification' of the economic process (a more economical use of resources and an increase in labour productivity) and by a slowdown in economic growth to bring about a reduction in imports combined with a spur for exports, even at the expense of domestic consumption, in order to improve the balance of payments. The expansion of domestic fuel production (coal) – though at the price of huge investment and pollution – also had to work in this direction. This strategy provided some breathing space, but only for a short time (Vintrová, 1984; Levcik, 1981; Urban and Lér, 1982; Kusín, 1982).

The only solution to the problems faced by Czechoslovakia was to restructure the economy: to stop the extensive growth of heavy industry in favour of a modernisation of the industrial branches with the potential of exporting products which were skilled-labour-intensive rather than material- and energy-intensive (Komárek, 1989). This was all the more necessary because heavy industry required more and more investment, which could have been used for better purposes. For a long time, the heavy industry lobby saw to it that the industry received investment funds even at the expense of light industry and services.

In one of its 1987 meetings, the CC[8] itself came to the conclusion that the existing structure of the economy was unsustainable because, among other things, it required investments which the economy could not afford. According to economic calculations, the further development of heavy industry and protection of the environment until the year 2000 would have required approximately three-quarters of all industrial investments. If the proposals had been accepted, few investment funds would have been available for new, high-tech industrial branches, and for the modernisation of light industry. The CC called mainly for the modernisation of the machinery industry (Soják, 1987; *Rudé právo*, March 20 1987).

Despite all the difficulties, Czechoslovakia had a good record in coping with inflationary pressures, incomparably better than Hungary, let alone Poland: open inflation in Czechoslovakia amounted on the average to 1.2 per cent annually in 1970–89 (see Table 8.1).

It also suffered from shortages, but these were not of the Polish magnitude and did not much affect the supply of consumer goods to the population. C. Kožušník (1991), a staunch supporter of a market economy, characterised the Czechoslovak pre-velvet revolution economy in the following way: 'Despite some recurring gaps, the shelves of our stores were not empty, inflation was moderate, foreign debt was bearable, employment was full and the standard of living rather stagnated, and as far as it declined, this was not alarming'.

In most of the 1970s real wages – an important indicator of the standard of living – grew; they achieved their peak in 1978. From then on they stagnated. If hidden inflation is disregarded, they were 3.6 per cent higher in 1989 than in 1978. Of course, if hidden inflation is taken into account, real wages in 1989 were lower than in 1978. In terms of per capita consumption the Czechoslovak population fared better. It increased by 15.5 per cent in the period 1980–9 (*SR*, 1985, pp. 24–5; 1988, pp. 23–4; and 1993, pp. 26–9).

The evolution of real wages and private consumption in themselves annoyed the population less than shortcomings in other indicators of the standard of living. The deficiencies in the delivery system of health-care services, as discussed above, was a permanent irritant. In Czechoslovakia the situation was worse than in the other two countries in that labour shortages were more extensive, and hospitals suffered from them more than other sectors of the economy, the main reason being wage policy. The slowness in satisfying the demand for housing was another reason for complaint. Perhaps a no-less-important factor which generated an anti-government mood was the fact that the selection of goods was falling behind that of Hungary, let alone Western countries. The public, in particular young people, were especially angered by the shortage of modern electronic products.

Limited possibilities for travel abroad was a special reason for anger and frustration, all the more because Polish and Hungarian citizens were not exposed to such restrictions.[9] The realisation that the restrictions were imposed in Czechoslovakia for political reasons did not increase the prestige of the CP and the government in public eyes. On the contrary, it hurt the credibility of both, which was in low esteem anyhow.

The Czechoslovak intelligentsia more than that of the other two countries had reasons for dissatisfaction. Czechoslovakia had the narrowest wage differentials for skill. In addition, the pension system, with its categorisation into three groups according to working conditions and the physical exactness of the work before retirement, put the intelligentsia in an unfavourable position. On top of this intellectuals enjoyed less freedom of expression and research than in the other two countries.

HUNGARY

Up to 1973 the Hungarian economy grew quite rapidly. From then on economic troubles started to pile up. In the middle of the 1970s Hungary was grappling with a slowdown in economic growth, a worsening of the terms of trade, a growing deficit in the balance of payments and the negative growth of the economically active population.

When the oil price increases started to affect Hungary itself the terms of trade became worse. Increasing Hungarian orientation towards Western markets, whence a growing portion of raw materials was coming, affected the terms of trade unfavourably too. In 1979 the terms of trade were at their lowest point of the 1970s; they had worsened by 24.8 per cent compared to 1970 (*SE*, 1980, p. 321). In the 1980s, the terms of trade continued to worsen but at a much slower rate than in the 1970s. In 1989 they were 6 per cent worse than in 1980 (*SE*, 1990, p. 206).

In 1973 Hungary owed Western creditors (mostly commercial) US $ 2118 million, whereas by 1980 the debt had increased to $ 11455 million and in 1989 to $ 20390 million.[10] Since interest rates were set according to changing market rates and, in the beginning of the 1980s, market interest rates went through the roof because of the restrictive monetary policy in the USA, debt-servicing obligations became an increasingly heavy burden on the Hungarian economy. In 1973, the interest on the loan amounted to 27 per cent of exports, in 1980 to 41.4 per cent and in 1986 it peaked at 75.1 per cent. After 1986 it started to decline (Merényi, 1993). Of the three countries Hungary has had the highest debt per capita.

The economic development of Hungary was much influenced by so-called central development programmes (energy, natural gas, aluminium, petrochemistry, computer engineering) which had a preferential claim on investments. These were designed not only to satisfy domestic demand, but also to meet the demand of CMEA countries. Many of these programmes, financed partly by foreign credits, were coming to completion at the time when the second oil-price shock occurred. The new development programmes meant an increased demand for oil and raw materials. This was at a time when the Soviets declined to increase oil shipments beyond the previously agreed quotas. In addition, the increased need for imports of raw materials from the West hampered the import of new technology (Csikós-Nagy, 1983; B. Kádár, 1983).

A great many industrial branches, which were given preferential treatment, were not really the most profitable; distribution of investment was, despite the 1968 reform, still based very much on what the planners believed should be given priority and on obligations resulting from CMEA agreements, and much less on profitability. Mining, metallurgy and electric energy swallowed up 36.1 per cent of industrial investments in 1975–80, and in 1981–5 as much as 46.1 per cent, whereas machinery and chemicals, which were quite profitable, could not increase to the extent needed because of a lack of sufficient investment. In 1975–80 their share of investment was 33.5 per cent and declined in 1981–5 to 30.4 per cent (Crane, 1991). Hungary was trapped in a situation from which it was difficult to extricate itself. It had to invest more in basic materials and to import more of them in order to be able to export machinery products to CMEA and developing countries, and also to export semi-finished chemical and metallurgical products and the products of light industry to the West. Hungary was not able to compete effectively with its machinery on OECD markets. And this contributed to a growing gap between Hungary and Western countries in the technology used (see B. Kádár, 1983).

This development was necessarily reflected in declining growth rates. In 1976–7 GDP grew on the average at 5 per cent, in 1978 at only 4 per cent, in 1979 even less (1.5 per cent) and in 1980 there was no growth at all (*SE*, 1990, p. 2). The Hungarian authorities concluded that something had to be done about the situation. The economic community was split into two camps: one advocated a continuation of the old strategy of economic growth and a mobilisation of all resources for this purpose, and the other preferred to focus on the elimination of the external disequilibrium, even at the expense of economic growth. J. Hoós (1981) maintained that the first suggestion overestimated Hungarian capacity, whereas the second underestimated it. According to him Hungary opted for a new path in economic growth strategy which, in my opinion, was somewhere between the two suggestions and closer to the second. The new growth strategy was supposed to be increasingly 'demand controlled growth'; namely, growth was to be based on demand arising from sales, preferably in demanding foreign markets, and demand which could be ensured in an efficient way. In other words, economic growth was to depend increasingly on the ability to increase exports. This was an almost revolutionary change in the strategy of economic growth, considering that previously fast economic growth was all but an article of faith. Supply was the only limit to growth.

This change in the growth strategy was substantiated by the need to import more and more raw materials and technology from non-socialist markets and for this purpose more and more adequate exports for demanding markets had to be produced in order to pay for the imports. However, it was difficult to find adequate markets for exports and therefore imports had to be slashed, as happened in 1982 (see Hoós, 1981).

The five-year plan for 1981–5 envisaged only moderate growth rates for national income produced (14–17 per cent for the whole period), and even much smaller rates for national income used (3–5 per cent) in order not to endanger external equilibrium. Investment was not to grow, and economic growth was expected from increases in productivity. No promises were made about increases in real wages and personal consumption. Only some increases in low pensions were promised (Havasi, 1981).

The planners assumed that a restriction of domestic absorption for two to three years combined with an increase in exports would improve external equilibrium to such an extent that it would be possible after some time to return to a dynamisation of economic growth (*Gazdaságpolitika* . . ., 1988).

The expectations for improvement did not materialise. On the contrary, the economic situation became worse in 1981–2 . The slump in the West, the result of the second oil-price explosion, made it more difficult for Hungarian exports, and therefore the export plan could not be achieved. As a result economic growth also remained behind target, but it still was much higher than in 1980 (*SE*, 1992, p. 2).

Polish events, the declarations of martial law and of insolvency, had created a small panic in Western financial markets and resulted in the imposition of a partial credit embargo on all East European countries. This probably prompted a sudden withdrawal of foreign currency, mainly by the Arab oil countries, from the Hungarian National Bank. The situation was aggravated by growing interest rates paid on foreign debts. Hungary was on the edge of insolvency (Csikós-Nagy, 1983; and Révész, 1990, p. 105).

Hungary managed to avoid the worst by imposing tighter import restrictions and, by giving enterprises various incentives, encouraged them and foreign trade corporations to increase exports to hard currency countries. In 1983–4 the economic situation in Hungary improved for a while, as it did in the other two countries. The economic recovery in the West must have helped too. The country managed to balance its merchandise trade, though there was no improvement in the terms of trade. In 1978 exports covered only 70.4 per cent of imports from convertible currency markets, whereas in 1983 it was 115 per cent. In 1983–4 the government also succeeded in balancing the state budget (Nyers and Tardos, 1984). There were also some other signs of improvement – in energy saving, in a reduction in material intensity per unit of production, etc.

The rapidly developing private or quasi-private sector, as a result of the legislative changes in 1982 which opened up new possibilities for private business, had a favourable effect on the economy. In the state sector there was no turnaround in economic efficiency, perhaps one of the reasons being that for many workers the work in a state factory was only one of two jobs, in some cases even three, which they held.

Encouraged by the two relatively successful years the Hungarian authorities decided to accelerate economic growth. They backed up their decision by making some changes in the economic mechanism, going beyond the principles of the new economic mechanism of 1968 (for more, see Chapter 7). The seventh five year plan for 1986–90 envisaged for the first years an increase in the annual growth rate of 2–3.5 per cent. This was a modest goal, but still higher than the rate achieved in 1981–5 (1.8 per cent). What is also important to mention is that the plan did not envisage a reduction in domestic absorption: on the contrary, it assumed a small increase, including an increase in investment. The planners also promised a small increase in real wages (Hoós, 1985).

One of the objectives of the new plan was to reduce foreign debt by achieving a surplus in the balance of trade. The planners wanted to prepare an environment for possible new loans if such a need arose. Furthermore, the plan envisaged the achievement of a previous goal – a restructuring of the economy in accordance with the needs of exports (*Gazdaságpolitika . . .*1988, pp. 97–8).

The five year plan was short-lived. The economy took a turn for the worse – but not instantly – so that the objectives in the plan became empty words, as many economists had predicted. In the beginning of 1988 the plan was abandoned, and the government embarked on a stabilisation programme. Soon after this, with the start of the crumbling of the socialist system, planning's role in guiding the economy started to crumble too.

The expectations of faster economic growth materialised only in the first two years of the plan (the GDP grew by 5.4 per cent). Later, the GDP started to stagnate and, with the transition to a market economy, to fall. In 1989 the GDP was only 15.3 per cent higher than in 1980. Neither was the government able to increase real wages as promised. In 1988 real wages declined by 5.1 per cent (*SE*, 1990, p. 56 and pp. 2 and 15).

Instead of decreasing, the Hungarian debt doubled in 1985–7 in terms of dollars as a result of dramatic changes in the exchange rate between the dollar on the one hand and the yen, mark and other Western currencies on the other hand. The expectations pinned to foreign trade did not materialise either. In 1987, the balance of trade was almost in equilibrium, and in 1988 there was even a surplus, but not sufficient to cover the interest payable on debts. No progress was made in restructuring the economy to the needs of exports (Csikós-Nagy, 1988; Révész, 1990, p. 143; *Gazdaságpolitika,*1988, p. 98).

Inflation, which from the end of the 1970s had accelerated and ranged from 6 to 8.6 per cent, amounted in 1988 to 15.9 per cent and continued to increase in the following years (*SE* 1990, p. 14). The introduction of a value added tax was corresponsible for the surge in inflation in 1988.

The worsening economic situation from the second half of the 1970s necessarily had its impact on the standard of living. The slightly declining standard of living gradually undermined the credibility of the government. No doubt this was one of the contributory factors in the collapse of the socialist system.

The decline in real wages was not as dramatic as it has been in the transition to a market economy. In the period 1978 (when real wages reached their peak) to 1989 the real wages of blue- and white-collar workers declined by 9.6 per cent; of this the greatest decline was in 1988 (see Table 8.1). In other years real wages declined minimally. The government tried hard for political reasons not to allow much erosion of real wages. To this end it used a portion of foreign loans to support consumption. However, workers, who were used to annual real wage increases, soon felt the difference and did not like it.

At the same period real incomes, which also include transfer payments, increased by 15.1 per cent. Private consumption per capita (computed in constant prices of 1980) increased by 11.4 per cent in the period 1980–8. (*SE*, 1990, pp. 14 and 214). Private consumption – as well as real incomes – reflects not only incomes from the principal job, but also from the second and in some cases the third occupation. Furthermore, it includes incomes from private activities, whether legal or illegal. Apparently, if the trends in the standard of living are judged simply on the basis of incomes as a whole, then one can hardly argue that there was a decline. In my opinion, not only the benefits of economic activities, namely incomes, should be considered, but also costs in terms of expended labour, energy, etc. Two jobs, which were performed by a large portion of the population, could not be carried out without a negative effect on the health of the population and family life. Health statistics confirm this.

Average pensions grew faster than earnings in the period discussed. New pensions were higher than the old ones, while at the same time low pensions disappeared with the dying off of old pensioners, and for this reason the average pension grew. Since the compensation for inflation lagged much behind the rate of inflation in most cases, the purchasing power of most pensions declined. In addition, the conditions for pensioners' extra earnings worsened in the course of time.

It is often argued that social programmes[11] in the countries under review were a great burden on the economy. I have come across comparative figures for Hungary only. It can be assumed that figures for the other two countries were not much different. In 1981, according to E. Gács (1986), who compared Hungary's social expenditures with those of OECD countries on the basis of figures published by that organisation, Hungary's social expenditures made up 20.8 per cent of GDP, one of the lowest in Europe. What is quite surprising is Hungary's government expenditure on health care – only 3 per cent of GDP. Expenditures on health care in 1983, when statistical yearbooks started to publish figures on health care alone, made up 4.2 per cent of government expenditures and 4.8 per cent in 1988 (*SE*, 1986, p. 330, and 1990, p. 319). Of course, real expenditures on health care were much higher: none of those computations include gratuities paid by patients to doctors.

On the other hand, expenditures on pensions compared favourably with OECD countries. They made up 7.8 per cent of GDP, which was more than in Britain, Canada and the USA (Gács, 1986).

CONCLUDING REMARKS

In the 1980s the economies of the countries under review performed poorly. This was true primarily of Poland, which experienced a huge decline in economic growth in 1979–83. Taking the period 1980–9 as a whole, it can be said that economic growth in the three countries was marked by stagnation. Neither Czechoslovakia nor Hungary suffered a decline in economic growth of the magnitude they suffered in the transition to a market economy.

Naturally, the poor performance in economic growth had an unfavourable effect on the standard of living, especially on real wages. In this regard Poland, if shortages are also considered, fared the worst and Czechoslovakia the best. In Poland there was a huge decline in real wages in 1982, but in the following years workers managed to obtain increases so that in 1989 real wages were almost on the level of 1980. However, the real wage pertaining to the countries discussed should be taken with some qualification, mainly with regard to Czechoslovakia, because in their computation hidden inflation was not taken into consideration. On the other hand, it should be borne in mind that consumption per capita was more favourable.

Of course, real wages alone are not a good indicator of the standard of living, if the availability of consumer goods is not considered. Of the three countries Poland had the worst record and Hungary the best with regard to the supply of consumer goods. Poland suffered from huge market disequilibria. As to inflation Poland was again worst off and Czechoslovakia the best.

The economic situation in the 1980s was thus bad, but there was no unemployment. Whoever wanted to work could easily find a job. Nevertheless people were very dissatisfied: the perception of the economic situation in the minds of the people was much worse than it was objectively. This was not only in Poland where the situation was especially difficult, but also in the other two countries. There were primarily two reasons for the popular perception mentioned. The economic stagnation lasted a long time and there seemed to be no prospect of improvement. In its propaganda the communist regime promised continuous improvement in the standard of living; even in the face of the economic difficulties the communist leaders continued to insist that there would be a turnaround, but there were no reliable signs that this would soon happen. In addition, the dissatisfaction was fuelled by the lack of access to the achievements of modern technology. People wanted to use their earnings according to their priorities. Those who could afford it wanted to be able to buy a car as soon as they had the cash and travel abroad without any administrative restrictions. They wanted to have access to a large selection of entertainment gadgets at affordable prices. They wanted to enjoy life like their peers in the West. The neglect of consumption by the socialist planners turned a great proportion of the population against the regime. It was to be expected that such a policy of neglect could not be pursued with impunity for long.

The second reason was that the anti-socialist propaganda managed to convince the public that its aspirations could be easily achieved if the socialist system was replaced by a market economy. And the transition to a market economy seemed to be painless according to the propaganda.

The only legitimacy of the socialist system was the promise that it could ensure a growing standard of living, full employment and an extensive safety net. When it turned out that the standard of living was stagnating, the legitimacy of the system was undermined.

9 Ownership Relations

INTRODUCTION

Marx and Engels believed that the communist economy would be a marketless economy, based on collective ownership of the means of production. In their *Manifesto of the Communist Party* (Marx–Engels Reader, 1978) Marx and Engels characterised bourgeois private property as 'the final and most complete expression of the system of producing and appropriating products that is based on class antagonism, on the exploitation of the many by the few' (p. 484) and suggested that the proletariat, as the new ruling class, would 'wrest, by decrees, all capital from the bourgeoisie' (p. 490). They also assumed that socialisation of the means of production was a prerequisite to many desirable changes in the economy and society. To them economic planning, which they advocated as a new coordinating mechanism for future society instead of the market mechanism, was possible only under collective ownership. They also believed that collective ownership would enable changes in the distribution of income. Finally, the institution of collective ownership was for them a precondition for the creation of a classless society and the elimination of the state as a political power in the second stage of communism.

Marx and Engels made it clear in their *Manifesto of the Communist Party* (pp. 484–5) that their call for the abolition of private property referred to bourgeois property. They assumed that the property of petty artisans and small peasants would be destroyed by industry. From the same work it is also clear that socialisation of the means of production should proceed gradually.

It can be assumed from their writings that nationalisation of the means of production was for them only the first step in the process of socialisation of the means of production. Since their objective was to create associations of producers which were self-managed, it is only natural that in their concept producers were supposed to have control over the means of production.

NATIONALISATION

The Bolsheviks seized power in 1917 with the intention of crushing capitalism and building a socialist system in its place. Socialisation of the means of production was regarded as one of the most important means of achieving this goal. The Bolsheviks intended to carry out socialisation in non-agricultural sectors first in the form of nationalisation, which in the Soviet and later in East European practice meant confiscation. Only foreign owners got some compensation after long negotiations. Agriculture was not regarded as ripe for socialisation for political (in order not to endanger the alliance with the peasantry) and economic reasons (because of its huge dispersal into many small holdings). However, one of the first decrees of the Bolshevik government in 1917 confiscated large estates, formally nationalised agricultural land and limited the amount of land peasants could hold to their capacity to cultivate it.

The Bolsheviks did not intend to implement nationalisation right away after the seizure of power. The first provision in this area was only a decree on Workers' Control (14 November 1917), which entrusted workers with the right to supervise management and control production (Dobb, 1966, p. 83). The Civil War, which accelerated the already-existing chaos in the economy, was instrumental in precipitating nationalisation. There is some evidence that the Bolsheviks wanted to limit nationalisation to a certain number of enterprises of great importance and to preserve a mixed economy for some time (Nove, 1982, p. 54). Even the leftists of that time, Bukharin and Preobrazhenskii, suggested leaving small scale production out of nationalisation. Though there were no good economic reasons, small-scale production was also nationalised by the end of 1920 (Nove, 1982, pp. 69–70, 77) and, with this, the preconditions for the working of market forces were largely eliminated.

The new economic policy (NEP) meant a change in nationalisation. A 1921 decree returned all enterprises with less than 20 workers to their original owners, or allowed such businesses to be leased to other people. Some medium-sized enterprises were taken over jointly by the state and private persons. Private enterprise started to play a very important role, mainly in retail trade (Dobb, 1966, p. 142). At the same time, compulsory requisitioning of grain, which united the peasantry into a dangerous opposition to the regime, was abolished. It was replaced, first, by a tax in kind and later (1924) by a money tax. Peasants were given the right to trade their surpluses in the market.

The two provisions (partial denationalisation and abolition of compulsory deliveries) meant a restoration of market relations including a revival of money circulation in much of the economy. This process was strengthened by the introduction of a new stabilised currency (1923). The fact that large enterprises, though they remained in the hands of the state, were given quite considerable autonomy and were operated on the profit principle, also fostered market forces.

NEP came to an end, and with it coordination of the economy by market forces, with the start of the planned economy and with the collectivisation of the means of production in agriculture (private plots are disregarded here). The first five year plan with its problems and difficulties in grain supply was instrumental in putting the intended collectivisation on the agenda earlier than had been expected.

The Soviet pattern of socialisation of the means of production was in substance adopted by East European countries. However, it was not carried out in its entirety right after the Second World War. At that time, the Soviet Union was interested in maintaining good relations with the West, and therefore tried to avoid measures which might tarnish these relations. Also, the CPs, for internal political reasons, did not want to disrupt the coalition with non-communist parties which existed at that time in most countries, all the more because the question of 'how' and 'when' political power would be seized was not clear. For all these reasons, the CPs embarked basically on a two-stage nationalisation programme. In the first stage, soon after the Second World War, the CPs pushed through a programme of nationalisation limited to key industries, banks and other financial institutions. The post-war radicalisation of the population and all the propaganda made it very difficult for non-communist parties to reject the programme of nationalisation, all the more because the CPs assured the public that they were interested in a strong private sector.

As soon as the CPs seized political power (in 1948–9), they forgot their promises. A drive for fully-fledged nationalisation came into motion, a drive which included a variety of methods, ranging from tightening the tax screw and barring access to raw materials to pressure and intimidation. In a relatively short period of time, the private, non-agricultural sector was liquidated in most countries. True, a small part of the private sector was turned into cooperatives; however, they were subordinated to the control of the state bureaucracy too.

Soon after the start of the second stage of nationalisation, a big push for the collectivisation of agriculture started. Though East European countries did not use as much violence as the Soviets did, collectivisation was not free of pressure and intimidation. As in the USSR, members of the collective farms were allowed to own a small private plot where they could keep animals as well as cultivate certain crops for their own needs and mostly also for sale.

All-embracing nationalisation meant also an elimination of many small factories and service businesses in the hope that their production would be transferred to larger and more efficient units. Socialist countries were from the beginning attracted to the idea of concentrating production as a way to simplify the organisation and administration of the economy, and to harness the advantages of economies of scale. In the course of time (in the smaller countries in the late 1950s and 1960s, in the Soviet Union later) the countries, as already mentioned, became obsessed with concentration, some viewing it as a substitute for a genuine reform. Needless to say, concentration of production strengthened the monopoly position of suppliers, with adverse consequences.

In reality, the structure of production, which had evolved through many decades, was broken up by nationalisation and was not properly replaced. In a market economy, producers incessantly scrutinise existing or potential market demand and adjust their productive capacity to it. Therefore, under peaceful conditions, a newly developed demand will usually be satisfied rapidly. In the traditional system, the central planners determined what the needs and possibilities of the economy were, and enterprises produced in substance what the planners told them to produce. With the best will in the world, the planners could not have all the existing million and a half products in evidence. Their interest was focused on large-ticket items and what in their eyes were items of central importance. In addition, enterprise managers were primarily concerned with the fulfilment of plan targets. The leeway they had in determining the product mix and quality of products was used according to their interest. If market demand coincided with their interest, enterprise managers would satisfy it. If not, as has been shown, they would act *contrary* to market demand since their financial well-being, as well as that of their employees, did not depend on satisfying market demand.

The way that collective assets were operated also contributed to the failure of the system. It was expected that collective ownership would eliminate the alienation of workers and instil in them a feeling of co-ownership; this in turn would be translated into good care for the use of resources and an encouragement to do hard and quality work. Such expectations turned out to be an illusion. The communist elites made little provision for expectations to turn into reality. Nationalised enterprises were turned into state enterprises without workers being given a real voice in decision-making about the use of the means of production. Meetings called by managers to inform workers about the fulfilment of the plan and to hear their comments were regarded by the workers as a sham. Neither was there an incentive system which would demonstrate to workers the advantage of being co-owners of the means of production. In some countries it took the authorities many years to come up with an incentive system which gave workers a share (in the form of bonuses) in the financial results. Since the bonuses were quite small, they did not have much of an effect .

The CPs were reluctant to give workers a say in the utilisation of the enterprise assets. Their resistance to any real workers' participation increased once the Yugoslavs started to introduce a self-management system which was anathema, mainly to the Soviet leaders. In the final analysis they saw self-management as a serious threat to the leading role of the Party.

For all the reasons mentioned workers did not feel themselves to be co-owners of state enterprises; to a great extent they viewed state ownership as property belonging to no one and treated it accordingly. They did not fight waste and theft; instead many of them participated in thefts.[1]

Sweeping nationalisation was one of the contributing factors to shortages, low-quality goods and low productivity.

THE IMPACT OF THE ECONOMIC REFORMS

I have discussed economic reforms in Chapter 7. Here I will discuss their impact on the approach to ownership. But, before I start to discuss the topic, several paragraphs will be devoted to the changes in policies *vis-à-vis* the private sector before the reforms started.

The first change in policy towards private ownership occurred in 1953 after Stalin's death. The ambitious medium-term plans adopted by the three countries brought about great imbalances in the economy. Shortages of raw materials as well as of consumer goods emerged; the latter resulted not only from neglect of consumer goods industries, but also from the forced collectivisation of agriculture. The situation was compounded by the decline in the standard of living. In all the three countries dissatisfaction and tension were spreading. The authorities decided to act: they made changes in national plans, reduced investments and released more resources for consumption. What was also important was that they allowed collective farms to be dissolved. In Czechoslovakia, where only a small percentage of collective farms took advantage of it, the breakup of the farms was only a temporary phenomenon. Soon the authorities started to push collectivisation again. In Hungary the breakup of collective farms and the flight from them started in 1953 and was accelerated after the 1956 uprising.[2] In the beginning of the 1960s, collectivisation was resumed, though in a way which was more acceptable to the peasants. In Poland collectivisation proceeded much more slowly than in the other two countries: in 1955 it encompassed only 9.2 per cent of the agricultural production area, with 205 000 members. In 1965 the number of members in collective farms was only 21 000. The predominant part of Polish agriculture remained private (Jezierski and Petz, 1988, pp. 213 and 302). In 1960, when collective farms in Czechoslovakia were active on 84.2 per cent of the cultivated area, the figure in Poland was 1.1 per cent of the total arable land (Brus, 1986, p. 80).

In 1956, after the Polish riots and the Hungarian uprising, small private ownership got a reprieve in the two countries mentioned. The Polish CC in October 1956, several months after the riots in Poznan which brought about a new leadership of the CP headed by W. Gomulka, decided to ease the rise of private small-scale production, as long as the supplies of materials were not at the expense of state enterprises and cooperatives. According to Aslund (1985, p. 55), the permission to expand private businesses had four objectives: to create new job opportunities, increase the standard of living (probably by satisfying demand), utilise free resources and develop backward regions. As a result of this policy, the small private sector, mainly retail trade, increased considerably. Later, some restrictions were imposed, but still the private non-agricultural sector survived.

In Hungary, too, the government tried by various measures, including tax relaxation, to encourage the expansion of the private sector. It also allowed some shops as well as catering outlets to be leased. The main purpose of this action was to reduce the political tension which the suppression of the uprising produced and also to alleviate shortages (Petö and Szakács, 1985, pp. 317–18).

The reforms of the 1960s did not bring about a substantial change in attitude to private ownership. However, small private ownership was allowed to expand. This was also the case in Poland without a major economic reform. Even Czechoslovakia, where nationalisation and collectivisation were almost complete, allowed some room for private ownership. Yet in all the three countries collective ownership remained the foundation of the economic system. Few dared to challenge collective ownership because in doing so they challenged socialism. The majority of even the most radical economists did not take the position that the functioning of the market presupposes pluralisation of ownership, or more precisely private ownership. They believed, as has already been mentioned, that the market could be made workable if enterprises were given full autonomy.

The permitted expansion or resurgence of small businesses, mainly in services, was combined more with political considerations and the desire to cope with shortages than with the intended supplementation of planning by the market as a coordinating tool of economic activities. For example, the Czechoslovak Action Programme of the CP, which was adopted in April of 1968 and which was a programme of reforms, reads: 'in the sphere of services small businesses have their justification . . . they should fill in the gap in the market' (*Rok . . .*, 1969, p. 129).[3]

The situation changed in the 1980s, mainly in the second half, but only in Hungary and Poland. In Czechoslovakia, compared with the other two countries the changes can be characterised as marginal.

In Hungary the private sector in agriculture as well as in the non-agricultural sphere was slowly growing. In 1978 245 000 people worked in the legal private non- agricultural sector; of them, 44 per cent were independent small-business people and 22 per cent performed business activities besides their full-time job. People working in the private sector had quite good earnings; they did not have to undergo so much competition as before the seizure of political power by the communists. Since in practice the issuance of business licences was limited, and many were afraid for various reasons to apply for one, those who had a licence were in a sense in a monopoly position (Gábor and Galasi, 1981).[4]

In Hungary in 1981 a considerable expansion of the non-agricultural private sector occurred as a result of new legislative measures. It should be made clear right away that these measures were not a challenge to state ownership, though they brought changes to what had been previously thought to be the place and the role of the state sector. The 1981 legislation created conditions for small cooperatives and private producers as well as for work teams within state enterprises. The small cooperatives, which could include 15 to 100 people, could work in various sectors other than agriculture. They differed from the well-known large non-agricultural cooperatives in several respects. In the large cooperatives the ownership question was pushed into the background: the cooperative members were viewed by the authorities as caretakers of the property rather than as owners. In the case of small cooperatives the members were the real owners. To become a member of a small cooperative it was necessary to pay a membership contribution amounting to at least two weeks' basic wage. In the decision-making all the members were to take part; representative decision-making, applied in large cooperatives, was not permissible in small ones (Falusné Szikra, 1986, pp. 178–80).

Private artisans could work in different areas. What was new was that the issuance of permits was simplified and that artisans were allowed to employ three non-family members and could perform jobs for state enterprises. The latter was a great concession and a sign that the authorities were moving in the direction of putting both the state and private sectors on a more equal footing. In the past the authorities had insisted that the two sectors should be strictly separated. They had some ideological as well as practical reasons for this. They were afraid, and rightly so, that the cooperation between the two sectors would open the door to various phenomena of corruption and theft.

Work teams were an entirely new institution. In brief, work teams were small self-managed units, comprising 2 to 30 workers and technicians, to whom enterprises contracted out work which was performed after regular work time. Initially, work teams consisted of the best and most respected blue- and white-collar workers. The contracted-out work was performed with enterprise machinery and equipment; originally no rent was paid for their use, later some rent was introduced. The work teams were allowed to bargain directly about the work to be performed and the price of the contract. Originally it was assumed that the work teams would perform different work after work time than in their regular work time. Wage regulation did not refer to the activities of the work teams, a circumstance which considerably reduced the opposition of many managers to their creation.

The rise of the work teams was motivated by labour shortages and maybe even more by the desire to counter the spreading discontent over the decline in real wages and to introduce a new element in wage differentiation. The much higher earnings made by work teams than it was possible for workers to achieve in overtime work for one hour of work benefited primarily the labour elite. And this was not accidental. The authorities hoped that by gaining the support of the elite they could influence the rest of the workers.

The work teams helped to solve some economic problems, such as coping with labour shortages and fulfilling delivery contracts, but at the same time they contributed to the worsening of labour discipline and tensions in enterprises. Many workers who wanted to, but could not, participate in the work teams were angered. Their anger was increased when they learned that work teams received higher earnings for the same work which was performed in normal work time (for more about work teams, see Adam, 1989a; Kővári and Szirácki, 1985; and Révész, 1986).

In 1983 a new private business form came into being: economic labour cooperation (*gazdasági munkaközösség*). Members of this new form could continue working in the socialist sector and perform private activities after work time, like the work teams, with the difference that they had to perform their activities outside state enterprises. In addition, they were allowed to hire a limited number of employees and the participants in this new form were liable for any debts to the extent of all their assets (Falusné Szikra, 1986, pp. 182–3).

Needless to say, work team activities as well as activities in the private sector outside enterprises, which were performed by many as a second job, had a negative impact on health and family life.

The above-mentioned legislative changes created preconditions for a rapid development of the private sector. Of course, besides the legal second economy, a large illegal economy existed, primarily in house construction and apartment maintenance. According to some estimates the number of people engaged in such activities amounted to 275 000. Most of the illegal activity was performed as part-time work. Part of the illegal activity was the work of the legal private sector; it resorted to such activity for two reasons, one being that the licence it had did not allow it to be engaged in the activities it desired, and the second being to avoid taxes (Falusné Szikra, 1986, pp. 214–15).

In Poland in the middle of the 1970s the private sector got new stimuli to expansion. Some of the measures were enacted before the aborted price increases in 1976, and some afterwards. The authorities increased their support for private agriculture. Specialised agricultural units were given various advantages in order to encourage increased production. What is perhaps no less important is that private farmers were put on the same footing as state employees for social security provisions, with certain qualifications. In order to get a pension they were obliged to sell a certain amount of output to the state procurement agencies (Mizsei, 1990, pp. 111–12; Lammich, 1978).

The government came up with several provisions aimed at encouraging the expansion of small private enterprises. It loosened the taxation screw and allowed artisans to employ, besides members of their own family, three people (one fully employed and two pensioners). Before, artisans had not been allowed to employ non-family members unless they received special permission. In addition, social security provisions for artisans were improved. Domestic trade organisations were allowed to lease trade units to private persons (Lammich, 1978; Aslund, 1985, pp. 106–8).

In 1976 the Polish government for the first time invited foreigners to invest in Poland. It took, however, several changes in the conditions for investment before the invitation started to attract foreigners (Mizsei, 1990).

The 1981 reform in Poland did not bring any changes to the role of state ownership; neither did Solidarity challenge it in its official statements before martial law was declared. Perhaps the reform proposal of NET (a grouping of Solidarity organisations in large enterprises) (1981) went furthest when it suggested allowing the expansion of the private sector. However, even this called for certain limitations (no specifics were mentioned), and once these limits were achieved, private enterprises should have been turned into mixed enterprises in order 'to reduce incentives to luxury consumption'.

Yet the 1981 economic reform brought about favourable conditions for the expansion of the private sector. In 1982 the government decree (*Reforma Gospodarcza*, 1983, p. 59) allowed the sale of small businesses as well as service outlets to private persons. Those interested in such sales were extended low-interest credit in order to be able to pay for the purchase.[5]

Of course, parallel with the expansion of the legal private sector was a booming illegal private sector in Poland. Its expansion was fuelled by the growing shortages which were quite large in 1981 and 1982, by obstacles to entry into the private sector and by the expectation of huge profits on which taxes would not be paid (cf. Mizsei, 1990, pp. 174–5; Kaminski, 1991, p. 183). The black market with foreign currencies, which started to develop in the middle of the 1970s, took on huge proportions in the 1980s and increasingly undermined the *zloty* as a medium of exchange and store of value. The black market in currency was indirectly supported by government hard currency shops and made possible other illegal transactions, such as the smuggling of goods from abroad.[6]

Self-management

The expansion of the private sector did not bring about a change in the state sector and, moreover, it was not a challenge to the latter. The introduction of self-management in state enterprises in Poland in 1982 and in Hungary 1985 meant a change in the exercise of property rights, but not in ownership itself; state enterprises remained the property of the state. In Czechoslovakia, unlike the other two countries,[7] self-management was introduced for the first time in the middle of 1968, but lasted only for a short time; with the ousting of Dubček and the dismantlement of the economic reform, self-management was abolished. It was reintroduced with the reform of 1987.

The concept of self-management varied in its application in individual countries. In Czechoslovakia in 1968 the self-management bodies had very limited authority; rather they performed an advisory role. In the beginning of 1969 workers in many enterprises pushed through a self-management concept which gave workers a much greater role, but it was short-lived.

In Poland and Hungary in the 1980s the instituted self-management system meant a real change in management structures, where it was applied according to the spirit of the law. The legislation on self-management gave self-management bodies important decision-making rights. In substance there were two groups of decisions which were delegated to the new management bodies: one referred to the strategic policy of enterprises and the second to the appointment of top managers. The first group of decisions was already largely in the hands of enterprises in Hungary; the changes approved in 1984 by the CC lay in this group of decisions being expanded and formally transferred to the new self-management bodies, though not in its entirety. The self-management bodies in Hungary were given the right to approve the annual plan of their enterprises, make decisions about splitting their enterprises or merging with other units, about the founding of branches etc. (see CC decision, *TSz*, 1984, no.5). In Poland the self-management bodies received similar rights (see *Reforma Gospodarcza*, 1983, pp. 18–20). Since Poland did not go through such far-reaching reform as Hungary did in the 1960s, its enterprises did not enjoy the kind of autonomy the Hungarian enterprises did, and therefore in Poland the institution of self-management meant in substance a transfer of rights from the ministries to self-management bodies.

The second group of decisions was transferred directly from the ministries. It referred on the one hand to appointment of top managers and on the other to the evaluation of their performance. On the appointment of top managers, the solution was not the same in the two countries. In Hungary, the ministry (the founder) had in fact the right of veto in the case of appointment as well as dismissal of top managers.

In Poland, the appointment of top managers was in the hands of self-management bodies in less important enterprises only. The evaluation of the performance of top managers was left to self-management bodies in Hungary.

The far-reaching economic reforms of the 1960s in Hungary and Czechoslovakia meant a transfer of certain property rights from the authorities to enterprise managers. The introduction of self-management in Hungary and Poland in the 1980s was a further transfer of property rights; this time primarily to self-management, or top management where self-management bodies were not able or willing to use the rights which were given to them. The ownership of enterprises remained, of course, in the hands of the state. Managers or self-management bodies were entrusted with the use of resources in the hope of their more efficient use. F. Havasi (1984), the Economic Secretary of the Hungarian CC, wrote the following about the changes in 1984: 'The purpose of the change is that, while maintaining the state character of ownership, the mode of disposal of property and the exercise of the employer rights should be made more efficient'.

Managers and self-management bodies were given not only rights to use resources more efficiently for the sake of a better performance, but also certain rights to the results (usufruct rights) of enterprise activities. But I do not think that this gave managers a title to future benefits from the resources used, so-called vested rights, as it is argued in the *Economic Survey of Europe* (1992, p. 202). Never was such a promise made. It was always understood that, once managers quit the enterprises which were entrusted to their management, they had no claim to any enterprise assets. There were suggestions that dividends should be extended from investment to employees of enterprises after they quit their jobs. This arrangement was supposed to aim primarily at older employees in order to increase their interest in investment. As far as I know, there was no attempt to turn this idea into reality.

Self-management was introduced in the hope that this would enhance the autonomy of enterprises and turn the old socialist promise of industrial democracy into reality and thus instil a feeling of co-ownership in employees. However, self-management did not greatly change the attitude of workers to state ownership. There were several reasons for this. In neither of the two countries was the self-management institution very active. According to some estimates employees in 15–30 per cent of enterprises took advantage of the rights given to them by the legislation. Most workers were not interested in participation, and many were discouraged by the fact that it was difficult for the self-management bodies to assert their rights in the face of resistance by the top management.[8] In addition, the authorities in both countries were not eager to turn self-management into an effective institution. In Hungary the institution did not have much support among the leading economists; they believed in B. Ward's conclusions (1958) about self-management with regard to unemployment and investments and were afraid that self-management would generate inflationary pressures. For them the idea of self-management did not have emotional connotations as was the case with many Polish economists. Nor was it an article of ideology, and therefore they were not willing to pay a price for industrial democracy. The increasing problems with self-management in Yugoslavia diminished the attractiveness of the idea. When the fight for private ownership became the agenda of the day, self-management lost its appeal almost entirely, primarily in Hungary. In the transition to a market economy self-management was slowly liquidated in both countries. (For more about self-management see Adam, 1989 and 1993).

The Second Half of the 1980s

As already mentioned in Chapter 7, Poland and Hungary came up with new reform programmes in 1987 which promised changes in ownership relations, though not dramatic ones. The promises opened the door to discussion about state ownership, which had been more or less sacrosanct until that time.

The Polish Theses about the second stage of the reform (Supplement to *Rzeczpospolita*, 17 April 1987) promised to create legislative and economic conditions for the development of the small-scale private sector in retail trade, catering and services. It also promised to facilitate the rise of mixed enterprises, in which private persons and private business could take part, but no details were mentioned. But the Theses made it clear that state ownership was continuing to be the basis of the system.

The publication of the Theses caused quite a lot of resonance, some critical and some positive. It is interesting that there was no great criticism of the approach of the Theses to ownership. In its position paper regarding the Theses the Association of Polish Economists did not even mention the private sector (*ZG*, 1987, no. 19). The situation soon changed in Poland; the attempt to mitigate the existing market disequilibrium by price increases failed, as has already been mentioned in Chapter 8. Workers reacted to price increases by demands for higher wages, demands which they backed up by strikes and strike threats. Being politically in a weak position, the government retreated. The end result was that market disequilibrium became even worse. In addition, the price manoeuvre changed the power relations between the government and Solidarity. The latter, which had gone into a decline, became active again and its influence and prestige grew fast. The increasing feeling that communist rule was coming to an end made social scientists think about the transition to a market economy. In 1988, the first studies about privatisation appeared.[9]

Needless to say, the expansion of the private sector in Poland continued; on the one hand new businesses were established and on the other hand, the government continued renting and selling small-scale businesses. In the period 1980–7 employment in the non-agricultural private sector (included are only employees whose main employment was in that sector) grew by 77 per cent and amounted to 6.2 per cent of the total employment in the economy (*RS*, 1988, p. 390). However, the share of the private sector as a whole, including agriculture, in employment declined because of the considerable flight from agriculture, which was private in Poland. The growth of the illegal private sector was even faster. Kaminski (1991, p. 183) estimates that the share of the second economy in total personal incomes tripled between the 1970s and 1986 (from 5 per cent to 15 per cent).

In 1989 the government concluded that the only way out of the political crisis was a dialogue with its rival, Solidarity. In the ensuing round-table dialogue the two rivals agreed on a free pluralisation of ownership (*TL*, 7 April 1989).

The 1987 Hungarian reform programme adopted by the CC, and the government programme based on the CP programme (*Nsz*, 4 July and 19 September 1987, respectively), did not mean a breakthrough in privatisation. The CP stressed only that private activities were an integral part of the socialist economy and that there should be cooperation between small-scale and large enterprises. It indirectly stressed that collective ownership should play a decisive role in the economy.

Radical reformers went, of course, further than the government. The already mentioned study 'Turning Point and Reform' (1987) demanded the opening of the door to all forms of ownership. Soon Hungarian economists, perhaps with greater caution than their Polish colleagues, came up with suggestions on how to privatise the economy.[10] In 1988 the government approved a new corporation law which gave managers, in cooperation with self-management bodies, the right to make enterprises fully autonomous and under certain conditions to privatise them (Stark, 1991).

As in Poland, the private sector in Hungary also continued to grow and with it the underground economy, primarily in construction. In the period 1980–7 employment in the private sector as the main employer grew by 59 per cent and in 1987 amounted to 5.2 per cent of the total economy (*SE*, 1986, p. 55). Of course, the number of people involved in the private sector was much higher. The same phenomenon existed in Poland.

In Czechoslovakia, the private sector was negligible and had no effect on the fate of socialism. In 1980 the share of employment in this sector in total employment was 0.003 per cent and increased to 0.005 per cent in 1986 and to 1.3 per cent in 1989 (in the Czech republic), the year of the velvet revolution (*SR, 19*87, p. 191, and *SR*, 1993, p. 181).

PRIVATE OWNERSHIP AND THE COLLAPSE OF THE SOCIALIST SYSTEM

There is no doubt that the legalisation of the private sector did not undermine the socialist system. On the contrary, it helped to stabilise it; it aided in minimising or overcoming shortages in the economy which the state sector with its excessive concentration on producer goods could not handle. It mitigated the unsatisfied demand for services. It also gave satisfaction to a segment of the population which was always interested in entrepreneurship. In this sense it brought not only an improvement in the economy, but also stabilised the system politically. This is true about the 1960s and the 1970s.

This is not to say that allowing the private sector had only positive effects from the viewpoint of the regime. The expansion of the private sector could be seen as an admission on the part of the communist leaders that the private sector was indispensable for the good working of the economy and that the predictions about the superiority of collective ownership had not materialised, at least not to the extent promised. It goes without saying that the expansion of the private sector fuelled anti-socialist propaganda: it was argued that the communists were abandoning socialism and adopting capitalism. Even some Westerners who sympathised with socialism expressed concern as to whether the expansion of the private sector might not open the door to capitalism.

As has already been indicated, in the 1980s, particularly in the second half, the legal, and even more the illegal, private sector expanded rapidly in Poland and Hungary. This was at a time when in both countries, particularly in Poland, the economy found itself in a crisis. In addition, again mainly in Poland, the communist leaders were increasingly losing their grip on the country. The question can be asked whether the private sector in the changed conditions was still a stabilising factor or, on the contrary, contributed to the collapse of the socialist system. Due to the different economic and political conditions in the two countries the impact of the private sector was different to some extent.

In Hungary many believe that the expansion of the private sector was one of the factors which brought down the socialist system. This is also the view of I. Szelényi (1990a), who in an interview maintained that 'Over a period of several decades, a radical embourgeoisement process disintegrated the communist fabric, restructured the bureaucratic system's consciousness and life style and undermined its ability to govern'. According to him embourgeoisement, which was brought about by the sale of products produced on private plots on the market, was a no-less-important factor in bringing down the system than the economic reforms and their architects, the intelligentsia.[11] He also denies that Gorbachev's reforms should be blamed or given credit for the collapse.

He also believes that the private sector was a stabilising factor in the 1960s and 1970s, and even maintains that it was able to compensate for government failings. However, in the 1980s it was no longer able to offset the increasing failings of the socialist system. There is some contradiction between his thoughts mentioned in the previous paragraph and those in this one in relation to the 1980s. If embourgeoisement was one of the factors, which brought down the system, how could it offset the government failings? If embourgeoisement was such a stabilising factor how could it bring down the socialist system? An interview is not a scientific piece, and a contradiction can easily creep in.

Some believe that the private sector should not be blamed for the collapse. A former member of the Hungarian CP politburo told me that the communist leadership did not view the private sector as a threat to the system and was determined to expand its activities.

In my opinion it is necessary to distinguish between the private sector in agriculture and that outside agriculture, when the role of the private sector in bringing down the socialist system is discussed. The

Hungarian private sector in agriculture (meaning primarily activities of collective farmers on their private plots) was no threat to the system. In Hungary more than in other countries with collectivised agriculture, the private sector had easy access to the market (Waedekin, 1985, pp. 443–4) and did quite well. Probably collective farmers who were engaged in producing for the market did not like the regime, as Szelényi argues. However, the same farmers were members of collective farms and as such the majority had no good reason to be in opposition to the regime. None of the socio-economic groups in Hungary fared as well as collective farmers. Most collective farms were engaged in activities outside agriculture which added income to that which they had from their main activity (which on the average was not much lower than in industry) and provided employment to many members during the off-season. In addition, farmers got credit with very favourable conditions for the construction of housing. The fact that most farmers are at present in favour of maintaining cooperatives is the best evidence that they did not fare poorly under the old system.

The Polish private sector (meaning primarily farmers who derived their earnings from working on their own land) was in a different situation. The agricultural reform of 1981 met many of the complaints of the private sector (among others it enabled better access to investment goods and purchase of land) (see Cook, 1986, p. 66), but at the same time its financial situation worsened. The private sector was not spared the general decline in the economy and earnings. Compared to 1978 (equal to 100), when the real earnings of private farmers achieved their peak, they amounted in 1987 to only 73.5 per cent. (See *RS*, 1988, p. 300.) Under such conditions one cannot expect that private farmers would be great supporters of the regime.

The non-agricultural private sector in Hungary was in a different position than the agricultural to some extent. In the 1960s and 1970s it did not have good reasons to oppose the regime, though it did not like the limitations imposed on it and the tax screw. As mentioned, the private sector had a monopoly position due to the barriers to entry. In the 1980s the private sector involved a majority of the population to different degrees.[12] However, only a small proportion of employees involved in the private sector had their main income from that sector. A majority, including many small employers, continued to be employed in the state sector and supplemented their income from compensation received for services to the private sector.

Of course, such an arrangement did not have a positive effect on the population's attitude to the socialist system. This appeared to them to be evidence that the socialist system was no longer able to ensure a reasonable income. What was no less important was that two and sometimes three jobs meant a great claim on working time and human energy, which in many cases was an irreparable threat to health. In addition, it is also important to remember that unlike the West, where services provided by the underground economy are cheaper than those provided by the legal economy, in socialist countries services purchased from the private sector, whether legal or illegal, were much more expensive than those from the state sector. This was so because the state sector was not able to provide the services or could only provide them with great delay, and the quality of services provided was often poor. Services provided by the private sector were mostly not accessible to low-income groups, a situation which generated aversion to the sector by these groups. The private sector by its very existence strengthened the propaganda argument that the socialist system had exhausted itself and was irreformable.

In Poland, the situation was in essence similar to the one in Hungary with regard to employment in the non-agricultural private sector. This Polish sector played, however, a much more active role in the disintegration of the socialist system than in Hungary. It was bigger, and the illegal sector was much more powerful. The activities of the latter were a testimony to the government's mismanagement of the economy and were a powerful factor in discrediting the system.

Thus in the 1980s the non-agricultural private sector in both countries was no longer neutral, unlike a large part of the private sector in the 1960s and 1970s. It saw the system as an obstacle to its expansion and joined the forces which brought down the system.

CONCLUDING REMARKS

The small countries did not manage to instil a feeling in workers of being co-owners of capital assets, which might have manifested itself in a commitment to responsibility for the performance of the economy. Perhaps the most important reason for this failure was that the communist leaders were not willing to involve workers in the decision-making process about the use of the means of production. They were apparently afraid that once workers were involved, they would exert pressure for the extension of the jurisdiction of enterprises, which might in the final analysis reduce the leading role of the Party. When the CPs finally agreed to the introduction of self-management, it was already too late to bring about a turnaround in the attitude of workers to state ownership.

Had the Soviet Union, after World War II, allowed at least small-scale private businesses to exist without impediment and had East European countries followed suit, socialist countries could have avoided many of the economic difficulties they experienced – shortages, the low quality of goods and a narrow product mix. The private sector would have competed with and complemented the state sector. Not only this, but the private sector would have expanded market relations with many of the associated advantages: it would have strengthened incentives and pushed for a more rational allocation of resources.

The non-agricultural private sector, if handled properly, might even have been a politically stabilising factor by its contribution to a better performance of the economy. In addition, it would have met the aspirations of people who desired to make a living as independent entrepreneurs. True, not all small entrepreuners would have been satisfied with the limitations on ownership, but there is no reason to think that they would have been as much of a danger to the system as they were in Poland and Hungary in the second half of the 1980s. There the private sector, mainly the illegal one, could play the role described because the economies of both countries, particularly in Poland, were in deep crisis in any case and, in addition, the socialist system was in the process of disintegration.

10 The Soviet Factor

INTRODUCTION

It is clear to every observer of the socialist camp that the collapse of socialism in the countries under review was only possible because the Soviet Union explicitly or implicitly allowed East European countries to go their own way. In other words, the countries could abandon socialism because the Soviet Union no longer insisted on Brezhnev's doctrine. Was it so because the Soviets were weakened to such an extent that they were no longer able to control events beyond their borders, or did the Soviet leaders become so enlightened that they no longer wanted to impose their will on other nations and therefore allowed East European countries to decide their own fate, or was it because they were under strong pressure from the West in a situation in which, for political and economic reasons, they wanted to be reconciled with the West? As will be shown, all three factors played a role. It is difficult to say which was the strongest so soon after the events. Mainly it is difficult to evaluate the West's role when access to the archives will be impossible for a long time to come, but this does not mean that there is no knowledge at all about the West's role.

ECONOMIC DEVELOPMENT

The Soviet Union, like the three countries under review, grappled with many similar economic problems, though there were also differences. The Soviet economy also exhibited declining growth rates from the second half of the 1970s. Of course, if we take the 1950s as a basis for a comparison, then the 1960s and 1970s could also be characterised as declining decades in economic growth. In my opinion, the 1950s are not an appropriate base because they can be largely regarded as a postwar reconstruction period. In the 1960s and the first half of the 1970s economic growth was in the order of 6.5 per cent, as reflected in national income produced. Even in the first half of the 1960s when the

180

rate of economic growth in most East European countries declined (in Czechoslovakia there was an absolute decline), the Soviet economy exhibited a robust economic growth.

In the second half of the 1970s the economy took a turn for the worse and continued to decline in the 1980s with some interruption. The decline in the growth rate was caused to a great degree by the exhaustion of the extensive factors of economic growth. Employment in the economy grew by 3.8 per cent annually in the period 1961–70 and 2.5 per cent in 1971–5. This figure declined to 1.4 per cent in 1976–80 and to 0.7 per cent in 1981–5. In the period 1986–90 the figure grew by only 0.2 per cent (see *SEzh*, 1981, p. 410 and Table 10.1).

Net fixed investment in the economy grew by 2.6 per cent in 1976–80 and declined absolutely in the following years. In 1986–90 it decreased on the average by 6.7 per cent (see Table 10.1). If one considers that productivity indicators also worsened, then there is a clear answer to the question about the reasons for the declining economic growth rates.

The declining productivity growth rates were caused by various factors. One of the reasons for this was probably that the share in employment of non-European republics, where the labour force was less educated and less skilled than the national average, was increasing (see *NK*, 1987, p. 365).

Table 10.1 Some indicators of performance in the former USSR (annual growth rates in per cent)

	1976 –80	1981 –5	1986 –90	1985	1986	1987	1988	1989	1990
National income produced*	4.3	3.2	1.3	3.2	2.6	1.7	4.1	2.4	−3.9
Industrial production	4.4	3.6	2.5	3.4	4.4	3.8	3.9	1.7	−1.2
Agricultural production	1.7	1	1.9	0.2	5.3	−0.6	1.7	1.3	−2.9
Number of employed	1.4	0.7	0.2	0.6	0.6	0.4	0.1	0.5	−0.6
Net fixed investment#	2.6	−1.7	−6.7	n.a.	−4.9	5.7	−7.4	−6.7	−20.0
Nominal wages	3.6	2.4	7.6	2.1	2.9	3.7	8.3	9.3	14.2
Retail price index	0.6	1.0	2.1	1.0	2.0	1.3	0.6	2.0	4.8

* The GNP figures listed by CIA for 1981–5 are much smaller, on the average 1.75 (Noren and Kurtzweg, 1993, p. 14). Figures listed by Khanin (1992, p. 78) on national income are also lower. According to them national income in 1990 was 3 per cent lower than in 1981.
# The figures for 1986–90 and 1990 are estimates.
Sources: Figures for investment and prices for individual years except 1985 are from *The National Economy of the USSR* (1990). The rest of the figures are from *NK*, 1990, pp. 6–8 and 36; *SEzh*, 1984, p. 282 and 1986, pp. 288 and 385.

Considering that the Soviet press from the 1970s on devoted great attention to labour discipline and called for its strengthening (Spulber, 1991, pp. 95–6), one can assume that there was a decline in the work ethic, which must have affected productivity negatively. The further loosening of discipline due to Gorbachev's reforms certainly had a similar effect.

The decline in capital productivity was caused by the slow retirement of used capital. The plans for capital retirement did not keep up with the level of technology development, but even these modest plans were not fulfilled. On the other hand, there were cases where new machinery lay idle in warehouses for a long time.

High material intensity of products was another reason for low capital productivity. According to Khanin (1992, p. 78) material intensity increased by 17 per cent in the period 1981–90.

The high material intensity of products in the USSR affected not only the economy of that country, but also had an effect on the economies of the three countries under review, which satisfied most of their demand for raw materials from imports from the USSR. The increasing domestic demand for raw materials made it more difficult for the USSR to satisfy the growing demand of the smaller countries, all the more because extraction of raw materials was investment intensive.

Compared to the smaller countries, which were importers of oil, the USSR had a tremendous advantage in being an exporter of oil and its derivatives. The explosive price increases in oil of 1973 and 1979 had a destructive effect on the economies of the small countries, though not immediately since they were cushioned from the price increase effects by the CMEA price formula. On the other hand, for the USSR the price increases meant a bonanza, which it did not manage to use effectively for the development of the economy. This was a good opportunity to modernise the civilian economy, the consumer goods industries in particular, and thus alleviate the shortages in modern durable goods, mainly electronic products. Such a policy would also have helped East European countries and probably reduced the need for borrowing in the West, which turned out to be fatal for the system. But the Soviets did not seize the opportunity: faithful to their old policy, they used a large part of the unexpected profits to strengthen the military. This policy of increased military spending was followed until 1989 (Rush, 1994). Needless to say, it had a negative effect on economic growth.

In addition, the Soviets did not consider seriously enough in their economic policy strategy the possibility that the high oil prices might be only a temporary phenomenon and that an opposite trend might set in. The decline in oil prices in the beginning of the 1980s found them unprepared to such an extent that their manoeuvring freedom was paralysed. And this had far-reaching consequences for their trade with East European countries. The Soviet Union was very much the engine which drove the East European economies because it was able to absorb huge imports and to export goods, mainly raw materials and oil, in return. In the beginning of the 1980s, the Soviet engine slowed down significantly and, as a result, trade relations with East European countries weakened. This aggravated not only the economic situation of the East European countries (Nyers, 1989), but also made it for Soviets more difficult to exercise control over Eastern Europe. After all, the control resulted not only from Soviet military might; economic dependence on the huge Soviet market and raw material deliveries also had much to do with it.

The Achilles heel of the Soviet economy was primarily agriculture. The country was not able to feed itself; it had to import huge amounts of grain in order to satisfy the demand of the population. This phenomenon is of importance in light of the known fact that agriculture fared quite well in Hungary and Czechoslovakia. True, Hungarian collectivisation in the beginning of the 1960s was quite different from the Soviet. But the Czechoslovak was not very much different and still performed quite well. The best proof of this is that collective farms have resisted various measures of the present democratically elected governments, intended more or less for their liquidation. Had collective farming been so bad for farmers, they themselves would have tried to liquidate the collective farms.

In the Soviet Union, despite great efforts and huge investments, amounting on the average to one third of total investments since the beginning of the 1970s (see *The Economy of the USSR*, 1990, p. 40[1]), the performance of agriculture did not improve noticeably. In the second half of the 1970s and in the 1980s growth rates of gross agricultural production were low (see Table 10.1). According to *The Economy of* . . . (p. 4), which uses figures received from Soviet sources, the performance of agriculture was worse than indicated in Table 10.1. Agriculture suffered from many problems. The main reason for the need to import agricultural products was due to waste and great losses of food. 'Substantial food losses arise because of shortages of packaging material, storage facilities, outdated processing technology and inadequacy in, and disruption of, transport' (p. 40).

According to Khanin (1992, p. 78) there was a remarkable economic recovery in 1983–8 (an increase in national income of 11 per cent, an increase in labour productivity, and a halt in the decline of capital productivity), after a decline in national income in 1981–2 (4 per cent). He attributes this recovery to Andropov's provisions and Gorbachev's first year measures. Maybe their measures had an effect, but since in 1983–6 a simultaneous recovery was experienced in Poland, Czechoslovakia and Hungary, one can speculate that the recovery was the result of cyclical development to a great extent.

In the following years, the growth rates of national income again started to decline and in 1990 there was an absolute decline in economic growth. In other words, Gorbachev's reform did not cause a turnaround.

STANDARD OF LIVING

At the time when the Iron Curtain was tightly closed the Soviet propaganda portrayed the Soviet standard of living as one of the highest in the world and Eastern Europe backed it up. In reality, the Soviet standard of living was very modest; it was lower than in the countries under review.

After the Second World War real incomes per capita as well as real wages grew relatively fast, primarily the former in the 1950s, 1960s and the 1970s. The fast expansion of the economy was reflected in growth in the standard of living. The slowdown in economic growth in the second half of the 1970s and the 1980s (or decline, according to Khanin) was not reflected extensively in real incomes and wages. The Soviets used a portion of their receipts from sales of oil to maintain the standard of living.

This is not to say that everything about the standard of living was in order. The Soviet economy suffered from shortages which had their origin in the structural disequilibrium of the consumption fund. The Soviet planners had no great difficulty in planning a balance between the global income fund (minus expected savings) and the real consumption fund. But the planners had tremendous difficulty balancing incomes and demand for individual or for groups of consumer goods because of lack of information and the cumbersomeness of the planning system. In enterprises a negative role was also played by the incentive system, which prodded enterprise managers to meet the targets regardless of the situation in the market. The supply situation was compounded by the shortcomings of the distribution system which allowed, in many cases, some products to be in abundance in one region while (an)other region(s) suffered from shortages. Needless to say, the Soviets could have mitigated shortages had they wanted to use prices to balance demand with the supply of goods. However, the Soviets were not willing to give up their rigid price stability policy in order to stave off the possibility of inflation.

In addition, the consumer goods mix was narrow and of shoddy quality compared with Western goods or even with Hungarian. The Soviet market mainly lacked modern electronic goods. Despite shortages, the supply of consumer goods was tolerable and exhibited an improving trend in the 1960s and 1970s.

In the second half of the 1980s, mainly in the last three years of Gorbachev's administration, a dramatic change for the worse occurred in the supply of consumer goods. Due to the balance-of-payments deficit the Soviets were forced to slash imports of consumer goods. Soon a new factor aggravated the supply situation. Gorbachev wanted to increase incentives to work by widening wage differentials. The 1987 wage reform, aimed at widening differentials, was based on the idea that enterprises would be allowed to take advantage of it provided they were to pay for the increased wage costs from their own resources by achieving higher economic efficiency. Obviously, self-management bodies did not respect this rule, and the government was lax in enforcing it. In addition, there were increases in wages for non-productive services which came from the budgetary sources (Schroeder, 1992, p. 98; and *The Economy* . . ., 1990, pp. 7 and 10).

The income increases,[2] though they were justified in many cases, primarily for qualified workers if the narrow wage differentials were to widen and thereby to create stronger incentives, nevertheless contributed to the intensification of shortages. Income increases were matched neither by production increases in consumer goods nor by adequate import increases.

In 1990 and more so still in 1991, the shortages took on dramatic dimensions. The line-ups became longer and more time-consuming, and were often in vain. Apart from the reasons mentioned, there were also new ones. The increasing bickering among the republics and the loosening of discipline, which undermined the distribution system, were two of them. The situation was aggravated by the Moscow and Leningrad mayors, who forbade shopping for non-residents in their cities, a provision which triggered retaliation from other regions. The growing trade deficit, which forced the USSR to slash imports of consumer goods, was another important factor in the growing shortages. Last but not least, considerable food hoarding, which was triggered by the government announcement of its intention to increase prices, made the situation even worse (Kondratenko, 1991).

ECONOMIC REFORMS

The 1965 reform was a minor reform, which did not exceed the framework of the traditional system of management, let alone the 'perfections' of the system of management under Brezhnev. Even the 'reforms' under Andropov do not deserve the name reform.

Gorbachev's economic reform in 1987 was a major reform, but not a far-reaching one, considering what was happening in the smaller countries under review. It resembled very much the Hungarian 1968 economic reform,[3] though in a watered-down form, combined with some organisational elements of the East German system. The reform also contained some components from the Chinese reform.

The main objective of the reform was to make enterprises work more efficiently and produce higher-quality goods in response to demand by giving them greater autonomy and making them adhere to the principle of self-financing. Enterprises were given greater decision-making powers in matters of output mix, price, wage, incentives and investment determination. The central planners were to use more indirect methods in steering enterprises.

The reform was in substance formulated in the Law on State Enterprises (*P*, 1 July 1987). According to it, enterprises were allowed to work out and approve their own five-year and annual plans. However, five year plans had to be worked out on the basis of non-binding control figures, state orders (contracts), limits and normatives. The control figures, which had an informative function for enterprises, included indicators of production in value terms which were to serve as a basis for concluding contracts between producers and buyers, profit, indicators of technological progress, etc. State orders (contracts), which were compulsory, referred to defence, centralised investment projects, important kinds of production, significant technical pro-grammes, etc. They could be distributed by tender. They were supposed, apparently according to Chinese example, to take up only part of enterprise capacity; the rest of the capacity could be used by enterprises according to their choice. In contrast to the Chinese, where this dual system in the use of enterprise capacity was combined with a dual system in pricing, only one pricing system existed in the Soviet reform for both state contracts and enterprise choice of production. The planned state orders for 1988 took up most of the capacity of many enterprises and thus became another form of assigned targets. Limits referred to inputs and some investments. Because of shortages, allocation of inputs was to be only gradually eliminated. From the foregoing it is clear that output mix was to be, to a great extent, determined from above. This was not supposed to deprive enterprises of options or the possibility of selecting partners for contracts.

Gorbachev's reform put great stress on economic normatives, which were not a new instrument; they were introduced for the first time in 1979. Long-term normatives had to be set for the distribution of profit between the state and enterprises, for determination of the wage bill, for the incentive fund of enterprises and the development fund.

Gorbachev's reform promised quite far-reaching changes compared to the traditional system. The mutual linkage of domestic price circuits (between wholesale and retail prices, and between agricultural procurement and wholesale prices) was to be restored. Fixed prices were to be limited to goods of national economic and social importance. Otherwise contractual and even free prices were to be applied.

For the first time in post-war history the 1987 reform made changes in the rigid state monopoly in foreign trade. Many ministries and associations were given the right to engage directly in foreign-trade operations.

What was quite surprising was that the idea of enterprise self-management, which had been resented by the previous communist leaders for fear that it might reduce the power of party organisations, was introduced by Gorbachev's reform. The self-management bodies were given quite considerable rights; they were, however, to be steered by CP organisations. Apparently, Gorbachev agreed not to antagonise CP organisations.

The process of concentration in industry continued in the 1980s; the number of associations (groups of enterprises) grew fast. Gorbachev's reform did not stop it; on the contrary, it seems to have strengthened it.[4]

Gorbachev's reform also brought about some changes in agriculture; however, they were not very radical. It seems that, here too, Gorbachev followed the Chinese example but with small success. Cooperatives were allowed to lease land to farmers, and thus family farms arose (Aslund, 1991, pp. 102–3). However, in the USSR the agricultural changes never took on such importance as in China.

There was also some concession to private ownership. Individuals or families were allowed to produce consumer goods after normal work time in their main job. In other words, private small businesses were not allowed to employ non-family members. Later, the newly permitted cooperatives in the non-agricultural sector were allowed to employ non-members and in such a way they became a cover-up for private enterprise (for more, see Hanson, 1990, pp. 83–94).

Some of the changes mentioned were to be implemented instantly, some gradually, but the whole reform was supposed to be in force in 1991.

The reform was, no doubt, an improvement over what had existed before. Yet many important elements of the traditional system remained. The assignment of targets was not eliminated; it was replaced by state orders whose role was supposed to diminish in the course of time. However, the institution of overfulfilment was done away with. Rationing of inputs continued because of shortages. There was a promise to switch to a market for inputs within four or five years. All this meant that the authorities continued to interfere with the day-to-day operations of enterprises with all the consequences of bureaucratic arbitrariness and bargaining, and strains on self-financing. Nevertheless, the rights of enterprises expanded substantially.

The authorities tried to regulate some microeconomic tools with the help of stable long-term normatives, an undertaking which raised doubts about its practicality, especially with regard to wages and incentives. A five-year period is too long for realistic normatives to be set.

The idea of self-financing was not new in the history of Soviet efforts to improve the working of the economic mechanism; it can, however, work only under certain conditions. And the Soviet reform did not produce these conditions.

I have mentioned only some contradictions built into the reform itself so that it could not achieve even its limited goals. As will be shown later in connection with the discussion of the restructuring of the political system, even the potential pluses of the reform did not materialise. Further developments in the Soviet Union made the reform obsolete.

In the fall of 1989 the Supreme Soviet passed a bill on the transition to a market economy. This did not mean that the authorities wanted to drop planning altogether. In the CC resolution of February 1990 (*Towards a Humane* . . ., 1990, p. 29) there was still talk of a planned market economy. It did not take long for planning to be relegated to an adjunct of the market mechanism and later dropped altogether.

Once the decision was taken to make a transition to a market economy, an array of proposals on how to carry it out emerged. The two best-known proposals were Shatalin's 500 days programme (*Perekhod* . . ., 1990) and the Yavlinski–Allison reform plan (1991). The first proposal was prepared at the request of Gorbachev and Yeltsin, a remarkable event considering that the two politicians were engaged in a power struggle. Shatalin's programme, which was based on republican sovereignty, was welcomed by Yelstin, but rejected by Gorbachev who wanted to sustain the Union, though in a loose federation. The programme was unrealistic in any case; it was an illusion to put the Soviet Union on the path to a market economy and carry out privatisation of a major part of the economy within 500 days.

The Yavlinskii–Allison programme was more realistic in that its planned implementation was spread out over a longer period (1991–7). However, it was based on the assumption of Western help. Its departure point was sovereignty of the republics, but it assumed that there would be a single market for the Soviet Union with a uniform monetary policy and a Central Bank. The political events in the Soviet Union, which resulted in its collapse, made the Yavlinskii–Allison programme useless (for more, see Adam, 1993, pp. 209–13).

In all three countries the 1987 Soviet economic reform had an impact. In Czechoslovakia, where the leaders were rather anti-reform minded, they nevertheless decided to follow the Soviet example and introduced more or less a similar reform as in the USSR. In Hungary and Poland, the economic reforms introduced earlier went much further than in the USSR. But the 1987 Soviet reform seemed still to have an effect. In 1987 a second stage in reforms in both countries came into being, reforms which meant an important leap in the direction of marketising the economy. These changes were probably only possible because of changes in the USSR. Seeing what was happening in the USSR, the opposition in both countries was emboldened to a further push for radical changes in the economic system. Additionally, the governments in both countries did not have to resist the changes because of possible criticism from the Soviet Union.

POLITICAL REFORM

Unlike his predecessors Gorbachev combined his economic reform with political reform. He realised that the economic reform could be successful only if it was combined with changes in the political system. Only by giving people greater freedom and rights could it be expected that they would reciprocate with greater effort, initiative and dynamism. Probably he realised that the rigid, authoritarian regime was untenable in the long run and unnecessary. If the CP was serious in its rhetoric, namely, that what it was doing was for the good of the people, then it should not be afraid of the people. Distrust of the people necessarily leads to distrust of government in a great part of the population.

Did Gorbachev have a well thought-out concept of the political reform? It is not entirely clear how far he wanted to go in the democratisation of the system. It is not clear to what extent the real development in the political system was in tune with his concept and to what extent he was pushed by forces which his reform generated

It is obvious that Gorbachev wanted to maintain the socialist character of the Soviet Union and that he did not want to turn the Soviet Union into a capitalist state. After all, Gorbachev even now professes to be a socialist. There is also no doubt that Gorbachev wanted to sustain the integrity of the USSR. It is not clear whether he realised that a far-reaching reform, particularly of the political system, concealed within it great dangers for socialism and the integrity of the USSR. He should have known that such a reform is equal to walking on the edge of a cliff and therefore caution should have been used in pacing and coordinating the political with the economic reform.

Gorbachev started out with economic reform. But he soon turned his attention to political reform. In his report to the CC in June 1987, which contained a proposal for a radical economic reform, he did not mention the need for a radical political reform. He suggested only the need for the democratisation of the political system, as an important precondition for a better working of the economy and elimination of the alienation people felt about the Soviet regime. At that stage it was not clear what Gorbachev meant by democratisation and how far he was willing to go. True, there was already a considerable relaxation of press censorship, people were no longer afraid to vent their dissatisfaction, the power of the police was curbed, etc. It is known that during the reforms of the 1960s Czechoslovak and Hungarian politicians also talked about the need for democratisation, but in fact they were determined to maintain the leading role of the CP and not allow any changes which might endanger it in the long run. What they were willing to do was to make changes at the edges of the political system by eliminating excesses in the working of the system, and by making the judicial system more independent. In brief, they wanted to give the system a more human face.

The Nineteenth Party Conference, which took place from 28 June to 1 July 1988, was an important milestone in the reform of the political system. At the conference the shortcomings of the political system were discussed and proposals suggested on how to reform it. Soon a resolution was approved to reform the electoral system by giving the public more say in the choice of candidates and by allowing more candidates to be fielded than there were seats. The new electoral system was not based on the idea of a multi-party system. Nevertheless its structure meant the rise of a multi-party system in an embryonic form: the electoral law allowed groupings of voters of 500 or more to nominate more than one candidate. At the same time the electoral system allowed representation for social groups, such as the CP, trade unions, the academy of science etc. a provision which was in effect a violation of democratic principles of elections (White, 1992, pp. 31–4, 46–7). The idea behind the special treatment of social groups was probably dictated by the desire to make sure that the political leaders would be elected, and thus avoid an embarrassment which might have occurred if the leaders had to go through a democratic election. In order to conceal the real intention of the special treatment, it was not confined to political leaders. The 1989 elections to the Congress of People's Deputies took place according to this law. In many republics, including the Russian, in the elections to their Congresses, which took place in 1990, the special treatment of social groups was dropped, and candidates were allowed to form blocs (White, 1992, p. 59). In other words, these elections can be regarded as free, democratic elections.

In 1990 political parties started to emerge and in a short time there were parties with right, centrist and left programmes. There was no shortage of monarchist and anarchist groupings. The February 1990 meeting of the CC more or less sanctioned such development. Its resolution submitted to the Twenty-eighth Party Congress, which was held in July 1990, read:

The democratisation of our society is accompanied by the emergence of new sociopolitical associations. The development of society does not preclude the possibility of forming parties ... The Communist

Party of the Soviet Union does not claim a monopoly and is prepared for a political dialogue and cooperation with everyone who favours the renewal of socialist society (*Towards a Humane* . . ., 1990, p. 33).

The resolutions of the Twenty-eighth Congress stated 'The entire political superstructure is being radically altered, and true democracy is taking root, asserting human rights, free elections and a multi-party system' (*Documents.* . ., 1990 p. 96).

Of course, the rise of new parties threatened the leading role of the CP. Gorbachev and his associates saw a solution to this problem in the institution of the presidency with broad powers. Such an arrangement had to allow the president to curb the possible rise of forces which might endanger the system. In addition, it had to allow the president to be independent of the CP, mainly if the president was elected by the population. The law on the institution of presidency envisaged a popular vote, but for the first presidency an exception was made. Gorbachev was elected by the Congress of People's Deputies in March 1990 (White, 1992, p. 66). The institution of the presidency was combined with a transfer of some power from the central authorities to the Soviets as the local authorities.

The changes in the political system were much more radical than in the economic system. Gorbachev failed to coordinate the two reforms adequately. It was easier in the Soviet system to bring about radical changes in the political system, which found approval amongst the public, than to improve the economy through changes in the economic mechanism. Gorbachev took over a strict authoritarian regime and every relaxation was gladly received.

The political reform eroded to a great degree the working of the economic mechanism which was in the process of reform. As is known, the old system was strictly hierarchical; orders were transferred from the centre through the chain of command down to enterprises. Discipline and obeying orders and instructions was crucial for the working of the system. If one of the links in the chain of command failed, the system could not work effectively. Larger breakdowns in the command system could endanger the whole system. The political system loosened discipline at the time when there was a transition to a new economic mechanism which still relied heavily on discipline.

Because political reform was combined with an unsuccessful economic reform which deepened the malaise of the economy, Gorbachev, who was very popular abroad, was gradually losing support at home at a time when he needed it very much in order to transform the Soviet Union, be able to change the economic system, and win the power struggle with Yeltsin. The changes in the political system eroded the leading role of the CP. With the rise of new parties the influence of the CP declined. In addition the Party discipline was weakened which found its expression in the emergence of strong factions within the Party (Gill, 1994, pp. 144–53). A process of rapid disintegration of the CP started.

The political changes had their impact on the nature of the changes in the programme of the Party. Without going into detail it is important to mention that the proposal for the Fourth Party programme – as explained in the session of the CC of the Soviet CP by Gorbachev (*P*, 26 July 1991) – was imbued with social democratic spirit. It stated that the Party was a party of democratic reforms and that revolutionary methods in the new conditions were no longer necessary. The idea of communism was left out; Gorbachev substantiated this step by arguing that the programme was intended to be a realistic document. The proposal also contained the idea that Marxism–Leninism should not be the exclusive ideological arsenal of the Party.

THE TRANSFORMATION OF THE UNION

The democratisation provisions, mainly those allowing freedom of speech, brought to the surface various grievances which had been dormant for decades. The worst grievances stemmed from the long suppression of national and ethnic aspirations. Political freedoms opened many old wounds, and gave a good opportunity to politicians to base their political careers on the rising nationalism, and they therefore fanned nationalistic sentiments. There were many justifiable grievances; some of the republics had been forced to join the Soviet Union; the Baltic states were the last case. The rights promised in the constitution to individual republics and autonomous regions were ignored by Moscow to a great degree. The attempts to impose the Russian language at the expense of national languages was resented. There were not only grievances *vis-à-vis* Moscow; there were also unresolved national problems among the republics or within republics. The most classic conflict was and is between Armenia and Azerbaijan about an enclave (Nagorno–Karabakh) which is inhabited by

Armenians. The Baltic states were the first to demand the restoration of their independence.

It was assumed that the Ukraine would be the greatest obstacle to maintaining the Soviet Union's integrity. In reality, it turned out that it was Russia, under the leadership of Yeltsin, which brought the Soviet Union to an end. Gorbachev made a big mistake in not putting the solution of ethnic problems among his first priorities. He must have known that, once the political system was reformed and human rights were restored to a great degree, the Soviet Union, a country made up of many nations and nationalities and largely held together by force, would face the danger of disintegration.[5] Therefore it was necessary to act quickly before local politicians could fan nationalistic sentiments to the extent that an agreement was impossible.

This required a restoration of independence to the Baltic states without delay. True, Gorbachev was afraid that the restoration of the independence of the Baltic states would encourage other republics to demand independence. Perhaps such a danger existed, but it could have been countered by showing that the occupation of the Baltic states was an act dictated by the danger of a German attack on the Soviet Union, which really happened. The reluctance to respond quickly to the demands of the Baltic states festered old wounds and strengthened forces in the West which wished for the disintegration of the Soviet Union.

Gorbachev and his associates apparently themselves recognised that they had neglected the nationality problem of the USSR, for they allowed criticism of this point to appear in the resolutions of the Twenty-eighth Congress (unless, perhaps, it appeared against their wishes). The resolutions read: 'top leadership have failed to realise the magnitude of the deformations and contradictions in the national policy promptly enough, to anticipate their impact on the course of perestroika' (*Documents* . . ., 1990, p. 125). The Congress decided that the Soviet Union should be transformed into a Union of sovereign states in the sense that all the republics would enjoy equal rights in the renewed union. The worked-out union treaty was approved in principle by the Congress of People's Deputies in December 1990 and in April 1991 by a referendum in which 9 republics, including Russia and the Ukraine, took part. It is interesting that there was no mention of socialism in the treaty; the republics only committed themselves to the principles of democracy, human rights and social justice.

After difficult negotiations Gorbachev managed to work out with the republics a final and concrete compromise union treaty, according to which defence, foreign policy, transport, communications, energy and the central budget would be decided in consultations between the centre and the republics, whereas all other issues would be decided by the republics. The signing of the treaty was scheduled for August 20. However, it could not take place because on that very day a *coup d'état* was attempted, with the apparent purpose of preventing the signing of the union treaty because the plotters opposed the weakening of the Soviet Union. However, the plotters' action brought about the opposite to what they intended to achieve: one republic after another declared independence. After the collapse of the coup Gorbachev again tried to put together the union treaty, but failed. The coup opened the way for Yeltsin – who on the one hand organised a successful resistance to the plotters and, on the other, destroyed the union by his intrigues – to outmanoeuvre Gorbachev.[6] The Commonwealth of Independent States, which Yeltsin put together, meant an end to Gorbachev's presidency (for more, see White, 1992, pp. 175–83).

GORBACHEV'S AND YELTSIN'S STRUGGLE FOR POWER

The conflict between Gorbachev and Yeltsin was fateful for reforms and for the survival of the USSR. If not for Gorbachev, Yeltsin would have probably remained a little-known politician. Gorbachev gave him the political base for his political growth and influence in appointing him the first secretary of the Moscow Party organisation. Yeltsin used this position for two purposes: one, to blacken the leadership of the CP for not proceeding fast enough with reforms and for not liquidating some of the old privileges of the communist elite and second, to endear himself to the masses by criticising the shortcomings in the supply and the quality of goods. As could be expected he was soon involved in a clash with Gorbachev, who relieved him from his function in the Party, but Yeltsin still got a cabinet position. He was already being treated in the new spirit.[7]

Yeltsin was not discouraged; he cleverly started to build a political base from which he could challenge Gorbachev and eventually defeat him. He started to clamour for equal rights for Russia, arguing that Russia did not have all the institutions that other republics had and that Russia subsidised other republics (cf. White, 1992, p. 173). Russian nationalism became his trump card; he tried and with success to whip up Russian nationalism and to present himself as its protector. Considering that Russians occupied the most important positions in the CP and government, his trump card was a strange one. But Yelstin managed to make it work, and this was important.

In the first elections to the Russian Congress of People's Deputies, which took place in March 1990, Yeltsin was elected deputy and chairman with a huge majority. In order to increase his prestige, he wanted to become the president elected by popular vote. His ambitions were fuelled by the realisation that a presidential post achieved through a popular vote would give him an advantage in his power struggle with Gorbachev, who was not elected by the people. The Congress was against such an election for fear that this would give him too much power. However, Yeltsin found an ally in A. Rutskoi, who was the leader of a moderate faction of the CP, and with his support he gained a majority for his presidency plan in the Congress. Rutskoi was rewarded for his services by becoming the vice-presidential candidate on Yeltsin's ticket. Both were elected in June 1991.

The presidency gave Yeltsin a powerful springboard for his power struggle with Gorbachev. And he used it to his advantage. That the unity of the Soviet Union as a loose federation or confederation became a victim in this fight for power was not a high price for Yeltsin to pay.

Yeltsin understood that his success was contingent to some extent on the West, mainly the USA. In addition, he was jealous of Gorbachev's popularity in the West. His first trip to the USA in 1989 was a disaster. This was largely due to his own doing, to his unusually rough behaviour, and the American underestimation of his capabilities. Yeltsin wanted very much to see the president, but the latter was not eager to meet him lest it should offend Gorbachev. In addition, Bush did not hold Yeltsin in high esteem. According to Beschloss and Talbot (1993, p. 103) Bush thought 'Yeltsin to be a loose cannon on the slippery, rolling deck of Soviet politics, with his reputation for heavy drinking, intemperate behavior and impolitic outbursts'. Judging from the monologue Yeltsin presented to Scowcroft (national security assistant) and Baker (Secretary of State), it is clear that he wanted to show the president that he had a better plan than Gorbachev for transforming the Soviet economy. After the meeting with Scowcroft, to which Bush and Quayle dropped in for a short period, Yeltsin told the press corps that he presented a plan to the president on how to rescue perestroika. His presentation was not appreciated very much because he manifested little knowledge of economics (ibid., pp. 104–5).

It has already been mentioned that Gorbachev and Yeltsin could not agree on the concept of economic reform. There were some differences in how they envisioned the transformation of the economy to a market economy, but these were not decisive. The main reason for disagreement, which was also reflected in each one's distinct approach to economic reform, was that the two politicians had different views on the transformation of the Union. Gorbachev wanted to maintain a loose Union whereas for Yeltsin this was not a priority because it would have kept Gorbachev in his position as president. The aborted coup solved the problem, as already mentioned above, in Yeltsin's favour.

GORBACHEV AND THE SMALL COUNTRIES

Being dependent on Moscow, East European communist leaders followed changes in the leadership of the Soviet CP and government with great interest and anxiety. This was mainly true of countries which did not want to follow the Soviet model in all respects, which were engaged in economic reforms and which were considering some political changes. The permanent question in their mind was: how will Moscow react? Gorbachev's ascendancy to power was also received in the capitals of Eastern Europe with curiosity and apprehension. It was soon discovered that with Gorbachev the Soviet Union had received a new type of leader. He was young, energetic, and what was more important he had a new approach to people and problems.[8] Unlike his predecessors who had avoided direct contact with ordinary people and mostly talked about problems in slogans, Gorbachev sought opportunities to talk to people and reacted to the problems brought up concretely, and was not afraid to criticise mistakes. In addition, he soon made it clear that he was going to reform the Soviet system. For the leaders and dissidents alike of the countries under review, the direction of the reforms and how they would influence the relationship of Moscow to the small countries was of great importance.

In the first years of Gorbachev's tenure there were no great changes in the relationship between Moscow and the small countries. The latter still consulted Moscow if they intended to make important decisions, in domestic as well as in foreign policy, and Moscow's view still could not be ignored. There is some evidence that even at the beginning of 1989, when the process of disintegration of the one-party state had progressed quite far in Poland and Hungary, Moscow was still consulted and listened to.[9] In his book about the 1989 political events,

I. Pozsgay (1993), who was the leader of the opposition within the Hungarian CP, talks about his intention to split the Party by leaving it and taking his supporters with him. But before doing so he consulted A. Yakovlev, a member of the Soviet politburo, whom he met in Rome at the congress of the Italian Communist Party. When Yakovlev advised him to support Grosz, the general secretary of the Hungarian CP of the day, Pozsgay abandoned his plan for the time being (p. 122). However, several months later, in September 1989, the Hungarian government in consultation with the West German opened the borders to East German tourists, an event which, as already mentioned (see p. 217), had far-reaching consequences for the socialist system in Czechoslovakia and other socialist countries, and the government did this without consulting Moscow. M. Németh, the prime minister of the day, maintained in an interview that he did so because he was convinced, on the basis of a talk with Gorbachev in the beginning of 1989, that Moscow no longer stuck to the Brezhnev doctrine (*Nsz*, 8 September 1994).

During the tenure of Gorbachev's predecessors, the reform-minded leaders of the small countries had good reason to be apprehensive of Soviet pressure; under Gorbachev the situation changed. Once he put his mind to political reform and progress was made in this respect, he soon got ahead of the old reformers in the small countries.

In Hungary the opposition to the regime came, as already noted, chiefly from within the CP. The political changes in the Soviet Union, the substantial elimination of censorship, the extension of human rights – all these innovations in the USSR were a great encouragement to the opposition within the CP.

Soviet political reforms also emboldened opponents of the regime outside the Party to intensify their organisational and recruitment activity. Opposition activity which had bubbled below the surface for some time started to surface. The first semi-public establishment of the Hungarian Forum Party, which was until the 1994 elections the ruling party in Hungary, occurred in 1987. What is interesting is that the forum for this action was created by a member of the politburo of the CP, I. Pozsgay (Pozsgay, 1993, p. 82). All this happened at a time when Kádár was still in power. Once the first signs of the rapid weakening of the authority of the Party became apparent, the anti-communist ranks started to swell with genuine dissidents, opportunists and also people who were looking for cover. The growth of anti-communist parties was encouraged by an increasing demoralisation in the ranks of the CP apparatus.

In Poland, the developments in the USSR strengthened the hand of Solidarity. The movement, which was forced underground and had its influence reduced considerably, got a powerful boost from the events in the USSR. In 1981 the Polish government was afraid not only of the political ambitions of Solidarity, but also of the economic and military threats coming from the USSR. It felt that failure to restrain Solidarity would not only result in economic punishment, but might endanger the sovereignty of Poland. The concern about a negative reaction from the USSR was no longer an issue. In 1989, when the Polish CP decided to legalise Solidarity and to engage in a Round-Table discussion about the further development of political and economic life in Poland, it had the support of Gorbachev (see Beschloss and Talbot, 1993, p. 53).

The Czechoslovak CP tried to ignore the political developments in the USSR. It was determined to maintain the *status quo*, all the more because the opposition was weak. It was embarrassed when the Soviet Union, which was portrayed in the propaganda as a friend whom it is worthwhile to imitate, started to dismantle the authoritarian regime, but nevertheless the Czechoslovak CP was not willing to budge. Even the promise of a political reform and the adoption of a new electoral system by the Soviet Congress of People's Deputies in 1988, which allowed the nomination of candidates by popular groupings, did not impress the Czechoslovak leaders. The developments in Hungary and Poland which brought about the end to the communist regime had, of course, an impact in Prague. Still, in September 1989 Jakes, the First Secretary of the Czechoslovak CP, said in Prague to the visiting M. Rakowski, the Secretary General of the Polish CP of the day, that as long as the stores were well stocked, the opposition would not have its way (Rakowski, 1991, p. 257). He turned out to be wrong: the domino effect soon brought down the Czechoslovak regime. Once people went into the streets at the call of the opposition, the Czechoslovak CP agreed to a dialogue which eventually led to a relinquishment of power by the CP. That the opposition dared to call the people into the streets and that people followed that call, was possible because in the neighbouring countries the communist regime had fallen without the Soviets taking any counter-measures.

THE ROLE OF THE WEST

Gorbachev and his associates wanted to achieve an increase in economic efficiency by the economic reform they had introduced and thus a turnaround in the economy, not only because they desired to better the material situation of the population and to strengthen the reformed regime, but because they also saw the reform as a response to recent developments in the international arena. Their main rival, the USA under Reagan's administration, embarked on a huge expansion of its military might, taking advantage of its technical superiority, with the apparent intention of forcing the Soviet Union into a stronger armament race in the hope that the latter, due to its much weaker economy, would exhaust itself.[10] I doubt that Gorbachev hoped that an economic reform would bring such a turnaround in the economy and in technological progress that would enable the Soviet Union to respond to the American challenge. Gorbachev probably knew that the Soviet Union could not win the race with an increasingly ailing economy and did not regard such a race as being in the interest of the Soviet Union. In addition, the arms race was anyhow a big burden on the economy which could not be increased without bringing about a further worsening of the performance of the economy and a decline in the standard of living. Unlike his predecessors, he was looking for reconciliation rather than confrontation with the USA. Needless to say, reconciliation on terms favourable to the Soviet Union depended very much on the strength of the economy[11] and the economic reform was supposed to strengthen the economy.

The economic reform was also intended to strengthen the Soviets' standing in the world. The lag in technological progress behind the West undermined the Soviet position in the eyes of East European countries and many Third World countries, though the USSR extended generous assistance to several of the latter. The economic reform was supposed to cure this problem too.

To convince the USA that in the Soviet Union a change in thinking and attitude to international problems and the West, especially the USA, had occurred, it was necessary to make some concessions to the West. Therefore Gorbachev made many concessions to the USA in the disarmament agreement by, among other things, accepting an asymmetrical reduction in conventional forces and weaponry and an unconditional withdrawal of the Soviet army from Afghanistan.

There is no doubt that the West, primarily the USA, supported the oppositions in East European countries, mainly the Polish Solidarity.[12] But it also leaned on the Soviet Union in regard to Eastern Europe, mainly when signs of the disintegration of the socialist system showed up in Poland and Hungary. Beschloss and Talbot mention in their book (1993, pp. 13–14) that, on his visit to Moscow at the end of 1988,

H. Kissinger, the former Secretary of State, handed a letter from Bush to Gorbachev which contained, among other things, a proposal for a deal about Eastern Europe. The proposal, which was the work of Kissinger himself, suggested that if the Soviets promised not to use force against reforms and accept liberalisation in Eastern Europe, the West would commit itself 'not to exploit the economic or political changes that occurred there at the expense of "legitimate" Soviet security interests' (p. 13). Gorbachev did not give a direct answer to this proposal. Allegedly, his adviser for Eastern Europe, the philosopher G. Shakhnazarov, was in favour of the proposal and suggested accepting it (p. 16). Needless to say, this was not the only proposal which exerted pressure on Gorbachev not to interfere in the developments in Eastern Europe and to leave it to its fate. It was difficult to resist American pressure at a time when the Soviets wanted to show that they meant seriously their statement of new thinking. Gorbachev was all the more responsive because he was very busy with internal affairs, fights within the CP, and the effort to sustain the integrity of the Soviet Union. Attempts to stop developments in Poland and Hungary, the two countries where the disintegration had progressed the furthest, probably would have led to great tensions. In addition, the Soviets could no longer rely on finding reputable allies among local leaders in the two countries who would be willing to assist in stopping the collapse of the socialist system.

M. Rakowski (1991, pp. 247-8) maintains that the Soviet decision to let East European countries go their own way was the result of a desire to give priority to its own interests. In the 1970s and 1980s the Soviets subsidised East European countries. By allowing them to make decisions independently about their destiny the Soviets absolved themselves from any material responsibility for East European countries. For this reason Gorbachev's statement in Kiev in February 1989 that Soviet relations with East European countries must be based on 'unconditional independence . . . full equality and strict non-intervention in internal affairs' was not accidental (*P*, 24 February 1989).

One can speculate that Bush offered a reward in the form of support for the integrity of the Soviet Union if the Soviets relinquished Brezhnev's doctrine. This might have been the reason why Bush discouraged the Ukraine from seeking independence, by denouncing nationalism in a public speech in Kiev in August 1991 (Beschloss and Talbot, 1993, p. 418). Perhaps up to the *coup d'état* Bush supported Gorbachev and indirectly his efforts to sustain the integrity of the

Soviet Union, though some of the American president's advisers opposed this because they believed that Yelstin had a better chance to gain the upper hand in the power struggle. In addition, they believed that Yelstin was prepared for more far-reaching reforms than Gorbachev. After the aborted coup the US administration shifted its support to Yelstin and indirectly and directly supported the disintegration of the Soviet Union.

CONCLUDING REMARKS

There is no doubt that, without the explicit or implicit approval of the Soviet Union, Poland and Hungary would not have been able to change their economic system, and the domino effect would not have come into play. That the Soviet Union agreed to such a development in the two countries was only possible because it itself had started to change radically. This is not to say that Gorbachev wanted capitalism. In my opinion he aspired to market socialism, but his policies and the rivalry with Yeltsin caused the political power to slip from his hands.

Gorbachev did not manage to coordinate properly the economic and political reforms. The political reform was carried out at a much faster pace than the economic reform and in addition the latter was a failure. All this contributed to the economic crisis, which was one of the contributing factors to the collapse. The political reform loosened discipline, introduced uncertainty and resentment in the ranks of the elites, and aroused fear in the minds of bureaucrats for their positions. All this happened at a time when the traditional system, which was based on strict hierarchical discipline, was already undermined, but not yet replaced by a new reformed system. Later the arguments about the transition to a market economy made the situation worse. Gorbachev himself later acknowledged that the improper coordination of the two reforms was a great mistake.

Of course, the worsening economic situation and increasing difficulties in supplying the population with consumer goods and services contributed to the collapse of the system. The arms race, competition with the USA for spheres of influence in the Third World countries, and the adventurous and costly war in Afganistan – all drained the resources of the USSR and contributed to the worsening of the economic situation.

Another mistake Gorbachev made was that he delayed the reform of the structure of the Soviet Union too long. It would have been prudent to start political reforms with the restructuring of the Soviet Union into a genuine federation or confederation in which all the republics would be given equal rights. To a large extent such a step would have deprived many politicians, including Yeltsin, of the possibility of using genuine republican grievances to fan nationalistic sentiments.

The struggle for power between Gorbachev and Yeltsin was no doubt fatal for the integrity of the Soviet Union and also one of the main reasons for the disintegration of the CP and thus for the collapse of the socialist system. The power struggle also contributed to the failure of the economic reform. The two competed for support within and outside the country. In the competition within the country Yeltsin had the advantage of being in opposition to Gorbachev, who was responsible for the performance of the economy and the well-being of the population at a time when both were rapidly declining. In addition, Yeltsin managed to position himself at the head of Russia, where Gorbachev also had residence, which meant that once the Soviet Union disintegrated, Gorbachev lost his power base. Once this happened the competition for outside support was also decided.

The implicit, public relinquishment of Brezhnev's doctrine came in February 1989. It can be assumed that already earlier, the Soviets had decided not to interfere if some of the small countries left the socialist camp or if some of the countries did not want to engage in reforms. This change in relationship to the small countries of CMEA was motivated by several considerations. Perhaps the most important was the desire to improve relations with the West and thus to slow down the armament race which was imposing an increasing financial burden on the Soviet Union. A change in thinking about the importance of the small countries for the Soviet security strategy and about the relations between sovereign countries probably played a role too. Internal infighting, which absorbed a lot of time in Gorbachev's administration, was also a factor. And finally, the lack of funds to help the smaller countries to extricate themselves from their difficult situation was given some consideration when new Soviet relations with smaller countries were determined.

Part IV
Conclusions

Conclusions

There is no doubt that the collapse was the result of not one, but many causes, systemic, economic, political, social, psychological etc. The causes were directly or indirectly linked.

ECONOMIC FACTORS

Economic factors, understood very broadly, were no doubt one of the main causes of the collapse. Of the economic factors four should be specially stressed: the increasing gap between the East and the West in the level of technology, the unfavourable development of the standard of living, the excessive socialisation of the means of production, and the growing indebtedness.

The increasing gap in technology resulted from the inability of the small countries as well as the USSR to match the West's pace of technological progress. The slow technological progress turned out to be an insufficient substitute for the exhaustion of the extensive factors in economic growth. And this was one of the chief reasons for the declining economic growth rates and the unfavourable development of the standard of living. The slow technological progress was reflected primarily in civilian production and even more in private consumption. All this meant that the socialist camp was losing the competition with the West.

The unfavourable evolution of the standard of living was of course a powerful factor for several reasons. Most people judge systems and governments according to the welfare effects they get from them. People in socialist countries were promised that the standard of living would continuously increase. The communist leaders were not only unable to meet their promise, but the standard of living was declining slightly or at best stagnating. In addition people believed that the standard of living they achieved in terms of real incomes or private consumption was much below the potential and blamed the socialist regime for this.

With the exception of Hungary which, thanks to its economic reform, was able to ensure a smooth-running supply of consumer goods to the population (though not in the rich mix which exists in the West), the countries under discussion, mainly Poland, suffered from shortages. In Poland the shortages became so widespread in the second half of the 1980s that the government had to resort to rationing of certain products. People were angry with and tired of the permanent searching for products in short supply and of standing in line-ups. They felt, and rightly so, that they had a right to an uninterrupted, smooth supply of a large selection of products.

One of the greatest blunders the Soviet communist leaders committed was the socialisation of *all* the means of production. This concept was taken over by Czechoslovakia and more or less by Hungary; only in Poland did most of the agricultural land remain in private hands. It is understandable that a socialist system could not leave large and certain middle-sized enterprises in private hands, but it was a gross mistake to nationalise small businesses. Had they left them in private or genuine cooperative hands from the early stages of the system, they might have helped to supply consumer goods and services and enrich the selection of goods, and thus they might have functioned as a tool against shortages. Needless to say, such a treatment of small businesses would have had a politically stabilising effect, also because the communist leaders promised before the seizure of power that they would not touch the small private sector.

The revision in the attitude to the small private sector in the 1960s in connection with the economic reforms still had on the whole a stabilising effect. In the second half of the 1980s the private non-agricultural sector, in tandem with a black market, became a contributing factor to the breakdown of the socialist system in Poland and Hungary. The rapidly expanding private – legal and illegal – sector was proof for the majority of the population that the socialist system had failed in its economic tasks. Since this development was combined with higher prices, low income groups were affected the most, and this did not endear the regime to the public. In addition, the private sector which in the 1960s and 1970s was neutral *vis-à-vis* the socialist system since the system created monopoly conditions for it joined the opposition in the second half of the 1980s, because it felt that the socialist regime meant an impediment to its expansion. In Czechoslovakia the private sector could not play so important a role because it was very tiny.

Growing indebtedness to the West was greatest in Poland and Hungary, the two countries where the movement away from socialism had started and was strongest. There is no doubt that the large indebtedness turned out to be – contrary to expectations – an impediment to economic growth and in this way was a contributing factor to the collapse of the socialist system. The loaned funds were not used effectively: much of them was used to boost consumption. Due to the high interest rates a large portion of exports had to be used to pay for servicing the debt. As a result imports of investment goods from the West had to be restricted, and this had a negative impact on economic growth.

The critical economic situation was due to systemic factors and also to the applied economic policy. The traditional economic mechanism was not adequate for solving the problems which faced a modernising society, and was doomed to failure. The detailed planning of the economy from the centre was highly inefficient and necessarily created market disequlibria, one reason being that the price system was irrational. The incentive system, which was an integral part of the traditional economic mechanism, was not effective enough to make people work hard and produce quality products. For these and other reasons the reforms were a necessity. Poland and Hungary, which first rejected the socialist system and started a transition to a market economy, and caused a 'domino effect' in other East European countries, had been engaged in far-reaching reforms for some time. This is not to say that the reforms brought down the socialist system, though reforms are always dangerous to an authoritarian regime. However, the economic reforms of the 1960s in Hungary and Czechoslovakia, when it was the best time for reforms because people still believed in the reformability of the system, were halted in the former and reversed in the latter. Disregarding the minor Polish reform of 1973, it can be said that in the1970s no real reform activity was going on. When economic reforms started again in the first half of the 1980s in Hungary, and when Poland joined in, the environment for reforms was quite different from the one in the 1960s. Both countries found themselves in an economic crisis. Poland experienced a huge decline in the level of production and was not able to meet its obligations to service its foreign debts. Hungary was production-wise much better off than Poland, but also groaned under the burden of foreign debts. Doubts about the reformability of the socialist system slowly started to take root, but still most of the elite, mainly in Hungary, believed in the reformability of the socialist system. In the second half of the 1980s the non-believers in the reformability of the system gained the upper hand. They continued to push for economic changes, not to salvage the system, but rather to destroy it. The communist elites started to introduce market socialism under pressure from the opposition, but it was too late to salvage the socialist system. Thus market socialism had no chance to stand the test of time.

The traditional and reformed economic mechanisms should not alone be blamed for the failure. Also to blame are *the economic policy*, as it manifested itself in the industrialisation drive with great stress on heavy industry at the expense of consumption and services, and the social welfare policy. The industrialisation drive was largely motivated by security considerations. Participation in the military race on the side of the Soviet Union affected negatively many aspects of the economy. The countries had to spend a relatively big portion of their GDP on armaments, funds which could have been used for the modernisation of the civilian economy and for increases in the standard of living. In addition, the most talented professionals were lured to the military industry from civilian production and services.

The socialist governments were not able to cash in goodwill points for the social welfare they had built up. The social welfare policy – as it was manifested in the full employment policy, the narrow skill differentials, the housing policy, the subsidised retail prices of essential consumer goods and shelter, and social security – worked in many respects against the efficiency of the economy. Some of the programmes were not designed properly, such as full employment. Some, such as price subsidies, were not really needed; their objective could have been achieved much more effectively by other methods.

The importance of full employment was depreciated by the inability of the socialist leaders to achieve a combination of full employment with a good work ethic and quality of products, and therefore the economy was hurt. In the final analysis the undemocratic nature of the socialist system was to blame for the reluctance of the authorities to take proper measures against the abuse of full employment. This reluctance was also responsible for the improper labour–management relations.

Reports that in the West an unemployed worker was getting more in compensation benefits than a worker in socialist countries in regular employment did not help make people appreciate full employment. People frequently appreciate advantages only when they lose them.

The significance of health care was depreciated by the system of tips paid to the doctors, the slow progress in technology and the lack of most modern drugs. Great housing shortages also created a lot of dissatisfaction with the regime.

POLITICAL FACTORS

In my opinion, internal and external political factors, understood very broadly, including instruments used for exercising political power and for pursuing political objectives, played a more important role, or at least as important a role as, economic factors in bringing down the socialist system. Capitalist countries go through a deep recession from time to time; nevertheless the capitalist system is in no danger of collapse. True, in the 1930s, during the Great Depression, the capitalist system was in great danger. The New Deal and other reforms rescued it and simultaneously made it depression-proof to a great extent. An integral part of the New Deal was the commencement of the build up of a social safety net which in the course of time developed into a comprehensive welfare system. This made the socialist system less attractive and protected the capitalist system from social unrest.

Of the political factors the focus here will be on the lack of legitimacy, the erosion of ideology, the anti-socialist propaganda, the disintegration of CPs, the dropping of Brezhnev's doctrine and the role of the West.

Perhaps lack of legitimacy was one of the most important causes of the collapse of the socialist system. Legitimacy, as it is reflected in a pluralistic political system, is perhaps the most important protection of the capitalist system. If people are frustrated with the government of the day because it could not prevent a recession or created one by its policy or for some other reason, they can punish the ruling political party at the next election by dumping it and giving their trust to a rival party. Both parties usually take the same position on decisive systemic issues, such as capitalism, democracy, ownership, market, etc., and differ only in their attitudes which do not transcend the framework of capitalism. Nevertheless the voters feel some satisfaction at least for some time. After a while they may be tired of the new government and wait for the time when they can get rid of it. (See for example the rotation of the Conservative and Liberal Party in Canada, or the Christian-Democratic Party and Social Democratic Party in Germany, Conservative and Labour Parties in Great Britain, etc.)

The capitalist system is also protected by the media, which is mostly in the hands of corporations, the foundation of the capitalist system. The owners of the media see to it, mostly with the help of subtle methods, that the media serves the capitalist system. Because the media is pluralistic it has tremendous influence on public opinion.

The socialist countries did not have a pluralistic system, and therefore the only way to punish the CPs for mismanaging the economy was to change the system. It is worthwhile to quote Fukuyama's view (1992) on the importance of legitimacy. 'Some have compared legitimacy to a kind of cash reserve. All governments, democratic and authoritarian, have their ups and downs; but only legitimate governments have their reserve to draw on in times of crisis' (p. 39).

The erosion of the socialist ideology and the spread of capitalist ideology were further reasons for the collapse. The communists started out with an ideology which was contrary to the potential reality in many important aspects. Therefore it was changed several times in important points and with every change it was brought closer to capitalist ideology, a phenomenon which could not escape the notice of even the less educated segments of the population. In addition, people heard and read about prosperity in the West and the great gap in the standard of living between East and West. And domestic and foreign propaganda made the public believe that prosperity was within reach once the countries abandoned socialism and opted for capitalism. When the socialist ideology lost its influence, it was no wonder that people began to pin their hopes for a better life under capitalism.

Anti-socialist propaganda also had a share in the breakdown of the socialist system. Propaganda machinery, fuelled by the opposition, increasingly grew inside the countries against the system. It was strongest in Poland and weakest in Czechoslovakia. In this activity *samizdat* literature played an important role. Perhaps rumours about the great prosperity in the West compared with the poor conditions in socialist countries had an even greater effect. Tourists, who were lucky to get to Western countries, provided much of the material for the rumours.

One contributing factor to the effectiveness of the anti-socialist propaganda was that Russia was the dominant factor in the Soviet Union. The very nations which spearheaded the movement to eliminate socialism, namely Poland and Hungary, had good historic reasons for not liking the Russians. The latter were the ones who had thwarted or helped to thwart their national aspirations in the past. Resentment of the USSR, as the successor to Russia, was reinforced by the fact that it had used the liberation of East European countries to impose its own political and economic system on them. Socialism was therefore viewed as a foreign product, imposed from outside by a country which had been an enemy to national aspirations in the past. Regular interference by the Soviet Union made the situation even worse.

Additionally, powerful communication machinery beamed subtle but well thought-out propaganda from Munich, which on the one hand portrayed the economic and political situation in socialist countries as being worse than it really was and, on the other, depicted the situation in the West in rosy colours on the whole.

The gradual disintegration of the Party and government apparatus was also a very important factor. There were several circumstances which led to the disintegration. One was the change in the personnel structure of the apparatus: more and more the jobs in the apparatus were occupied by people from a new generation who were more educated, less ideologically oriented and as a result also less committed to socialism and more pragmatic than the ones whom they replaced. The incessant crises in the 1980s, primarily in Poland, frustrated and demoralised the apparatus and many politicians alike, to the point that a feeling of tiredness, impotence and indifference began to set in. Poland went through martial law and a substantial decline in performance: in 1983–5 it seemed that the economy was on the way to recovery and Solidarity was muzzled; soon the economy plunged again into a crisis and a huge market disequilibrium set in and Solidarity started to flex its muscles. In Hungary, infighting within the CP, which was provoked by the worsening economic situation, removed Kádár, the old leader, in 1988 and brought on the scene an ambitious politician who was willing to accept market socialism. The removal of Kádár did not mean an end to the infighting; on the contrary it continued with greater intensity and resulted in a split in the CP. Only in Czechoslovakia was the infighting less intensive and the collapse the result of a 'domino effect'.

The members of the intelligentsia, primarily those who were not in positions of responsibility within the CPs and governments, played an important role in bringing down the regime. One of the reasons why they turned against the regime was the shabby treatment which they had received from the authorities. Even in Poland and Hungary, where the intellectuals were relatively better treated, they could not be satisfied with their position. They were long denied the principal freedoms, essential for their self-realisation. More than other segments of the population, the intelligentsia was troubled by the encroachment on national sovereignty and the lack of democratic institutions and human rights. In addition, it had serious grievances: it felt that it was discriminated against in the process of income distribution and not given the social status in society it deserved. It regarded the narrow wage differentials for skill as disrespectful of its professions and interests. All this was sufficient to make the majority of the intelligentsia resentful of the socialist regime. On top of this, there was the institution of nomenclature, which excluded for political reasons well-educated people from positions of responsibility. This was only to some extent true of Poland and Hungary in the second half of the 1980s.

Of course, the West can be given some credit for the collapse. It exercised pressure on the USSR not to interfere with the disintegration process in the small countries. It also contributed by helping to win over a great segment of the intelligentsia for a capitalist economy; to this end it used very subtle methods such as invitations to conferences and research stays in the West, which were designed to show the participants the advantages of capitalism. No doubt, the Western intelligence services, mainly the CIA, had their share in converting the countries under review to capitalism.

The Brezhnev doctrine was declared in 1968, but it had determined the relations between the Soviet Union and East European countries, with the exception of Yugoslavia, since the end of the 1940s. The Soviet Union made it clear that it would not allow a genuine or assumed threat to socialism in Eastern Europe. The Soviet Union proved that it meant business when it suppressed the 1956 uprising in Hungary by force, occupied Czechoslovakia in 1968 and threatened to occupy Poland in 1981. Knowing that the Soviet Union was not bluffing and wanting to avoid a nuclear war, the Western countries did not interfere.

The communist leaders in the small countries felt secure against domestic upheavals or external interventions from the West. They knew that they were protected against such eventualities by the Soviet Union and they were willing to pay the price, which they could not avoid anyhow, to follow Moscow's guide. The non-reform-minded leaders could use Moscow's shield as an excuse for staying away from reforms. On the other hand, leaders who had Moscow's trust could engage in reforms if they managed to present them as a useful experiment not threatening socialism. This was the case of Hungary in 1968.

After having held for some time the post of Secretary General, Gorbachev embarked first on economic reform and later on political reform. Both non-reform-minded as well as reform-minded leaders in small countries might have been scared. Both felt that Gorbachev was pushing too far and this contributed to the disintegration of the CPs. Once Gorbachev dropped Brezhnev's doctrine the political leaders were no longer shielded against domestic opposition. The Czechoslovak leaders tried in vain to enlist help from Moscow against domestic opposition.

In sum, the collapse was primarily the result of many internal economic and political factors. The coincidence of the gradual far-reaching political changes in the Soviet Union with the disintegration of the socialist system in Poland and Hungary was a very important factor. If in 1985 a less reform-minded leader than Gorbachev had been elected, perhaps the socialist system would still be around.

Notes and References

1 Thoughts on the Causes of the Collapse of the Socialist System

1. Brzezinski is using the term the communists used to characterise the capitalist system.
2. In his review of Fukuyama's book M. Rustin (1992) calls the author's interpretation of history a liberal version of historical materialism.
3. 'The Mechanism is, in other words, a kind of Marxist interpretation of history that leads to a completely non-Marxist conclusion' writes Fukuyama (131).
4. According to the author, Schumpeter (1950) *Capitalism, Socialism and Democracy* and Nelson and Winter (1982) *An Evolutionary Theory of Economics* belong to the group of evolutionary economists and to the second which professes a conservative political philosophy, Burke, (1790) *Reflections on the Revolution in France*, Popper (1971) *The Open Society and its Enemies* and Oakeshott (1962) *Rationalism in Politics and other Essays*.
5. I do not think that Murrell is correct when argues that ' . . . gradually policy returned to its natural path in ensuing months'. He has apparently in mind the Polish attempt to stimulate the economy in the second half of 1990. Once the stimulation brought about an increase in inflation, the policymakers returned to their old policies.
6. As in other places of her book, here too, she is not very specific about what she means by anarchy.
7. A good overview of Lange's views as well as of the debates about market socialism is given in the introduction to the volume of papers edited by Bardhan and Roemer (1993).

2 The Traditional Economic Mechanism

1. Some economists distinguish the two terms, but I will use them interchangeably.
2. I cannot cite all or most publications on the topic mentioned. Therefore only a few names will be given. Bornstein and Fusfeld (1970); Gregory and Stuart (1989); Kornai (1992); Nove (1980) and Spulber (1991). With the exception of Kornai's book all others deal with the Soviet system. As is known, the traditional system in the countries under review was more or less the same as in the USSR.
3. This right of choice of job did not exist from the start of the system. For a long time employees could not move freely from one job to another. It is interesting that the freedom to quit a job was instituted first in the USSR and only later in East European countries.

4. Gross value was computed in constant wholesale prices and included for a long time the value of the final products, semi-finished products and the value of subcontracting services for other enterprises.
5. For example the 1967 price reform in Czechoslovakia brought about a huge increase in wholesale prices, but this did not affect consumer prices.
6. In many consultations I had about the reasons for the collapse, the following two stood out: the large overestimation of planning's ability to coordinate the economy and insufficient incentives. Here I would like to mention specially the names of two scholars who stressed this point, J. Mujżel and G. Révész.
7. It is known that many people in the line ups were employees who were supposed to be at their jobs.
8. This is not to say that enterprise managers did not have room for manoeuvring; as has already been shown, the authorities made their decisions on the basis of information they received from enterprises.
9. The last three paragraphs rely very much on Berliner's study (1981).
10. It is also known that the allocation of inputs to enterprises and the monopoly position of suppliers generated a lot of corruption.
11. A. Bajt (1971) gave a good survey of the theories of cycles under socialism which were published before 1971. In 1981 T. Bauer, a well-known Hungarian economist, made an important contribution to the theory of cycles under socialism.

3 Economic Policy

1. When Y. Malenkov, the new leader of the Soviet Union after Stalin's death, stated in his programmatic speech that the new leadership would put greater stress on the development of light industry, he was reminded by N. Khrushchev in an article in *Pravda* that the growth of the economy required the law of preferential development of producer goods to be respected.
2. In 1990 Shevardnadze used the figure 25 per cent for the USSR (Fukuyama 1992, p. 345).
3. This manifested itself in very high participation rates.
4. The offering of an increase in the wage bill for an overfulfilment of plan targets was not a necessary component of the traditional system. It is known that in the 1965 Soviet economic reform, which did not go beyond the framework of the traditional system, the institution of overfulfilment was restricted. Also the Polish government limited it at one time to instances of approval in advance (see Adam, 1973; Fick, 1964).
5. I have heard from several friends who had family members hospitalised in the 1980s in Czechoslovakia that they themselves cleaned the rooms where their relatives were lying ill, and the toilets. They did these jobs voluntarily because of the shortage of cleaning staff at the hospitals.
6. Stalin attacked wage levelling as a petty bourgeois idea. In his talk with Emil Ludwig, Stalin said: 'Only people who are unacquainted with Marxism can have the primitive notion that the Russian Bolsheviks want to pool all wealth and then to share it out equally' (quoted according to Lane, 1982, p. 22).

7. It can be assumed that in Hungary the situation was not much different.
8. This policy was not carried out consistently since other criteria which applied contradicted the social criterion.
9. Collective farmers' households spent relatively more on clothing and footwear than non-collective farmers. In addition, the non-rural population got compensation in the form of cheap utilities, city transport and shelter.
10. The cheapness of bread encouraged people to use it to feed animals.
11. In 1956 in Czechoslovakia the authorities initiated research to find out the extent to which the existing distribution of the turnover tax under the existing structure of consumption favoured individual income groups. The finding was that it makes little difference. The advantage which low-income groups per capita had from low prices of certain foodstuffs was offset by the advantages of high-income groups per capita which profited from low prices of certain products which low-income groups could afford only in small amounts (high quality cuts of meat are a good example).
12. In the 1950s in Czechoslovakia, the authorities tried to counter the growing practice of tipping by prosecuting health providers who accepted them, but later abandoned this idea. In Hungary the authorities legalised tips as long as they were given after the services were extended.
13. In Czechoslovakia, the action of moving the exponents of the old regime from large cities was already in preparation. At the last moment it was stopped.
14. The usual propaganda argument was that in the West unemployment benefits were higher than wages in the East.

4 Labour–Management Relations and Incentives

1. In the 1950s a French delegation visited the biggest enterprise in Prague. It had long conversations with managers and workers alike. The spokesman of the delegation, according to reliable sources, summarised his impressions by saying that there was a difference between France and Czechoslovakia: in France you are allowed to criticise the president of France, but not the foreman, whereas in Czechoslovakia the situation is the opposite.
2. In Canada and West European countries the position of the top manager is more restricted.
3. Not all socialist countries adopted the idea of one-man management. In China, up to the middle of the 1970s, collective management existed in enterprises.
4. This subchapter and the next rely heavily on two of my earlier books (1979 and 1984).
5. This is less true in unionised firms. However, their number has much declined in the past decades.
6. Political prisoners, who were forced to perform hard work, were assigned jobs.
7. Among the students expelled, many were in the last year of their studies. The aspirations of many young people were ruined.

8. I was forced to work for 7 years (1951–8) as a skilled worker in the biggest factory in Prague after being recalled from my diplomatic post, and therefore I intimately know how workers behaved. For example, many workers left their workplace 20–30 minutes before the end of the shift, often without having a replacement for the next shift. They used the time for their ablutions so that, when the shift was ending, they were already standing at the time clock.

9. The well-known classical saying of workers that the government pretends to pay us and we pretend to work reflected the situation quite well.

10. In the United States workers are afraid of losing their jobs because it is usually difficult to find new ones and also because in most cases they lose health care insurance at the same time.

11. The Hungarian 1968 economic reform introduced considerably differentiated bonuses. Top managers were entitled to bonuses amounting to 80 per cent of their basic salaries, whereas workers to only 15 per cent of their earnings. The division of funds earmarked for wages and bonuses between the two items was controlled by top managers to a great degree. Since top managers were interested in maximising bonuses, whereas workers wanted to maximise wages, a conflict of interest developed which threatened the peace of enterprises. Therefore the authorities soon modified the bonus fund (Adam, 1979, p. 153).

5 Foreign Economic Relations

1. CMEA was established in 1949. Needless to say, this institution was the result of Soviet initiative. The founders of CMEA were, besides the USSR, Poland, Czechoslovakia, Hungary, Rumania and Bulgaria. Albania and East Germany joined later. CMEA had also non-European members: Mongolia (from 1962), Cuba (1972) and Vietnam (1978). Yugoslavia was an associate member.

2. Šafaříková (1989) took a similar position when she argued that the international socialist market did not have the attributes of a real market ; it was rather a bidding place, where individual economies tried to sell their low quality commodities at higher than international prices to exporters of raw materials and semi-products, who accepted such deals for payment reasons.

3. To V. Shastitko (1990) the corrections did not reflect objective processes.

4. The reader who is interested in a short review of the debate should consult Brada (1991) and Lavigne (1991, pp.241–52).

5. Holzman also advances another possible explanation; this is based on custom union theory , which in my opinion is less convincing.

6. According to Kornai (1992, p. 358) CMEA countries agreed in 1975 on 'sliding' oil prices which meant that prices were adjusted each year on the basis of a five-year average.

7. To make an objective judgement about the advantages the small countries enjoyed from getting cheap raw materials, one would also have to take into consideration other factors, *inter alia,* the interest rate the exporters paid on investment credits.

8. These data are based on 1967 US dollars calculated from national data at the official exchange rate.
9. According to computations (see Gajdeczka, 1989, vol. 2, p.383) the total debt compared to exports in 1987 was 95 per cent in Czechoslovakia, 342 per cent in Hungary and 542 per cent in Poland . The debt in terms of per capita was the highest in Hungary.
10. It is worthwhile mentioning that if, in the trade of CMEA countries, market relations prevailed, some countries could not have afforded to produce cars.

6 Political and Ideological Factors

1. Whatever the name of the CP was, here it will be called CP. The Polish CP was called Polish United Workers' Party and the Hungarian was called Hungarian Socialist Workers' Party. Only the Czechoslovak CP had the word communist in its name: it was called the Communist Party of Czechoslovakia.
2. It is known that the CPs kept a close watch over the activities of the non-communist parties through their agents inside the parties. In Czechoslovakia, for example, each of the non-Communist parties had its own daily paper. But the CP determined the number of copies the non-Communist parties were allowed to publish. The quota was well below demand.
3. Most of the time there were informal factions which, of course, did not operate openly.
4. One Hungarian political scientist mentioned to me the excellent example of M. Németh, the last socialist prime minister. He was a member of the Party apparatus. In 1988 he was promoted to the powerful post of Party secretary for economic affairs and several months later to the post of prime minister. In his function he, no doubt, contributed to the rapid collapse of socialism. Apparently he felt that the regime was untenable and he wanted to have some credit for its fast demise. And indeed, he was rewarded by the West: he was appointed to the position of deputy managing director of the European Construction Bank. His 'commitment' to socialism was best manifested in his refusal to become a candidate of the Socialist party in the 1990 elections. He also earned the gratitude of the West, mainly Germany, by allowing East German tourists in Hungary in August 1989 to go to West Germany instead of East Germany. This provision, which was taken in cooperation with G. Horn, the foreign minister of the day and the present leader of the ruling Socialist Party, put into motion forces which accelerated the collapse of the socialist system in Czechoslovakia.
5. Z. Brzezinski (1989), not known as a great friend of communism, wrote the following about it: 'Communism thus appealed to the simpletons and to the sophisticated alike: it gave each a sense of direction, a satisfactory explanation, and a moral justification. It made its subscribers feel self-righteous , correct and confident all at once' (pp. 2–3).
6. What is also interesting is that neo-liberalism, a right-wing ideology which adheres to *laissez faire*, found many adherents in both countries, not only in the ranks of non-communists, but also in the ranks of ordinary

members and functionaries of the CPs, among them many former dogmatic communists. Some of the new neo-liberals were later elevated to high functions in the non-communist governments.

7. Because capitalist countries adopted social programmes which were first advocated by socialists and were first applied in socialist countries, many social scientists started to talk about a convergence of the two systems.

8. In Czechoslovakia, Charter 1977, an organisation of dissidents, used the Helsinki accord as a cover for its activity.

9. Of course, the West used other means too, to bring down the socialist system. See Chapter 10 for the diplomatic efforts made.

10. A critical analysis of Kádárism is given by two Hunagarian philosophers, F. Fehér and A. Heller (1990, pp. 71–87).

11. O. Šik (1990) gives a good insight into the rise of the 'Prague Spring' and the Soviet-led occupation. Z. Mlynář's book (1980) is of great importance because it sheds light on the Soviet scandalous treatment of the Czechoslovak leaders.

12. Fehér and Heller (1990, pp. 91–110) give an evaluation of the role of the 'Prague Spring' in the efforts of the East European emancipation.

7 Economic Reforms

1. This statement refers to Novotny's leadership; Dubček who came to power in 1968 was very reform-minded.

2. This was the view of a very well-known Polish economist who was critical of the regime. There were many others who were thinking in the same way.

3. In his review of Kornai's *The Socialist System* , W. Brus (1993) stresses in substance the same point.

4. In brief, the so-called Brezhnev doctrine meant that the socialist camp was responsible for the socialist development of its members. A strayer from the socialist path should be put back on track with the help of the camp. In other words it meant that the USSR had the right to intervene in the internal affairs of socialist states.

5. My explanation of the price changes is somewhat simplified, because I do not take into consideration the differences in the Czechoslovak and Hungarian reform.

6. The authorities in Hungary could interfere directly in the economy when the security of the country was involved and when deliveries to CMEA countries were threatened. In such cases they could make enterprises do what the authorities believed was necessary. Enterprises , however, were entitled to compensation, if such interference caused financial damage.

7. In the Czechoslovak reform of the 1960s, unemployment compensation was introduced, but not because the authorities intended to create a genuine labour market; it rather was intended as a provision in case some unemployment arose as a result of the economic reform or of the plan to liquidate obsolete and inefficient enterprises, a plan which was carried out to a very limited degree.

8. In his report to the CC meeting R. Nyers, who was the Economic Secretary of the CC and as such in charge of the economic reform of the

1960s, maintained that the market categories would be used in a planned way. According to him 'the labour force even in the future cannot become a commodity and not the market, but conscious, state planned management will have the decisive role in extended reproduction, in investment' (1968, p. 140).

9. T. Nagy, who headed the reform committees, mentioned in a 1988 interview (Ferber and Rejtő, 1988, p.25) that he was told by the secretary of the CC not to come up with, *inter alia* , a proposal for changing the organisational system. Apparently the CP leadership was afraid that this might antagonise the bureaucracy.

10. In Hungary, the founding body had to exercise its right of veto at the stage of selecting candidates for the position of top manager.

11. For example, the Hungarian economist T. Liska (1965) came up with the idea of entrusting the banking system with the running of state property. The banks lease the property to the highest bidder in organised auctions. Apparently Liska assumed that the utilisation of assets would be more efficient under the management of lessees than under state management. In my opinion this proposal could be applied to some small- and middle-size enterprises, but I have doubts about its practicality with regard to large enterprises. Nuti (1990) mentions the Liska proposal as one possibility. He also mentions large 'state shareholdings in private companies' as a form of management privatisation. Dréze (1993, p. 262) believes that labour-managed firms can be efficient 'in moderate capital intensity firms'.

8 Development of the Economies

1. It was not an infrequent phenomenon that newlyweds had to move in with the parents of one of the couple in a two-room apartment or to continue to live separately. What was even worse was that housing shortages forced divorced couples to continue to live in the same apartment, even if one of the former partners remarried. Needless to say, conditions which deprived people of privacy led to frustration and conflicts.

2. Workers were outraged by the intended price increases mainly for two reasons. They were frustrated by stagnating real wages in the 1960s in any case, and were not willing to accept a further decline in the standard of living. In addition, the price increases, which included a huge rise in the price of meat, were announced just a few days before Christmas, when meat is bought in relatively large quantities.

3. W. Jaruzelski (1992, p. 29) maintains that in 1980 Poland got credit to the amount of \$ 8.7 billion and paid out \$ 8.1 billion in interest.

4. In the beginning of the 1970s, the Polish leaders tried to appease the private peasantry with various concessions (abolition of compulsory deliveries, price increases for agricultural products, extension of social security to the peasantry). When the political situation was consolidated, the Polish leaders started to talk about the importance of socialised agriculture, and this scared the peasantry (for more, see Brus, 1983, pp. 35–6).

5. Even in a relaxed international situation the Soviets would have exerted pressure on Poland. With Reagan's decision to enter an enhanced arms race with the Soviet Union, the Soviet worries about Poland increased.

6. The US government was informed about the planned martial law by its agent in the Polish army general staff, Colonel Kuklinski. The fact that it did not pass on the information to Solidarity indicates that the USA also tried to prevent a Soviet invasion of Poland.

7. The estimates of how much Czechoslovakia fell behind Austria differ considerably. The estimate by the World Bank that Czechoslovak GNP per capita in 1990 was only US$ 3,300 and thus only slightly higher than 20 per cent of that of Austria (see Dyba and Svejnar, 1991) was probably based on the official exchange rate of the Czechoslovak crown, which was much undervalued. The best way to estimate the performance of an economy of a country, mainly its standard of living in comparison with other economies, is with the help of an exchange rate based on purchasing-power parity. (This is not to say that such calculations are without problems; nevertheless, if they are made with proper consideration of all the factors they can give an objective result.) According to V. Komárek (1989), who made such computations, the Czechoslovak per capita GDP in 1985 was only 15–25 per cent lower than that of Great Britain, Austria and Belgium, and 15–40 per cent higher than that of Greece, Portugal and Ireland. According to É. Ehrlich (1991), Alton et al. estimated the Czechoslovak GNP per capita in 1986 at US$ 7786. According to P. Havlik's computations (1992), the Czechoslovak GDP per capita in 1985 was 76.3 per cent of the Austrian.

8. This was a meeting of the CC which discussed, among other things, the Czechoslovak contribution to the integration of CMEA.

9. Travel abroad was mostly in large groups, organised by state travel agencies. Because of the high prices of such travel, its participants were mostly people who had gained money in illegal ways. This was another reason for dissatisfaction.

10. The figures listed are gross figures. The net figures were much smaller. Much of the credit which Hungary extended was not expected to be repaid.

11. Price subsidies on foodstuffs and services are not considered here.

9 Ownership Relations

1. 'Who is not stealing (meaning from state property), is cheating on his family'. This was a saying during the communist regime in Czechoslovakia which characterises quite well the attitude of people to state property.

2. In 1953 collective farms had 376 000 members; in 1958 the number of members declined to 169 000, to increase in 1961 to 1 203 900 (see Petö and Szakács (1985, pp. 257 and 445).

3. It is interesting that there was no mention of the private sector in the material of the Hungarian CC.

4. Gábor and Galasi (1981, p. 174) published earnings ranked by occupation. According to their figures, the earnings of a private retailer

were second in rank after those of a minister. Other private occupations are not far from the top of the list. It is probable that the private sector earned more than was admitted.

5. Those who took advantage of such sales gained property very cheaply. Inflation made the repayment of credit very easy.
6. One can speculate that the government itself, being short of hard currency, purchased hard currency on the black market.
7. We disregard here the self-management arrangements in Poland and Hungary in the 1950s.
8. The composition of the Hungarian self-management body (enterprise council), which pertained in most enterprises, was such that it easily allowed a manipulative manager who had good relations with his employees to dominate it: managers could sit on the enterprise council (self-management body) as representatives of employees and the council could be convened only once a year (Sárközy, 1985).
9. See Kawalec (1988), Krawczyk (1988), and Lewandowski and Szomburg (1988).
10. See, for example, Tardos (1988), and Kopátsy (1988).
11. I. Szelényi (1988, p. 217) has devoted attention to structural changes in agriculture in socialist societies, particularly in Hungary, over a long period. Researching the economic activities of collective farms, he came to the conclusion that in the 1970s a process of embourgeoisement started in collective farms, a small group of farmers starting on their private plots (he calls them mini-farms) to produce for the market. These small entrepreneurs were the same people or their offspring who were engaged in production for the market before the communist regime. According to him the emergence of this petty bourgeoisie was possible because the Party bureaucracy acknowledged that the system could be rescued only by allowing a private sector.
12. I. Szelényi (1990, p. 417) maintains that in the middle of the 1980s 70 per cent of the population were receiving earnings from the second economy.

10 The Soviet Factor

1. *The Economy...* (1990) is a joint work of four Western financial institutions.
2. In 1988 incomes increased by 9.2 and in 1989 by 12.9 per cent. At the same time the retail price index increased by 1 and 2 per cent respectively (Schroeder, 1992, p. 97, and *The Economy...*, 1990, p. 6).
3. Gorbachev himself acknowledged that his reform resembled the Hungarian one most of all (*New York Times*, 10 July, 1988, taken from Aslund, 1991, p. 151).
4. For more, see Hewett (1988, pp. 309–33), Aslund (1991, pp. 114–53), Adam (1989, pp. 169–89) and *The Economy...* (1990).
5. E. Shevardnadze, the former foreign minister of the Soviet Union, said to J. Baker, according to Beschloss and Talbot (1993, p. 379), that had Gorbachev offered the 1991 union treaty proposal in 1988 or 1989, even the Baltic states would have accepted it.

6. Before the coup Gorbachev had the promise of Ukraine leaders that they would join the union. After the coup a great number of deputies voted for independence for fear of Yeltsin (see *The Economist*, 7–13 May 1994).

7. When Khrushchev was ousted he became a pariah.

8. This new style, which was also used in dealing with foreign leaders, ensured him popularity and trust in foreign countries. After a meeting with Gorbachev, Mrs Thatcher declared that it was possible to do business with Gorbachev, a compliment which she never used about talks with former Soviet leaders.

9. It can be assumed that Gorbachev was consulted about Kádárs' ousting in 1988. It is not known what his answer was. One would not be surprised to hear that he agreed.

10. In his book W. Laqueur (1994, p. 67) takes a different position in maintaining that 'The arms race was regarded in Western capitals as a highly undesirable necessity rather than a deliberate strategy that would have dramatic results'.

11. Some social scientists argue that in Czarist Russia as well as in the Soviet Union security considerations triggered economic reforms (see Bova, 1992, pp. 46–7).

12. It is generally known that US trade unions and the CIA supported Solidarity financially.

Bibliography

For space reasons only full references to books, regardless of the language in which they are published, are listed. References to periodicals and newspaper articles are listed without titles unless they are published in English.

ADAM, J. (1973) 'The Incentive System in the USSR', *Industrial Relations*, no. 2, May.

ADAM, J. (1979) *Wage Control and Inflation in the Soviet Bloc Countries* (London: Macmillan Press).

ADAM, J. (1984) *Employment and Wage Policies in Poland, Czechoslovakia and Hungary since 1950*, London: Macmillan Press and New York: St. Martin's Press.

ADAM, J. (1989) *Economic Reforms in the Soviet Union and Eastern Europe since the 1960s* (London: Macmillan Press and New York: St. Martin's Press).

ADAM, J. (1989a) 'Work-Teams: A New Phenomenon in Income Distribution in Hungary', *Comparative Economic Studies*, no. 1.

ADAM, J. (1991) 'Social Contract', in J. Adam (ed.) *Economic Reforms and Welfare Systems in the USSR, Poland and Hungary* (London: Macmillan Press and New York: St. Martin's Press).

ADAM, J. (1993) *Planning and Market in Soviet and East European Thought, 1960s–1992* (London: Macmillan Press, and New York: St. Martin's Press).

ALTMANN, F. L. (1987) *Wirtschaftentwicklung und Strukturpolitik in der Tschechoslovakei nach 1968* (Munich: Olzog Verlag).

ASLUND, A. (1985) *Private Enterprise in Eastern Europe* (London: Macmillan Press).

ASLUND, A. (1991) *Gorbachev's Struggle for Economic Reform*, updated and expanded edition (Ithaca: Cornell University Press).

BAJT, A. (1971) 'Investment Cycles in European Socialist Economies: A Review Article', *Journal of Economic Literature*, March.

BARDHAN, P. K. and J. E. ROEMER (1993) *Market Socialism, The Current Debate* (Oxford University Press).

BAUER, T. (1981) *Tervgazdaság, beruházás, ciklusok* (Budapest: KJK).

BAUER, T. (1983) 'The Hungarian Alternative to Soviet-Type Planning', *Journal of Comparative Economics*, 7, pp. 304–16.

BERLINER, J. (1981) 'The Prospects for Technological Progress', in M. Bornstein (ed.) *The Soviet Economy* (Boulder: Westview Press).

BERLINER, J. (1992) 'Socialism in the Twenty-First Century', in M. Keren and G. Ofer (eds) *Trials of Transition, Economic Reform in the Former Communist Bloc* (Boulder: Westview Press).

BESCHLOSS, M. R. and S. TALBOT, (1993) *At the Highest Levels, The Inside Story of the End of the Cold War* (Boston: Little Brown Company).

BIELASIAK, J. (1983) 'The Party: Permanent Crisis', in A. Brumberg (ed.) *Poland, Genesis of a Revolution* (New York: Vintage Books).

BODZABÁN, I. and A. SZALAY (eds) (1994) *A puha diktaturától a kemény demokráciáig* (Budapest).

BORNSTEIN, M. and D. R. FUSFELD (1970) *The Soviet Economy, a Book of Readings* (Homewood: R.D. Irwin).

BOVA, R. (1992) *The Soviet Economy and International Politics*, in M. Ellman and V. Kontorovich (eds) *The Disintegration of the Soviet Economic System* (London: Routledge).

BRABANT VAN, J. M. (1980) *Socialist Economic Integration* (Cambridge University Press).

BRABANT VAN, J. M. (1987) 'Socialist and World Market Prices: An Ingrowth?', *Journal of Comparative Economics*, vol. 11, pp. 21–39.

BRADA, J. C. (1991) 'The Political Economy of Communist Foreign Trade. Institutions and Policies', *Journal of Comparative Economics*, vol. 15, pp. 11–39.

BRUS, W. (1983) 'Economics and politics: the fatal link', in A. Brumberg (ed.) *Poland, Genesis of a Revolution* (New York: Vintage Books).

BRUS, W. (1986) 'Economic History of Communist Eastern Europe', in M. C. Kaser (ed.) *The Economic History of Eastern Europe 1919–1975*, vol. III (Oxford: Oxford University Press).

BRUS, W. (1993) 'The Politics and Economics of Reform. Reflections on János Kornai's New Book', *Acta Oeconomica*, vol. 45 (no. 1–2).

BRUS, W. and K. LASKI (1989) *From Marx to the Market, Socialism in Search of an Economic System* (Oxford: Clarendon Press).

BRZEZINSKI, Z. (1989) *The Grand Failure, The Birth and Death of Communism in the Twentieth Century* (New York: Carles Scribner's Sons).

BURKE, E. (1790) *Reflections on the Revolution in France*.

CAMPBELL, R. (1991) *The Socialist Economies in Transition* (Bloomington & Indianapolis: Indiana University Press).

ČECH, J. (1959) *Plánovité rozmísťování pracovních sil v ČSR* (Prague).

CHASE-DUNN, C. (1992) 'The National State as an Agent of Modernity', *Problems of Communism*, January–April.

COOK, E. (1986) 'Prospects for Polish Agriculture in the 1980s', in *East European Economies: Slow Growth in the 1980s*, vol. 3 (Washington: US Government Printing Office).

CRANE, K. (1991) 'Property Rights Reform: Hungarian Country Study ', in Blommenstein, H. and M. Marrese (eds) *Transformation of Planned Economies: Property Rights Reform and Macroeconomic Stability* (Paris: OECD).

CSABA, L. (1990) *Eastern Europe in the World Economy* (Cambridge University Press).

CSIKÓS-NAGY, B. (1983) 'Liquidity Troubles and Economic Consolidation in Hungary', *Acta Oeconomica*, vol. 31 (no. 1–2).

CSIKÓS-NAGY, B. (1988) *Valóság*, no. 6.

DOBB, M. (1966) *Soviet Economic Development since 1917* (London: Routledge and Kegan Paul).

Documents and Materials (1990) (Moscow: Novosti).

DRÉZE, J. H. (1993) 'Self-Management and Economic Theory: Efficiency, Funding, and Employment', in Bardhan, P. K. and J. E. Roemer (eds) *Market Socialism, The Current Debate* (Oxford University Press).

DRUCKER, P. (1986) 'The Changed World Economy', *Foreign Affairs*, Spring.

DYBA, K. (1989) *PE*, no. 5.

DYBA, K. and ŠVEJNAR, J. (1991) 'Czechoslovakia: Recent economic developments and prospects', *American Economic Review, Papers and Proceedings*, May.

Economic Developments in Countries of Eastern Europe (1970), Volume of papers for the use of the US Congress (Washington: US Government Printing Office).

Economic Survey of Europe, 1991–1992 (1992) (Geneva: Economic Commission for Europe).

Economy of the USSR (1990) (Washington: World Bank).

EHRLICH, É. (1991) *Országok versenye (1937–1986)* (Budapest: KJK).

ELLMAN, M. and V. KONTOROVICH (1992) (eds) *The Disintegration of the Soviet Economic System* (London: Routledge).

ENGELS, F. (1969) *Anti-Dühring, Herr Eugen Dühring's Revolution in Science* (Moscow: Progress Publishers).

Essential Works of Marxism (1965) A. Mendel (ed.) (New York: Bantam Books).

FALLENBUCHL, Z. (1986) 'The economic crisis in Poland', in *East European Economies: Slow Growth in the 1980s* (Washington: US Congress).

FALUSNÉ SZIKRA, K. (1986) *Kistulajdon helyzete és jövője* (Budapest: KJK).

FEHÉR, F. and A. HELLER (1990) *Jalta után* (Budapest: Kossuth Könyvkiadó).

FEJTŐ, F. (1974) *A History of the People's Democracies* (Harmondsworth: Penguin).

FEKETE, J. (1983) 'Problems of International Indebtedness – as seen from Hungary', *The New Hungarian Quarterly*, no. 90.

FERBER, K. and G. REJTŐ (1988) *Reform (év) fordulón* (Budapest: KJK).

FICK, B. (1964) *ZG*, no. 1.

FLAKIERSKI, H. (1993) *Income Inequalities in the Former Soviet Union and its Republics* (Armonk: E. M. Sharpe).

FUKUYAMA, F. (1992) *The End of History and the Last Man* (New York: Avon).

GÁBOR, I. and P. GALASI (1981) *A 'második' gazdaság* (Budapest: KJK).

GÁCS, E. (1986) 'Hungary's Social Expenditures in International Comparison', *Acta Oeconomica*, vol. 36 (no. 1–2).

GAJDECZKA, P. (1989), 'Creditworthiness of Eastern Europe', in *Pressures for Reform in the East European Economies*, Volume of papers for the use of the US Congress (Washington: US Government Printing Office).

Gazdaságpolitika és gazdasági fejlődés Magyarorszagon (1988), Study of the Planning Office.

GAZSÓ, F. (1993) *TSz*, no. 5.

GILL, G. (1994) *The Collapse of a Single-Party System* (Cambridge University Press)

GOLDMANN, J. (1964) 'Fluctuations and Trends in the Rate of Economic Growth in some Socialist Countries', *Economics of Planning*, no. 2.

GOLDMANN, J. (1964a) *PH*, no. 11.

GRANICK, D. (1987) *Job Rights in the Soviet Union: Their Consequences* (Cambridge University Press).
GREGORY, P. and STUART R. (1989) *Comparative Economic Systems*, Third edition (Boston: Houghton Mifflin).
HANSON, PH. (1990) *Ownership Issues in Perestroika*, in Tedstrom, J. E. (ed.) *Socialism, Perestroika and the Dilemmas of the Soviet Economic Reform* (Boulder: Westview Press).
HAVASI, F. (1981) 'The Sixth Five-Year Plan of the Hunagarian National Economy (1981–1985)', *Acta Oeconomica* vol. 26 (no. 1–2).
HAVASI, F. (1984) 'Development of Economic Control', *Acta Oeconomica*, vol. 32 (no. 3–4).
HAVLÍK, P. (1992) *NH*, no. 3.
HAYEK, F. A. (1944) *The Road to Serfdom* (Chicago: University Press).
HAYEK, F. A. (1963) (ed.) *Collectivist Economic Planning* (London: Routledge & Kegan Paul)
HAYEK, F. A. (1989) *The Fatal Conceit, the Errors of Socialism*, Collected works, vol. 1 (Chicago: University Press).
HETÉNYI, I. (1969) 'National Economic Planning in the New System of Economic Control and Management', in I. Friss (ed.) *Reform of the Economic Mechanism in Hungary* (Budapest: Akadémiai Kiadó).
HEWETT, E. A. (1988) *Reforming the Soviet Economy, Equality versus Efficiency* (Washington: The Brookings Institution).
HÖHMANN, H. H. (1985) *Osteuropa Zeitschrift für Gegenwartsfragen des Osten*, no. 1.
HOLZMAN, F. D. (1987) *The Economics of Soviet Bloc Trade and Finance* (Boulder: Westview Press).
HOÓS, J. (1981) 'Characteristics of the New Growth Path of the Economy in Hungary', *Acta Oeconomica*, vol. 27 (no. 3–4).
HOÓS, J. (1985) *KSz*, no. 9.
HORVÁTH, L. (1970) *F*, no. 22.
HRON, J. (1968) *Změny v oblasti mezd v obdobi 1945–1953* (Prague: The Economic Institute of the Academy of Sciences).
JARUZELSKI, W. (1992) *Stan Wojenny Dlaczego . . .* (Warsaw: Polska Oficyna Wydawnicza).
JĘDRUSZCZAK, H. (1972) *Zatrudnienie a przemiany spoleczne w Polsce w latach 1944–1960* (Warsaw: Wydawnictwo Polskiej Akademii Nauk).
JĘDRYCHOWSKI, S. (1982) *Zadluzenie Polski w krajach kapitalistycznych*. (Warsaw: Ksiazka i Wiedza).
JEZIERSKI, A. and B. PETZ (1988) *Historia Gospodarcza Polski Ludowej, 1944–1985* (Warsaw: PWN).
JÓZEFIAK, C. (1981) *Odra*, no. 3.
JÓZEFIAK, C. (1984) in J. Mujzel and S. Jakubowicz (eds) *Funkcjonowanie Gospodarki Polskiej* (Warsaw: PWE).
KÁDÁR, B. (1983) 'Hungarian Industrial Policy in the Eighties', *The New Hungarian Quarterly*, no. 92.
KALECKI, M. (1963) *Zarys teoriii wzrostu gospodarki socjalistycznej* (Warsaw: PWN).
KALECKI, M. (1964) *Z zagadnien gospodarczo- spolecznych Polski Ludowej* (Warsaw: PWN).

KAMINSKI, B. (1991) *The Collapse of State Socialism, The Case of Poland* (Princeton University Press).
KAUTSKY, K. (1964) *The Dictatorship of the Proletariat* (University of Michigan Press). The original was published in German in 1918.
KAWALEC, S. (1988) in *Propozycje Przeksztalcen Polskiej Gospodarki* (Warsaw: Zeszyty Naukowe).
KHANIN, G. (1992) 'Economic Growth in the 1980s', in Ellman, M. and V. Kontorovich (eds) *The Disintegration of the Soviet Economic System* (London: Routledge).
KISIEL, H. (1984) *Finanse*, nos 7–8.
KOŁODKO, G. W. (1992) 'Stabilizacja, Recesja i Wzrost w Gospodarce Postsocalistycznej', in G. Kołodko (ed.) *Polityka Finansowa, Transformacja, Wzrost* (Warsaw: Instytut Finansow).
KOMÁREK, V. (1989) *PE*, no. 5.
KONDRATENKO, R. (1991) *PE*, no. 3.
KOPÁTSY, S. (1988) Unpublished paper.
KORBONSKI, A. (1989) 'The Politics of Economic Reforms in Eastern Europe: The Last Thirty Years', *Soviet Studies*, no. 1.
KORNAI, J. (1983) *Contradictions and Dilemmas* (Budapest: Corvina).
KORNAI, J. (1986) 'The Hungarian Reform Process: Visions, Hopes and Reality', *Journal of Economic Literature*, vol. XXIV, December.
KORNAI, J. (1990) *The Road to a Free Economy; Shifting from a Socialist System: The Example of Hungary* (New York: Norton).
KORNAI, J. (1992) *The Socialist System, The Political Economy of Communism* (Princeton University Press).
KORNAI, J. (1993) 'Market Socialism Revisited', in F. K. Bardhan and J. E. Roemer (eds) *Market Socialism, The Current Debate* (Oxford University Press).
KOUBA, K. (1968) in K. Kouba *et al.* (eds) *Úvahy o socialistické ekonomice* (Prague: Svoboda).
KOUBA, K. (1991), 'Economic Reform in Czechoslovakia', unpublished paper.
KÓVÁRI, G. and G. SZIRÁCKI (1985) *Mozgó Világ*, no. 1.
KÖVES, A. (1992) *Central and East European Economies in Transition* (Boulder: Westview Press).
KOWALIK, T. (1987) 'Three attitudes and three dramas', in G. Fink, G. Poll and M. Riese (eds) *Economic Theory, Political Power and Social Justice*, In honour of Kazimierz Laski (Wien: Springer Verlag).
KOŽUŠNÍK, Č. (1991) *NH*, no. 6.
KRAWCZYK, R. (1988) *Przeglad Katolicki*, no. 13.
KUDRNA, A. (1967) *Práce a mzda*, no. 7.
KUSIN, V. V. (1982) 'Husák's Czechoslovakia and Economic Stagnation', *Problems of Communism*, May–June.
LAMMICH, S. (1978) *Osteuropa Wirtschaft*, no. 1.
LANE, D. (1982) *The End of Social Inequality? Class, Status and Power under State Socialism* (London: Allen & Unwin).
LANGE, O. (vols 1 and 2 in 1973 and vol. 3 in 1975) *Works* (Warsaw: PWE).
LAQUEUR, W. (1994) *The Dream that Failed. Reflections on the Soviet Union* (Oxford University Press).

LAVIGNE, M. (1991) *International Political Economy and Socialism* (Cambridge University Press). Translation from French.

LENIN, V. I. (1967) *Selected Works* (Moscow: Progress Publishers).

LEVCIK, F. (1981) *Europaische Rundschau*, no. 2.

LEWANDOWSKI, J. and J. SZOMBURG (1988) in *Propozycje Przeksztalcen Polskiej Gospodarki* (Warsaw: Zeszyty Naukowe).

LIPOWSKI, A. (1986) *ZG*, no. 18.

LIPOWSKI, A. (1988) *Mechanizm rynkowy w gospodarcze polskiej* (Warsaw: PWE).

LIPTON, D. and J. SACHS (1990) 'Creating a Market Economy in Eastern Europe: The Case of Poland', *Brookings Papers on Economic Activity*, no. 1.

LISKA, T. (1965) *Ökonosztát* (Budapest: KJK).

MARER, P. and J. M. MONTIAS (1981) 'CMEA Integration: Theory and Practice', in *East European Economic Assessment*, Part 2 (Washington: US Government Printing Office).

MARRESE, M. and J. VANOUS (1983) *Soviet Subsidization of Trade with Eastern Europe* (Berkeley: University of California Institute of International Studies).

Marx–Engels Reader (1978) in R. C. Tucker (ed.) second edn. (New York: Norton).

MERÉNYI, M. (1993) *Nsz*, 3 February.

MEYER, A. (1965) *The Soviet Political System: An Interpretation* (New York: Random House.

MIESZCZANKOWSKI, M. (1984) *ZG*, no. 29.

MIESZCZANKOWSKI, M. (1988) *ZG*, no. 1.

MILIBAND, R. (1992) 'Fukuyama and the Socialist Alternative', *New Left Review*, May–June.

MISES VON, L. (1963) 'Economic Calculation in the Socialist Commonwealth', in F. A. Hayek (ed.) *Collectivist Economic Planning* (London: Routledge& Kegan Paul). It is a translation from the German original, which appeared in 1920.

MIZSEI, K. (1990) *Lengyelország. Válságok, reformpótlékok és reformok* (Budapest: *KJK*).

MLYNÁŘ, Z. (1980) *Nightfrost in Prague. The End of Human Socialism* (New York: Karz Publishers).

MOSÓCZY, R. (1979) *A KGST-országok gazdaságpolitikája 1976–80* (Budapest: Kossuth Könyvkiadó).

MURRELL, P. (1992)'Evolutionary and Radical Approaches to Economic Reform', *Economics of Planning*, vol. 25, pp. 79–95.

MURRELL, P. (1993), 'What is Shock Therapy? What Did it Do in Poland and Russia?', *Post Soviet Affairs*, vol. 9, no. 2.

NAGY, T. (1960) *Az árak szerepe a szocializmusban* (Budapest).

NET (Siec) (1981) *Biuletyn AS*, no. 34, 28–30 August.

NELSON, R. and S. WINTER (1992) *An Evolutionary Theory of Economic Change* (Harvard University Press).

New Party Program of the Communist Party of the Soviet Union (1965) reprinted in *Essential Works of Marxism*, A. Mendel (ed.) (New York: Bantam).

NOREN, J. and L. KURTZWEG (1993) 'The Soviet Economy Unravels: 1985–1991', in Kaufman, R. and J. Hardt (eds) *The Former Soviet Union in Transition* (Armonk: M E. Sharpe).

NOVE, A. (1980) *The Soviet Economic System*, Second edn (London: Allen & Unwin).

NOVE, A. (1982) *An Economic History of the USSR* (Harmondsworth: Pelican Books).

NOVE, A. (1991) *The Economics of Feasible Socialism, Revisited* (London: HarperCollins: Academic).

NUTI, D. M. (1990) 'Market Socialism: The Model that Might Have Been but Never Was', a paper presented at a conference in Harrogate, England.

NYERS, R. (1966) in *A gazdasági mechanizmus reformja* (Budapest).

NYERS, R. (1968) *Gazdaságpolitikánk és a gazdasági mechanizmus reformja* (Budapest: Kossuth Könyvkiadó).

NYERS, R. (1983) 'Interrelations between Policy and the Economic Reform in Hungary', *Journal of Comparative Economics*, 7, pp. 211–24.

NYERS, R. (1988) *Útkeresés – reformok* (Budapest: Magvető Kiadó).

NYERS, R. (1989) Interview, *Mozgó Világ*, no. 9.

NYERS, R. and M. TARDOS (1984), *Gazdaság*, no. 4.

OAKESHOTT, M. (1962) *Rationalism in Politics and Other Essays* (New York: Basic).

OLĘDZKI, M. (1974) *Polityka zatrudnienia* (Warsaw: PWE).

OSERS, J. (1977) 'First Attempts towards the Introduction of a Self-management System in Czechoslovakia ', *Economic Analysis and Workers' Management*, vol. XI (no. 3–4).

Perekhod k rynku. Kontseptsiia i programma (1990) (Moscow: Ministry of Information).

PETŐ, I. and S. SZAKÁCS (1985), *A hazai gazdaság négy évtizedének története, 1945–1985* (Budapest: KJK).

PETRAKOV, N. (1993) 'The Socialist Idea and the Economic Failure of Real Socialism', *Problems of Economic Transition*, June. Translation from Russian.

POPPER, K. (1971) *The Open Society and Its Enemies* (Princeton University Press).

POZSGAY, I. (1989) *Politikus-pálya a pártállamban és rendszerváltásban* (Budapest: Püski).

Program NSZZ 'Solidarność' (1981) *Tygodnik Solidarność*, no. 29.

RAKOWSKI, M. (1991) *Jak to sie stalo* (Warsaw: Polska Oficyna Wydawnicza).

Reforma Gospodarcza (1983) (Warsaw: Institut Wydawniczy Zwiazkow Zawodowych).

Report of the Consultative Economic Council for 1986 (1987) *ZG*, nos 7 and 8.

RÉVÉSZ, G. (1984) *Gazdaság*, no. 3.

RÉVÉSZ, G. (1990) *Perestroika in Eastern Europe, Hungary's Economic Transformation* 1945–1988 (Boulder: Westview Press).

ROEMER, J. E. (1993) 'Can There Be Socialism after Communism', in P. K. Bardhan and J. E. Roemer (eds) *Market Socialism, The Current Debate* (Oxford University Press).

Rok šedesátý osmý v usneseních a dokumentech ÚV KSČ (1969) (Prague: Svoboda).

RÓZSA, J. and T. FARKASINSZKY (1970) *Munkaügyi Szemle*, no. 4.

RUSH, M. (1993) 'Fortune and Fate', *The National Interest*, Spring.

RUSMICH, L. (1972), *PH*, no. 8.

RUSTIN, M. (1992) 'No exit from capitalism', *New Left Review*, May/June.

ŠAFAŘÍKOVÁ, V. (1989) *HN*, no. 20.

SÁRKÖZY, T, (1985) *Egy gazdasági szervezeti reform* (manuscript).

SCHÖNWALD, P. (1980) *A dolgozók élet- és munkakörülményeinek alakulása a munka-jog szabályainak tükrében 1951–1956* (Budapest).

SCHROEDER, G. E. (1992) 'Soviet consumption in the 1980s: a tale in woe', in Ellman, M. and V. Kontorovich (eds) *The Disintegration of the Soviet Economic System* (London: Routledge).

SCHUMPETER, J. A. (1950) *Capitalism, Socialism and Democracy* (New York: Harper & Row).

SHASTITKO, V. (1990) 'Pricing on the CMEA Market', *Foreign Trade*, no. 1

ŠIK, O. (1967) *Plan and Market under Socialism* (White Plain:International Arts and Sciences, and Prague: Academia Publishing House).

ŠIK, O. (1990) *Jarní probuzení – iluze a skutečnost* (Prague: Mladá fronta).

SOJÁK, Z. (1987) *HN*, no. 13.

SPULBER, N. (1991) *Restructuring the Soviet Economy, In Search of the Market* (Ann Arbor: University of Michigan Press).

STALIN, J. (1952) *Economic Problems of Socialism in the Soviet Union* (New York: International Publishers).

STANISZKIS, J. (1991) *The Dynamics of the Breakthrough in Eastern Europe. The Polish Experience* (Berkeley: University of California Press).

STARK, D. (1991) *KSz*, no. 3.

SZELÉNYI, I. (1988) *Socialist Entrepreneurs, Embourgeoisement in Rural Hungary* (University of Wisconsin Press).

SZELÉNYI, I. (1990) *Új osztály, állam, politika* (Budapest: Európa Könyvkiadó).

SZELÉNYI, I. (1990a) *Valóság*, no. 1.

TARDOS, M. (1988) *Gazdaság*, no. 3.

THERBORN, G. (1992) 'The Life and Times of Socialism', *New Left Review*, no. 194.

Towards a Humane and Democratic Socialist Society, Plenum of the CPSU CC (1990) (Moscow: Novosti).

Turning Point and Reform (1987). A study edited by L. Antal, L. Bokros, I. Csillag, L. Lengyel and Gy. Matolcsi, *KSz*, no. 9.

URBAN, L. and O. LÉR (1982) *PE*, no. 11.

URBAN, L. and O. LÉR (1986) *HN*, no. 7.

VINTROVÁ, R. (1984) in *Reprodukční proces v ČSSR v 80. letech*, Ch. 6 (Prague: Academia).

VINTROVÁ, R. (1989) *PE*, no. 5.

WAEDEKIN, K. E. (1985) 'East European Agricultural Trends and Prospects: European Perspective', in *East European Economies: Slow Growth in the 1980s*, vol. 1. (Washington: US Government Printing Office).

WARD, B. (1958) 'The Firm in Illyria: Market Syndicalism', *American Economic Review*, no. 4.

WHITE, S. (1992) *Gorbachev and After* (Cambridge University Press).
WOLF, T. A. (1977) 'East–West European Trade Relations', in *East European Economies Post Helsinki*, Volume of papers for the use of the US Congress (Washington: US Government Printing Office).
WHITE, S., GARDNER J. and G. SCHÖPFLIN (1987) *Communist Political Systems, An Introduction* (New York: St. Martin's Press).
ZWASS, A. (1989) *The Council for Mutual Economic Assistance* (Armonk: M.E. Sharpe).

Index

Note that some common items (e.g. Poland, Czechoslovakia, Hungary, the Soviet Union, the West and the East) are only indexed exceptionally, and many selectively. 'Cz' stands for Czechoslovakia, 'd' for definition, 'EE' for countries under review, 'H' for Hungary, 'P' for Poland, 'SU' for the Soviet Union.